The Art and *Science of* # BUSINESS PERSUASION

The Art and Science of

BUSINESS PERSUASION

Mastering the Power of Getting What You Want

GEOFF BURCH

A BIRCH LANE PRESS BOOK
Published by Carol Publishing Group

First Carol Publishing Group edition 1996

A Birch Lane Press Book
Published by Carol Publishing Group
Birch Lane Press is a registered trademark of Carol Communications, Inc.
Editorial Offices: 600 Madison Avenue, New York, N.Y. 10022
Sales and Distribution Offices: 120 Enterprise Avenue, Secaucus, N.J. 07094
In Canada: Canadian Manda Group, One Atlantic Avenue, Suite 105, Toronto, Ontario M6K 3E7
Queries regarding rights and permissions should be addressed to Carol Publishing Group, 600 Madison Avenue, New York, N.Y. 10022

Carol Publishing Group books are available at special discounts for bulk purchases, sales promotion, fund-raising, or educational purposes. Special editions can be created to specifications. For details, contact: Special Sales Department, Carol Publishing Group, 120 Enterprise Avenue, Secaucus, N.J. 07094

First published in Great Britain in 1994 by Headline Book Publishing, a division of Hodder Headline PLC.

Manufactured in the United States of America
10 9 8 7 6 5 4 3 2 1

Library of Congress Cataloging-in-Publication Data

Burch, Geoff.
    The art & science of business persuasion : mastering the power of getting what you want / Geoff Burch.
        p. cm.
    "A Birch Lane Press book."
    ISBN 1–55972–354–8 (hardcover)
    1. Business communication.   2. Oral communication.   3. Persuasion (Psychology)   I. Title.
HF5718.B772   1996
650.1—dc20   95-50089
                                                                    CIP

To my long-suffering best friend and missus, Sallie. To my boys, James and Simon, and in memory of my mom whose bizarre but profitable business adventures traumatized my childhood and taught me all I know.

Contents

Acknowledgments

To Gillian Bromley, my brilliant editor; to my mother-in-law, who read the first draft and raised an essential eyebrow at my excesses; and to all my super clients without whom this book would not have been written.

Introduction

The object of this book is to explain the value and power of persuasion and to arm you with an understanding of how it works. Persuasion is a sort of verbal martial art, which, if used correctly, will always give you the outcome you desire. This sounds like a wonderful state of affairs; however, like all martial arts, persuasion is open to abuse and misuse. It can be perverted by bullies to overwhelm the weak; and it can be misapplied to bring about an outcome that is desirable neither to persuader nor to persuaded.

"Icebergs? What icebergs? Believe me, if I thought there were icebergs out there, I wouldn't be encouraging you to go full steam ahead."

On the other hand, the potential benefits for business are immense: your customers all say yes, your staff are with you all the way, and the success you planned is within your grasp.

From a very early age I took pleasure in the fact that I could persuade anyone to do anything; as a result, on more than one occasion, my *Titanic* sank with all hands lost. Even now, when I know that the ability to persuade has to be treated with great caution, I still drop myself in it sometimes: that is why, on this lovely sunny afternoon, I am sweating away with inky fingers, trying to produce a book that I convinced a publisher I could write!

A young manager I know went on one of those high-fliers' weekend courses where you are sent galloping around snowbound trails with nothing but a jock strap, hockey boots, and an oil drum. He came back into the office on Monday morning full of vim and vigor to find his colleagues the same turgid, dismal crowd he had left on Friday. Nothing had changed, and he couldn't change them.

Failing to communicate his enthusiasm, he was swallowed back into the morass of everyday life and the value of his course was dissipated. If he could have persuaded his workmates into sharing his newfound ideas, he might have put them into effect. Great new working practices crash and burn with strike action because managers failed to persuade unions of their value. Wonderful inventions die on the vine, new businesses fail, and products languish unsold—all for lack of a bit of friendly persuasion. Over the next few chapters we will find out how it is done.

Beware the king's tailors

And, perhaps, how it is not done. I often come into conflict with the received wisdom of how the skills of business persuasion should be taught and exercised. When I was expelled from school as a disruptive influence, I thought the future looked bleak; however, recently, political correctness has come to my aid. In accordance with the idea that language should give offense to none, you are no longer "bald" but "follicly challenged," no longer "short" but "altitude disadvantaged"—and, joy of joys, I am no longer a "disruptive influence" but an "agent for change." All the same, and despite having now earned the impressive if ambiguous title of "business guru," my attitude has at bottom not changed much, and I have often been attacked for it.

Too often I find myself feeling like the little kid in the story of the emperor's new clothes. I have to say that I have always felt the outcome of that tale to be deeply unrealistic. I bet when the kid started shouting about the king being naked, they didn't really turn round and say: "Golly, you are right. What a clever little fellow." I bet the crowd would have kept their mouths shut and the con men would have kicked the child to death, thereby not only silencing him but also giving a warning to any other smartass who fancied his chances against them. I was just the sort of kid who jeered at naked kings and, as I said, I got booted out of school as a disruptive influence.

As the business world changes more and more rapidly, I see desperate management latching on to ever more bizarre philosophies in the hope of rescue when in fact the tide has left them stranded like beached whales and it is their own bulk and unwieldiness that is crushing them. As they gallop about with the latest book of wise words, dangle from ropes on a windswept mountainside or go to be rebirthed, they don't exactly welcome news of their nakedness or reminders of the fact that in this gritty existence, we have to do and make things and then sell those things at a profit. All other operations just involve us in costs.

Such was the reputation I gained as a boat-rocker that one of my colleagues once said that he would no longer let me meet the clients at a presentation. That wasn't fair, I said: they were all my creative ideas that were being presented and anyway I was, after all, the boss. As I was pulling rank, he found it very hard to tell me why he was so reluctant to let me "help" him with the presentation. I pressed him for an explanation and eventually he came up with a description of my approach which, although I profoundly disagree with it, has stuck.

"The trouble is," he said, "you piss on their yucca plants." Less picturesquely, another business consultant told me that I showed far too much cynicism towards my profession—and he had a point: if I smell flowers, I want to know where the funeral is. But questions need asking. I am very impressed by the business superstars and their works such as *In Search of Excellence, Up the Organization, The One Minute Manager,* and so on; but if their wisdom is correct, which much of it probably is, then why hasn't everyone who has read these books driven their companies on to ever greater heights of success?

I am accused not only of cynicism towards my own profession but also of failing to take it seriously. After one talk I had given I was accosted by a gray little man who said that I had used too many jokes and gave me to understand that I had in some way devalued the great god Business. Which of my tales had caused the most offense? I asked him. All of them, he said, and proceeded to repeat them back to me, word for word. I asked him if any other training session he had been on had put across a message that could be repeated so faithfully.

John Cleese, when similarly challenged, said: "You don't have to be somber to be serious." Humor is not only one of the best ways of staying sane, but also one of the best means of communication there is. If you find my style irritating, it may not mean I can't help you and your company; think of how a little bit of grit grows a pearl in an oyster through constant irritation.

Watch the little bald guy

I also believe that to teach effectively you need detachment. This is something I didn't at first appreciate when I nailed up my plate as a trainer in business ideas. My role model then was a godlike creature who swanned about in a white Rolls-Royce, wearing a white suit, dripping gold, and doused in several gallons of pungent aftershave. Businesspeople would sit at his feet, drink in his wisdom and shower him in riches. Seemed simple; and though I hadn't got the Rolls and I looked like a butcher in the white suit, clients did start to come in, albeit largely from the more rabid direct sale companies in odd investments or home improvements. But they didn't like me: I would start putting forward my views, and before long, out of the serried ranks staring at me with their arms folded and an expression of fanatical expectation on their faces, someone (usually called Alan) would start hassling me.

One Wednesday evening, while I was wondering where I was going wrong with these people, I happened to be watching a top soccer team training. It was late, wet, and cold, and here were these twenty-two men running up and down to the point of exhaustion, while a short, balding man with a cigarette hanging out of his mouth bawled at them, "Go on, get those legs up!" And they did. What's going on? I asked. Oh, they're training, was the reply. Well, who's the little bald guy? I persisted. The answer: Oh, he's the coach.

Eureka!

This was one of the best teams in the world; why did they need to train, what more could they learn, and who was capable of teaching them? They needed to train to *stay* the best. There is always something new to learn, some ability that has become dulled that needs honing, something that has been forgotten that needs bringing back into play. And who can teach them? It must, obviously, be someone who can train beyond his own ability, otherwise every sports superstar would have a coach who could outperform him, which is of course impossible. The relationship between coach and performer is also very special. Do you ever see a sports star holding out his or her racquet, stick, or ball to the coach and saying: "All right, if you are so clever, you do it?" Why not? Partly because the coach is detached, poses no threat or competition, and is often very unlike his or her protégé in attitude and appearance.

Which brings me back to Mr. White Suit and my snarling audiences. What I hadn't realized is that Mr. White Suit was what most of these people (including Alan) aspired to be; he intimated that if they did what he said, they might become nearly as rich as he was. Of course, if you talk down to people to tell them how to climb the ladder you are on, they can only reach as high as your feet. If they want to go on upwards, they will start trying to push you off to take your place on the top rung. The principle of informed detachment is just as applicable in business as in sport, and in both arenas one of the marks of a top coach is that the skill of the team is irrelevant: he might be working with top professionals one day and the Cub Scouts the next.

Armed with this insight, I had to tackle the problem of results. In these early days, some of the techniques, systems and rules I was setting out were traditional fare—widely accepted practice, in fact—and yet I would be greeted with the response: "Oh, we've done all that before." And it plainly hadn't worked; indeed, in some cases it had had a negative effect. So I started looking for inspiration outside the world of commerce and closer to home— with my own father. Dad was a dotty old Viennese shrink who specialized in homicidal maniacs. If there was someone with a strange smile sitting on our sofa holding a carrier bag, you could bet there would be a human head in it. Now, it stood to reason that if Dad could persuade these people to stop dismembering the general public and take up basket weaving instead, he must have some pretty fancy tricks up his sleeve. So I showed him all my material, and he tried to explain to me the psychology behind the techniques. After a lot of muttering about such arcane mysteries as Gestalt theory, he concluded that some methods were in fact sound and, with certain modifications, could be very powerful persuasive tools, while others were actually destructive and would dissuade rather than persuade.

All this was many years ago, since when I have come to focus even more strongly on the art of persuasion. In the rest of this book I will attempt to show why some techniques work and why some don't; and to show you how you can not only achieve your own objectives but increase your satisfaction a thousandfold by making others—actual and potential customers, colleagues, clients—happy in the process. Like any great performer, you should listen to the coach but then make up your own mind what you are going to do about it.

The Art and Science of
BUSINESS PERSUASION

1

The Gentle Art of Persuasion

All textbooks, training programs, and seminars set out to bring about change. To borrow a statement from the new psychology called neurolinguistic programming, "If you do what you have always done, you will get what you have always got. If you don't like what you are getting, then you must change what you are doing." This, of course, is a lot easier to say than to do. Most people are unhappy with some aspect of their life or business; but change can be hard and the prospect frightening. At the moment, you are probably thinking of how you and your company might change to become more successful, and how this book might give you some new ideas as the basis for your plans. I hope it will; but think too of the change you are aiming to effect every time you or one of your colleagues tries to sell something, to conduct a negotiation, to implement a set of new working practices. All of these activities, and many more in business and commerce, involve changing someone's mind; and it stands to reason that if you were mentally nodding a moment ago when I said that change can be hard and frightening, you might have a better chance of success in any of these situations if you could make the change you are aiming to achieve a little less hard and frightening for the other party.

Getting caterpillars airborne

This is one of the key principles underlying the art of persuasion. In my early days as an art college student in the sixties, I used to like the saying, "What the caterpillar calls death, we call a butterfly"—but try telling a quivering little green grub about the benefits of flitting about in the sunshine with glorious purple wings. Or, as the cartoon of a flat-capped caterpillar watching a butterfly pass overhead has him saying to his mate, "You wouldn't get me up in one of those things." It is in its approach to getting the reluctant caterpillar airborne that persuasion parts company with some of the more fashionable techniques of selling and negotiation.

Just as frightening as the prospect of bringing about change yourself is that of bringing about unwanted change in someone else. Remember the icebergs and my often-sunk *Titanic*? Here is another example of the dangers of successful persuasion. My wife came to me once saying that one of her friends was very upset because her husband had been going to massage parlors and generally behaving badly. Putting on what I believed to be my truly caring hat, I took this guy out for a drink and told it to him the way it was. I pulled no punches: I tore his behavior to bits and told him that he was being completely selfish and ignoring the deep responsibilities he owed to his family. As I ranted on I saw his previously irrepressible cockiness disappear to be replaced by a look of chastened penitence. He thanked me for my frankness and we parted.

About two weeks later, we met again and he grasped my hand, thanking me fulsomely and almost tearfully for my help and the way I had changed his life.

"That's what you did for me, Geoff," he said. "It's no more Mr. Nice Guy for me! You were right: I can get what I want, no matter who gets trodden on in the process. I was weak, you showed me, but I'm not going to be like that any more. Look out, world: I'm going to do the pushing around from now on!"

He left me with my jaw on my chest and the horrible realization that he had heard from me quite literally just what he had wanted to hear. He went on to greater excesses of awful behavior which, as in any decent Italian opera, led to his eventual downfall—for which I felt somewhat responsible. Since then, I have stopped quoting chapter and verse at people and offered my ideas on a strictly take-it-or-leave-it basis.

So, advice can be something of a loose cannon, and persuading someone to change their view carries a heavy burden of responsibility. Don't be put off by this. The crucial thing is to gain, and keep, *control* over the process. At the very beginning of this book I said that persuasion, if used correctly, *will always give you the outcome you desire.* In other words, it will enable you to control the outcome—to predict what would normally be considered unpredictable. That predictability is the very essence of successful persuasion. Professional gamblers are successful because they have learned how to create predictable outcomes from a sport or activity whose very nature seems to be its unpredictability. Interactions with people should not be a gamble; but most people do not plan an outcome, and the person who does is almost guaranteed success.

Paradoxically, perhaps, achieving this control does not mean going all out for the hard-hitting, attacking approach. Control is not the same thing as coercion. Persuasion is a powerful art, but a gentle one—I like to see it as almost cuddling your opposite number into agreement. I worry about this label "business guru," especially when it is applied to me, because I see other "gurus" and I really don't see myself as one of them. Many of them are highly respected (and even more highly paid). They tend to be aggressive, strident people who use words like *tough, win*, and *get.* I watched one the other day performing on a theme which had something to do with agreement. He was abrasive, abusive, and verbally violent. His audience loved it, and the company who hired him told me that his technique really works.

My approach is so different that I felt one of us had to be wrong, and I hoped it wasn't me. However, as hard as I tried, I couldn't fault either of us. He got the results he promised; I get the results I promise. Then it came to me: it wasn't the effectiveness of the techniques that needed examination so much as their repercussions after the initial objective had been achieved.

The monk and the mugger

Imagine encountering a huge thug in the street. You bar his way, stick out your chin and invite him to hit you. He of course joyfully accepts your invitation and flattens you. As you peel yourself off the pavement, you may then see him encounter a small Tibetan monk, who gently steps aside to let him past. The thug is having none of this and shoves and abuses the little monk. To the thug's surprise, the gentle, smiling man lays down in a puddle at his feet. He is astonished and bends over in puzzlement to examine the recumbent holy man. A split second later, the death kick erupts from the puddle, felling the aggressor like a broken tree.

Naturally, you will not want to break the neck of every potential customer; the point is that effectiveness does not depend on aggression on your part, yet makes use of aggression directed at you. If you are not faced with aggression, no violence will result. The problem is that if you are going to make this kind of approach work, you will need to develop the humility to lie in puddles. Most businesspeople would rather have their pedestals smashed from underneath them than lie in a puddle—or, to put it more plainly, would rather face ruin than step outside their own protected and self-justifying position to consider the point of view of the other party. Our monk achieved his end (safe escape) by being prepared to understand the mind of his attacker. Because he knew how the thug would react, he was able to control the situation and to bring about his own predicted outcome. Worth lying in a puddle for?

To look at this theme from another angle, let us turn briefly from the martial arts to the black arts. I live in a large, old house in the center of a most respectable town. It backs on to an even older and larger house which has been divided into rather smart apartments. For a while, the garden of this house was a regular meeting place for a group of devil worshippers, whom I saw from time to time cloaked from head to toe in black robes and chanting around a fire, complete with all the props: chickens, daggers, etc. They were quite entertaining, if somewhat noisy.

(On one occasion I threw a window open and shouted: "Hey, keep the noise down, I've got kids trying to sleep up here!" The Grand High Priest called back: "Sorreeee!" and from then on they continued their sinister rituals in whispers. Only around here could you get committed demonologists who are polite to the neighbors.) What bothered me, though, was why they were going to all this trouble? Why should anyone join a coven to practice black magic? I became obsessed with this mystery and at all my seminars I would tell the story and ask if anyone knew what the point was. A reply that kept coming up was that they were after power. But what sort of power? What was magic, and what sort of power did it give? Then I heard a famous personality who was being interviewed about the occult define belief in magic as "belief that you could influence future events through force of will."

That was it! The power to change the future. If you had a magic spell that would make you millions, when would you get them? Yesterday? Now? Or shortly after you used the spell? In other words, some time in the future? We spend a lot of time wondering what is going to happen to us, or to our businesses, and thinking what we would like to happen (or not): and yet we know, or think we know, that a lot of it is a matter of chance. Anyone may become rich, erupt into boils, or lose the will to live; what makes the prospect of magic exciting is the thought of making any of these things happen exactly where, when, and to whom we choose. This is precisely what perfect persuasion—or marketing, or selling, or negotiation—is all about: changing the future through force of will. Magic spells seem to require complicated rituals, precise ingredients and a great deal of faith if the desired outcome is to be achieved; some of these things are also necessary for successful persuasion. But think of the power!

First, of course, whether you are a magician, a company chairman, or a photocopier salesperson, you need a clear outcome in view. If you don't know what you want, how can you make it happen? You then proceed to take the appropriate action to make this outcome inevitable. We will go into this in more detail in the ensuing chapters; but for now, those of you who are scoffing at these parallels with superstitious practices and who live in the bright light of today's supposedly logical and rational commercial practices might like to think for a minute of how things might have been handled in the court of King Arthur a few centuries back. You might find some striking similarities.

Follow the instructions

King Arthur headed an organization which I suppose you could say was in the service sector. His stock-in-trade was administration and management services backed up by a workforce of bloodthirsty warriors. This profitable day-to-day business had to be protected from threats and trouble by a group of ancillary staff, namely the soothsayers and oracles who saw the problems coming and the witches and wizards who dealt with them. Modern counterparts are not hard to find. The cost accountants, finance directors, and market research departments would do nicely as soothsayers and oracles—after all, their function is the same. When your accounts department and market intelligence division get together to cast and interpret their rabbits' entrails, they should come up with information about the future. In a similar way King Arthur would consult his oracle, who might warn him of enemies in the dark wood. King Arthur, on the advice of his soothsayer, could avoid the wood and you, on the advice of your accountants, can avoid a collapsing kumquat market. Market intelligence, whether financial- or marketing-based, is there to tell you about the future.

It is when Arthur has recourse to the wizards that we see more powerful forces at work. Perhaps the King tells Merlin the wizard that his oracle has warned him of enemies in the dark wood.

"So what do you want me to do?" says Merlin.

"Get rid of them," says the King.

"Okay," says Merlin, "I'll turn them into toads."

And with a wave of the wand it is done.

Now your modern equivalent of Merlin is your sales and marketing arm. You should be able to go to them with the future threat, problem, or desire that your soothsayers have identified and expect them to be able to change the future. Accounts and research departments may be able to predict the future, but only your persuaders are able to change it.

"Collapse in the kumquat market? Then we will have to create a new one by selling kumquats to untapped markets."

Successful persuasion, like successful magic, changes the future by force of will.

A word of warning is in order here. Like lots of kids, when I was young I fancied my chances at casting the odd spell. One night I came toddling home from the library with a book of magic. All the spells seemed a bit complicated, but I picked one of the simpler ones that was about becoming irresistible to the opposite sex. Even this one had a rather tricky list of ingredients— cobwebs spun at midnight, bats' blood, and purest gold. Not to be

put off by such details, I poked about and found things that I thought were near enough—cotton wool, tomato sauce, and gold foil sweet wrappers. Of course, the spell didn't work, and this made me feel relieved that I hadn't gone to all the trouble of getting the right ingredients as it would all have been a waste of time.

The problem with this attitude came home to me years later, when a client told me what a disaster his advertising campaign had been. He said that he had wasted ten thousand on half-page black-and-white ads in the press.

"To think," he said, "Our marketing consultants wanted us to spend ninety thousand on full page, full color. At least I was able to stop that and save eighty thousand."

Apparently, during the Second World War, a fully laden bomber had to have its engines on full boost and revved nearly to destruction, just to clear the hedge at the end of the runway. What my client had just said was like taking that bomber at half throttle and when you crashed into the trees saying: "That could have been nasty, it's a good job we weren't going any faster!" To bring about the future outcome you want, you have to have commitment: half measures or toes in the water won't get you anywhere.

So: you've got your desired outcome in your sights, you're brimming with commitment, and straining at the leash to use your power over the future. Or are you? Are you perhaps feeling slightly nervous about this idea of controlling other people in order to get them to do something or, worse, buy something? Before we get too far into the details of how this fascinating art of persuasion might be exercised, we should take a look at what selling is. And isn't.

2

Selling Tanks to Genghis Khan

In the middle of any of my seminars I can strike terror into the hearts of normal, happy people merely by mentioning the high-pressure salesman. This ghoul is responsible for so many misconceptions about selling that I would like to exorcise it before we go much further. It is the notion of the high-pressure sale that fosters the pernicious and widespread refusal to believe that anyone in a commercial organization outside the sales department has anything to do with that rather grubby and regrettable business of "selling"—let alone that all their livelihoods depend on a healthy order book. So strongly do I hold the contrary view—that everyone in an organization not only can but should sell—that I have devoted a whole chapter later in the book to how this works. As we shall see, it goes way beyond saying "Have a nice day." After all, if you believe in the ideas, services, or products generated by your company, surely you will *want* to contribute to the company's growth and prosperity by selling them?

For the moment, then, let's put aside the kind of selling that everyone should be doing and address the kind of selling from which most people shrink. What, in fact, is a "high-pressure sale"? I ask this question a lot during seminars and courses and get a range of responses, from the textbook pomposity of "identifying needs and satisfying those needs with goods or services" to the more down-to-earth definition of a high-pressure salesman as someone who forces people to buy things they don't need and don't want.

You may remember that in the introduction I said that I intended in this book to show you how to achieve your own objectives and make your clients, customers, and colleagues happy in the process. This cheerful goal is clearly somewhat at odds with the steamrollering image we have just conjured up. So let us look at it more closely.

Making people want things

We should start by admitting honestly that people frequently don't want what you want for them. You may want to use the skills outlined in this book to settle a labor dispute, or to convince your employees that it would be nice to take a pay cut—an idea that you will have to sell just as strongly as you would your products. In the case of the pay cut, of course, you will most certainly be selling something that the intended recipients don't want, to the point that you may have to accept that a cut throat is something *you* don't want. The sad fact is that your whole future depends on dealing with aspects of resistance. You may sell Ferraris; the average person would not hesitate for a moment before saying that he wanted one, but what he does not want is to have to pay for it. Your persuasion must therefore be directed towards the area of resistance: you don't have to persuade anyone to do what they already want and intend to do. Persuasion, as we have already noted, is all about change: it is the art and science of changing attitudes and beliefs, and to use it effectively you need to target it accurately at the aspects of resistance or misunderstanding that are standing in the way of agreement.

This targeting of your persuasive efforts is strongly related to the need I have already emphasized to have a particular desired outcome for each transaction. Most people do not enter interpersonal transactions with such an aim; in other words, they do not intend to sell or persuade. When I go around with representatives, I say to them: "Why did you visit this man?" and they say to me: "To see if he wanted anything." Well, if he had actively wanted anything, surely he would have got in touch himself?

Perhaps he doesn't know what he wants, or doesn't know what is available that he might want? We are all in the business of making people want things. We must all intend to sell.

Lest this sounds horribly Machiavellian, let me tell you a story that makes my point perfectly. I once saw a poor little butcher struggling away in his modest shop. I guessed that a small secondary unit like his probably gave a turnover of no more than a few thousand, of which maybe just a third would be profit. As dusk fell, I saw this sad but proud person take off his overalls and pull down the shutters. My picture of stoical peasantry was then somewhat shattered as he swept off home in a brand new Jaguar.

In search of an explanation, I watched him at work. Imagine yourself as sales assistant in a butcher's shop. If someone came in and asked for a pound of bacon, you would probably give it to them, smile, and take the money. What have you just sold? The answer, sadly, is: nothing. Admittedly, you did nothing to obstruct the customer from buying, which is quite an advance on most shop assistants, but you also did nothing to promote sales. Now watch our butcher.

As a customer approached, his kindly ruddy old face would crack across in a huge friendly beam, and in a broad country accent he would greet her:

"Morning ma'am, what can I do for you today?"

"Pound of bacon please, Mr. Smithers."

"For your husband's breakfast, Mrs. Jones?"

"Yes."

"Cause I tell you why, I've just got in some of those lovely spicy breakfast sausages. Had a few m'self this morning, they're delicious, cooks themselves they do. Pop a couple of pounds of them in?"

"Oh, go ahead."

"Now," (wrapping up the sausages skillfully) "I've got a chance of some free range chickens, would you like me to put one aside for you for the weekend?"

Did Mrs. Jones *want* sausages or chickens when she entered

the shop? Will she feel aggrieved and coerced when she leaves? Would you call this a "high-pressure sale"? Or was the butcher using his excellent persuasive skills to make his customer want things that she would still feel she wanted when she had bought them? Mr. Smithers's customers love him and he probably loves them; but by intending to sell he more than doubles his turnover for virtually no increase in overhead. Don't we all wish we could do that?

Mr. Smithers, of course, would not be eating his own sausages for breakfast if he thought he was going to get food poisoning from them; in fact, he probably earmarks one of the nicest free range chickens for his own Sunday lunch. In other words, he believes in his products. Often when I am training salespeople in what are popularly believed to be high-pressure techniques—for example, cold calling on the telephone—one aspect of their reluctance that comes up again and again is their criticism and claims of unreliability against their own products. In other words, they feel they are being asked to sell not only something the client doesn't need and doesn't want, but something they don't have much faith in themselves. Given that ringing people up out of the blue is inviting rejection, which we all hate, anyone who is asked to do it will need a lot of support, both in terms of a friendly and encouraging atmosphere and in terms of reliable product backup.

But suppose the product is a real gem: a unique item and highly desirable to the customer, if only he could be brought to recognize this? Would the sales team feel that the high-pressure element they fear so much was reduced? I decided to conduct an experiment. The product I chose was a modern battle tank—a fully fueled and armed weapon of terror. The next step was to find a list of potential customers. A good place to start, clearly, would be bloodthirsty dictators. This list would include such names as Napoleon, Hitler, Ivan the Terrible, Attila the Hun, Genghis Khan. We pick Genghis Khan as our first target. (At this point I should warn any historians among you that you will have to suspend your disbelief for a bit.)

Where is our potential customer and what is his situation? He is out somewhere on the Russian steppes, it's pouring with rain, and he has just had a very bruising run-in with the Mongols. There he is, sitting on an upturned yak bucket, his chin in his cupped hands, watching the rain plip, plip, plipping into his discarded helmet. The phone rings. He snatches it up and yells: "Khan. What do you want?" It's you, and you want to sell him a tank. Well, go on; what do you say? You know he would love to have a tank, so go on, sell it to him; it should be like shooting fish in a barrel.

Perhaps a script would help. Even better, a script delivered in a high, robotically cheery voice: this seems to be de rigueur for everyone who gets me out of bed on a Sunday morning to discuss my desperate need for double glazing, and if it works for the home improvement industry, who am I to criticize?

"Hello, Mr. Khan, my name is Tracey from Tanks International, sorry to trouble you when you are so busy, but you have been selected as the lucky bloodthirsty dictator to receive a free demonstration of our new super tank. One of our consultants will be in your area in the next couple of days, if I could just trouble you for a few minutes…"

I don't see Genghis going for it somehow; but he should, this is madness. We know that when he gets his hands on the tank, he will go ape. All his dreams will come true. So where are we going wrong?

If they'll buy it, they can sell it

Perhaps Tracey from Tanks International has no belief in the thing she is selling. She might even secretly think she is conning poor old Genghis and be sneakily relieved when he tells her what she can do with her tank. When you approach potential customers, do you believe in your heart of hearts that you are offering them the best possible option and that they could not do better anywhere else? I am not talking about that hoary old chestnut "positive thinking," which often seems to be used as a kind of ploy to make people work harder for less; I mean *really* believe in what you're doing. There's a big difference. I was once working with a company over some period of time, helping them to sell their employees the idea of positive quality control for this whizzy whirly thing they built. The staff gazed at me with sympathetic but impervious amazement as I drivelled on about commitment and teamwork. It wasn't until I discovered that this whizzy whirly thing was a bit of helicopter that I found the solution. I took the team for a jolly day out culminating in a helicopter ride.

"Doreen, you know that thing you make?"

"Yes."

"Do you know what it does?"

"No."

I pointed to the whirly thing above our heads.

"Well, we are five thousand feet above the ground, and we are hanging from it," I said.

Doreen could see that the thing to which she sometimes gave a surreptitious whack with her hammer was now all that stood between her and a sticky end. The word spread, and quality control improved no end. Why? Because the product had come to life. None of us can be convincing if we don't believe. Look seriously at your own offer, be it a pay award to the union, a marriage proposal, or your product: Are you overflowing with confident enthusiasm? You ought to be. It really helps. If you aren't, it might well be worth working on it until it improves to the point where you buy it hook, line, and sinker, and can offer it with confidence. I am sure loads of you reading this believe that your product or service is the cat's pajamas and that either the customers are too thick to see it, your sales force are too lazy to sell it, or the rest of your team can't bring themselves to share your enthusiasm enough to promote it. So take your team, and sell it to them first. If they will buy it, they can sell it.

In a previous life I was in an arduous selling job that involved a lot of phone work, which I hated and at which I was outstandingly awful. The telephone frightens me to death, and the activity of generating brand new business in particular makes me break out into a cold sweat. Even now, if it ever becomes my turn to promote our consultancy by phone—which it rarely does because of my Machiavellian alchemy with rotas, dates, and leap years, not to mention the fact that I am the boss and set an example by making everyone else do the dirty work—I have terrible trouble embarking on the task. I set up the phone, a list of potential clients, a pad, and a pen. It's nine o'clock: no point in badgering people at the start of the business day, so I make a cup of coffee. Gosh, it's Wednesday: must toddle round to the store for *Motorcycle News*...half past ten already, better not interrupt people's breaks, have another coffee. Now, who to ring: have a little wander through the list. Mr. Savage, don't like the sound of that, Savage by name, savage by nature. I ring my mom just to break the ice. Then I ring someone we already work for and who I know loves us.

"Hi, Mr. Smith, Geoff Burch here."

"Oh, hello Geoff, what can we do for you?"

"Just checking you are still happy with everything."

"Oh yes, Geoff, everything's absolutely great."

"That's good. Well, I'll let you get on then."

Good grief, it's lunchtime already. I'm exhausted; I think that's enough telesales for one day.

Never mind that what I teach is of course entirely different—stand up while you're calling, it makes the voice richer and brighter, go through your list in order, one by one, don't rest between calls, just blip the button rather than putting the receiver down (even if your hands have to be taped to the handset to make you do this)—I hate it, and so do most people.

Anyway, one evening during the period in which I was having to do a lot of this, a friend mentioned to me that he was looking for a Triumph motorcycle.

"Never see them," I said helpfully.

The next night another friend asked me if I knew of anyone who wanted his Triumph Bonniville. I shot to the phone.

"Hey, Mike, great news, I've found you a bike."

"What is it? How much?"

"Only a grand, and it's a '65 Bonny."

"Oh, Geoff, that's great! Thanks!"

Mike was pleased with his bike, the other friend was pleased with his grand, and I got that nice warm feeling you get when you've done a friend a favor and they really appreciate it. I hadn't telesold a motorbike, you understand; good grief no, I was helping a friend. What's the difference? It existed only in my head.

If I'd truly believed at work that I was helping my customers by fixing them up with what it was my job to sell them, I would have been just as eager as I was the night I sold the bike.

The more acute among you will have spotted one important difference between my friend Mike and Genghis Khan: Mike knew that when I uttered the magic words "'65 Bonny" I was dangling in front of him *precisely* what he wanted. You could almost see the picture form in his mind of himself all decked out in new leathers clambering aboard his gleaming prize. Our curmudgeonly dictator, on the other hand, hasn't a clue what a tank is, so when dear Tracey of Tanks International gives him her spiel he hasn't the slightest idea why he should pay any attention to what she is saying. Yet we know that if he knew what a tank could do for him vis-à-vis the Mongols, he'd probably snap up the next six months' production. Genghis "doesn't want" a tank from Tracey, because he doesn't know what a tank is, and the way she is going about things he isn't going to give anyone a chance to show him. If we persist with him, are we going to run up against accusations of using high-pressure tactics to force him into buying something he doesn't want?

Don't sell a drill, sell a hole

Let's tip the whole thing on its head and think about what Genghis *does* want. Consider the old marketing cliché of the company that makes drills. What are they selling? No, not drills. If that is what they think, they are in deep trouble. What they are really selling is holes. When I buy a drill, I buy it because I want holes. If I could go to my local hardware store and pick up a pack of assorted self-adhesive holes—"just peel backing paper, place on wall and insert screw"—the drill industry would be decimated at a stroke. I made much the same point recently to a group of garden center managers. Who are your competitors? I asked them. They dutifully reeled off a list of other garden centers. When I asked whether the local football team was a threat to them, they laughed. I pointed out to them that garden centers are not just places where the green-fingered go for their potting compost, they are a weekend leisure activity. So is the local football team, which is therefore a very live competitor for their customers' leisure cash. Once you have grasped these points—what it is that your customer really wants, and what is your real competition—you will find that your initial approach to the customer changes.

Out on the medieval Russian steppes, the spear manufacturers are locked in introverted competition with one another, trying to undercut their rivals with bulk discounts, improved grip design, and new point design, little knowing that we are just over the horizon with a product that, if we can get near enough to Genghis to show him what it does, will give them a real competitive headache. They have spent so long in a world where people fight with spears that they think Genghis wants spears, whereas what he really wants is to wallop the Mongols.

So now you have to ring Genghis with a proposal that will tempt him. To help you, I will ask you again: What are you trying to sell him when you make this first phone call? Now, I know that after my little tirade you won't say "a tank"; you might even say "to wallop the Mongols"; in fact it is even simpler than that. Consider: he's hardly going to send you a check in the mail just because you make him what sounds like a fairly rash promise about the potential of your new gadget; what you really want is an appointment to see Mr. Khan. So, on that first call, restrict yourself to selling the appointment.

As I have said before, this persuasion thing is all about control. Even if it is gentle, it is still control. It is about getting the outcome you wish for, without any doubt. With this in view, you want to be able to choose the time and the environment for your conversation, demonstration, or whatever. I have seen many a situation screwed up because people haven't grasped this. Maybe you have called on a potential client on the off-chance. To your surprise, the receptionist tells you that he will see you, and within seconds you hear brisk footsteps approaching down the corridor. Your potential customer erupts into reception saying:

"Right, I'm very rushed but I can spare you a moment. What have you got to show me?"

At this point you hop about on one leg trying to open your briefcase, which responds by exploding like one of those Christmas toy bombs, scattering brochures, cheese and pickle sandwiches, and buns in all directions. You haven't got a hope. You should have asked him if there was somewhere quiet you could discuss your proposal. If he had repeated that he was too busy, you should have apologized for disturbing him and used the opportunity to make a proper appointment for another day. Exactly the same applies if you are buttonholed in the corridor of your plant by the works convenor. Be civil but firm in setting a more appropriate time and place for the discussion.

After all, you can imagine what is likely to happen to you if you gatecrash Genghis Khan's headquarters and catch him in a bad mood. The prospect should bring home to you fairly vividly the need to control each stage of this process.

As we will discover when we go on to look at the business of questions in Chapter 4, it is dangerous to assume that you know all about your customer; but for now I think we know enough about Genghis to have a good guess at what will appeal to him. Pick up the phone.

"Yo, Ghengis baby, we are talking world domination here, I mean death and destruction on a level that will gladden your heart."

"Oh, no, not another spear salesman."

"No way, come on Mr. Khan, just a few minutes of your time."

"Send me details, I haven't got time to listen to you now."

"Sure, whereabouts are you, Mr. Khan?"

"Outer Mongolia."

"Outer Mongolia, well I never, that's on my way home. I tell you what, I'll drop the details off to you and if you're not too busy, you can have a quick look at the tank."

"Oh, all right—but if you are wasting my time, I'll have your head off."

"That's great, Mr. Khan....By the way, what's that peculiar squealing noise?"

"Oh, that? That's me spit-roasting the last salesperson who wasted my time."

Drop the phrase book

I do beg you, at this stage, not to spend time classifying every stage of the process. Forget the labels; think instead of what you are doing and why. According to the classic repertoire of sales techniques, what we have just used is an opening benefit statement. Fine. Except that when you slap the label on it, you kill it stone dead. Some genius somewhere realized the rewards to be gained from telling the intended customer how the product or service will benefit them. They then took this rare orchid, which requires individual attention and sensitive nurture, ran off millions of copies, squashed them into bottles, and hawked them en masse to the rabid throng of salespeople who were baying for the Secret of Selling. The tragic result of this deformation is that we are all in constant danger, day and night, of some spotty twerp ringing up and saying:

"Oh, hello, Mr. Burch, can I ask you, do you want to make money/be happy/be admired?"

The received wisdom dictates that an opening benefit statement is irresistible and that I should therefore reply positively; instead, I think: What is he selling? and I say: "Get lost."

And yet this is perplexing, because the way I get successful results and the ideas behind how most salespeople are taught are not all that far apart. I have come to the conclusion that the problem is in the mind, in the attitude. Again and again in this book we will come up against the crucial point that you cannot learn selling, or negotiation, or any of these skills, parrot-fashion; persuasion doesn't come out of a phrase book. I often clash head-on with trainers who regurgitate all the gobbledegook about opening benefit statements, trial closes, and all sorts of other magic formulas, when what they should be doing is producing people who feel cheerfully confident that they can persuade without any guilt or other bad feelings. You can learn all the terminology you like, but if you don't know exactly what you are doing, and why, and what you are aiming to achieve in each individual case, *and believe in it,* you will always be more like Tracey of Tanks International than Mr. Smithers with his sausages and his Jag.

Back to the steppes. Your big moment is here at last: you are outside Khan's tent with your tank. We will deal in detail with demonstrations and customers' needs later on, but let's just run through the encounter. Off you go.

"Hello, Mr. Khan."

"SNARL."

"Things not going too well? What seems to be the trouble?"

"Those Mongols are driving me nuts."

"Where are they at present?"

"Over that hill, just out of spear range."

"Oh, Mr. Khan, that must be frustrating. I'm not sure, but I think perhaps our battle tank might be able to help you."

"What's that?"

"Well, Mr. Khan, that is a powerful twelve-cylinder diesel engine..."

Now remember, stay in control. Khan has a specific problem to solve that is going to make him buy the tank, and we don't want him distracted even by all the other goodies we know he will love.

"...and when you take delivery, our engineers will explain what wonders it will perform for you, but for now would you like to sit just here...?"

Even—or perhaps especially—with the technical demonstration, it is good to get people involved. I have had personal experience of a whizz kid trying to show me how a computer works with a blur of fingers that left my head spinning.

"Now, Mr. Khan, where did you say those Mongols were?"

"Over that hill!"

"Okay, Mr. Khan, now just look in this little glass box..."

Yes, a little glass box. To you it may be a high-definition liquid

crystal head-up display targeting system, but what Genghis sees in front of him is a little glass box. Don't distract, don't confuse. I once had a nightmare of a time working with a luxury car manufacturer whose sales force consisted of car salesmen. This may not appear on the face of it to be a problem; but car salesmen speak a foreign language. One day an elderly and obviously wealthy gentleman drifted into the showroom and inquired about a used top-of-the-range model. The salesman oozed into speech.

"A Waftomat 8000, sir. I've got the very motor. It's got wheels, windows, glass, music, and a roof, but sadly it's only flat paint. Still, what do you expect when it stands in four back from book?"

The intended victim tottered away with a glazed look in his eye and I, equally baffled, asked what on earth all that meant? Surely a car would have wheels, a roof, and windows, and I for one would be surprised if it had bumpy paint. Eventually I got the translation: the car had alloy wheels, electric windows, tinted glass, cassette player, sunroof, and nonmetallic paint, and was priced at four thousand dollars below the recognized retail price.

Are you ever guilty of this? Every industry has jargon which its members use to each other day in, day out, and it sometimes requires a conscious effort to avoid it.

Back to Outer Mongolia.

"What can you see, Mr. Khan?"

"Ooh look, it's the Mongols!"

"Great. Now just twiddle these knobs till the lines cross. That's right. Now press the red button marked Fire."

The Mongols are annihilated. Genghis is dancing with joy and gibbering.

"GIMME GIMME GIMME, OH YES GIMME!"

Now, was that high-pressure selling? We sold something to someone who definitely said at first that he didn't want it. As I said, you don't persuade people to do things that they already agree they want to do. This book is dedicated to the art of changing opinions and bringing people around to your point of view. Is that immoral or manipulative? I have often been told so. In fact, I think it is neutral: like all powers, its morality is determined by how you use it.

The single-minded crocodile

Having read this far, perhaps you are beginning to think that there is no such thing as high-pressure selling; at least, you will agree that the criteria we set up at the beginning of the chapter by which to define it do not apply. Still, I can feel your skepticism. The fact is, of course, that there *is* such a thing; it is just that it needs to be defined more accurately. In the pursuit of this definition, I watched all kinds of people selling all kinds of things in all kinds of ways, and finally I pinpointed it.

A high-pressure salesperson has only one aim and that is to take care of his or her own interests. That is to say, once they have sold to you they never want to see you again. They set out to take as much money off you as possible at the moment of contact and then they are off to the hills. You can recognize one of these

creatures as it gallops off down the road laughing manically, clutching a briefcase with crisp fifty-dollar bills fluttering out of it. When that vacuum cleaner salesman finally stitches you up and you say: "Okay, but what use is a three-hour guarantee?" he says: "It gives me a hundred-mile start."

I see this creature lurking when I visit some car showrooms. The experience reminds me of canoeing up the Amazon. For the very few of you who have never been canoeing, let me just remind you of the similarity to a modern dealership. It is warm, there are palms, there is bright light burning down, and there are many interesting sights and sounds. Should my native paddler make a mistake and tip me in, I should not be unduly worried as it is like a warm bath and I bob around practicing my backstroke. I feel just the same if I have inadvertently wandered into my local main car showroom. But then I notice out of the corner of my eye the native bearer on the bank leaping about in panic and shouting for me to leave the water, and fast. I don't need to look; I get that prickling feeling in the back of my neck, river or showroom, that tells me that something with a lot of teeth and a great big smile has slithered down the bank behind me and is heading swiftly my way. One rapid exit is required if I don't wish to lose an arm and a leg.

Again, I know the car salesmen (if not the crocodiles) are trained and trained and trained, in disciplines not a million miles from my own; so what is wrong? The distinguishing feature of these people is that they see the customer as prey. Just as in the cartoon movies, when the fox looks at the chicken, a thought bubble appears showing a sizzling drumstick, so when I see one of these salesmen I also see a bubble showing a ringing cash register or simply the phrase LUNCH TICKET. These predatory techniques sometimes work well for those who use them, and for the rest of us it is a case of let the buyer beware. If you don't intend to see the person or group you are persuading ever again, you may even wish to consider using these techniques yourself. But pause for thought: these methods may be devastatingly effective, but the chances are you *will* meet your victims again, and a lynch mob can be unsettling. Salespeople and politicians tend to forget this.

Frogs, vultures, and the special relationship

So what's the alternative? When I presented my theory about high-pressure selling to one business group, there was a huge communal sigh of relief.

"Thanks, Geoff, that's just what we needed to hear. We don't want to alienate our customers. We've been forced to train our sales staff in these methods and the results have been far more complaints, resentment, and cancelled orders. We are going to stop immediately."

"That's great. What are you going to do instead?"

"Oh we shall with honor and dignity and without complaint lie down and wait quietly for death."

For heaven's sake! I am in the business of bringing about change and showing other people how it can be done, and I do get annoyed by this kind of defeatist inertia.

Among all the learned tomes on business matters that I read, I came across Professor Charles Handy's theory about boiling frogs. He postulates that if you capture a large frog and place it in a container of water which you then place on the stove, the frog will sit there going "ribbit" as the water gradually heats up, eventually comes to the boil and kills it. What should the frog do? Obviously it should jump out, but at what point? It is in its familiar environment and it thinks it can sit it out.

A bank where I was doing some training was worried about the number of its clients' businesses that were failing, and asked me to visit firms that were about to have the plug pulled to see if the problem was with sales. The first sight that would greet me on one of these visits was a sales graph of the kind you see in cartoons, where the line declines till it comes off the chart, runs down the wall and vanishes through a hole in the floor. I started with the sales director.

"What on earth have you been doing?"

"Nothing different."

"I can see that. Didn't you notice that the market for gas-mantles has been declining since 1896?"

I would then be taken to see the Managing Director, and there was a great big green frog in a pinstripe suit.

"*Ribbit,* recession, lad? *Ribbit,* seen it before. *Ribbit,* sit tight and wait for the upturn. *Ribbit!*"

I could see the bubbles rising around him, but why should he jump?

We all fear change, but quiet acceptance of our fate is not my scene. I belong to the school of the vulture who turns to his mate and says: "To heck with patience. I'm going to kill something."

If you know what you want for your business, you must gear up to go out and get it. Waiting for the upturn is fatal.

So: we have agreed that high-pressure methods are not for us, and waiting patiently for our steamy end doesn't have much to recommend it. Where does that leave us? What we must do is set two targets and work positively towards them in conjunction. The first is still that of our own interests—that is, after all, why we are in business; the second, which demands as much attention as the first, is our relationship with the customer.

There is a great flurry of noise at the moment about customer care. We will be looking at this whole subject in detail later, but for now it is important to note the problems that arise if it is seen in isolation from your own business interests. If you worked on nothing but building a great relationship with the other party, whether it consists of employees, customers, or whoever, and you were quite sincere in your aims, you might end up having to give them help or advice that would work directly against your business interests. Perhaps you would find yourself telling the union that a strike against you would be best timed to disrupt a massive deal so that you would have to cave in quickly; or, even more simply, telling your customers that they could get the same goods more cheaply next door.

Of course you don't want to do that; so how does "customer care"—or, more accurately, the relationship with the customer— fit in with your business interests? The fact is that the relationship must be based on one of the simplest tenets of contract law, which states that a contract is null and unenforceable unless there is clear benefit to both sides. You can't have a deal in law that benefits only one party. In the same way, your business relationships should profit you in proportion to the effort you put into maintaining them.

You can be as tough as you like in pursuit of your own interests as long as you do nothing to damage the good relationship with the other party. If you decide that threatening to bean the customer with a baseball bat if they refuse to sign the new order will speed up the negotiations, that's fine as long as they subsequently say what a wonderful firm you are, that they will always do business with you, and that they will send all their friends to you. This is, of course unlikely: you will need to be kind, thoughtful, and understanding to build a genuinely durable relationship, but you should still be prepared to profit from it. Don't worry about putting pressure on the other party and striving to make the maximum profit; if you are aware all the time of the possibility of damaging the relationship, it becomes self-regulating. The other side will soon let you know if you have overstepped the mark.

To sum up: you cannot be accused of high-pressure selling if you build a positive relationship with your customers; on the other hand, you won't stay in business long if that relationship does not profit you. It doesn't matter that you always get what you want, as long as the other party remains happy and would be pleased to repeat the experience. Doing this is what this book is all about. It is not as easy as it sounds. Think about it.

3

Risky Business?

It so happens that I offer for sale these pungent-smelling felt pens that are known as magic markers. Naturally, they wouldn't be allowed to be called magic markers if they weren't, and I have discovered that they will, with a few minor adjustments and the right incantations, grant wishes. Some modification was necessary to the initial models, as when these were offered to people the recipients would smile piously and say that they would wish for universal happiness in the world. Well, that was obviously no use: I need some personal greed to work on, so it was back to the lab until I had a version that would simply produce one million in used bills. It won't do it for me, the manufacturer, only for the customer, and it will perform just the once. All the purchaser has to do is wave it about, repeat the incantation on the enclosed card, and the cash is theirs.

Now, dear reader, a few of these are still available and I would be prepared to offer you one. Just send me ten thousand today, in cash, and I will, by return, send you your magic marker.

Why are you hesitating? Most books like this seem to promise to tell you the secret of how to become a millionaire, and I bet you didn't think it would be this quick. But for some reason I don't seem to be getting a flood of nice fat little brown envelopes on the doormat. All right, let me make you another offer. I will send you the magic marker completely free of charge—there is nothing to pay at all. All I ask is that you go outside with it. (You need to be outside, or you will be buried in money.) Repeat the incantation on the card, and when the cash materializes, I want you to bundle up eight hundred thousand of it and return it to me. In other words, you will then have two hundred thousand that you would not have had before for no outlay whatsoever. That has got to be the better deal of the two—hasn't it?

Which of the two offers would you go for? If you jumped for the second, just consider what you have done and why. You have paid eighty times as much for the product as was originally quoted. If you had taken the first offer, you would have shown a profit of nine hundred and ninety thousand; now all you have is two hundred thousand. You must, surely, have made the wrong choice. Can you think of any circumstances in which your customer would pay eighty times as much for your product or service as it was first offered at? So what stopped you sending me that ten thousand I asked for in the first place? Was it that you had no use or need for a million? Was it because you are quite happy with your current supplier of magic spells? No. You didn't send me the ten grand because you sincerely believed that once you had, you wouldn't see me, the money, the magic marker, or the million ever again. With the second offer, however, you have nothing to lose, so why not try it?

A fascinating insight emerges from this. It concerns not what the customer wants, but what they want to avoid. They want to avoid *risk*. In fact, they want the biggest possible gain for the smallest possible risk. My first offer held out the prospect of a huge gain, but required you to risk a lot. My second proposal offered a lesser but still substantial gain, but no risk at all.

Ousting the horse and cart

This insight has clear implications for the process of persuasion, and neatly identifies a problem you will be bound to have as you go round the world peddling your marvelous new idea or gleaming new product. Who are your potential customers? One group, of course, consists of people who have never seen or used anything like this before, and are not meeting their need with an alternative or substitute idea/product. This combination is rather unlikely, so we will move on to consider those people who are already using something. You might have just invented the motor car, but you will still come up against the horse and cart or good old walking—and, what is more, against a lot of people who profess themselves perfectly content with these ways of getting themselves around. There is a law of physics that states that all space except a vacuum is occupied by something. If you wish to occupy that space, you must displace what is already there.

What are you offering? Perhaps your super system can double your client's income, perhaps it can revolutionize working conditions or make people lastingly happy. I'm sure you sincerely believe this; but what about their current arrangements? In nearly every situation in which you apply persuasion, you are trying to displace something, and if you are going to be able to do this, you have to understand the desire to avoid risk. So when your potential client says "No thank you, we are quite happy with the people we have got," try to resist putting your hands round his throat, and don't scream that he is too stupid to see the benefits you are offering him. After all, you wouldn't send me my ten grand, and all the while I was fuming in a red mist of frustration because I knew it would make you rich. I've still got a few, as it happens; it's not too late to take up that first offer. Still reluctant? What have I got to do to convince you?

That is the key: *What have you got to do to convince them?* What will reduce the element of risk in their mental equation?

One thing we can get out of the way right away is price. Whenever I or my colleagues have brainstorming sessions with the commercial powers that be, the linked themes of price, cost and competition always seem to take center stage. But price can only be a factor when you are comparing like with like, which may explain why we have found that people are far more likely to haggle over price *after* they have decided to buy than before. The car trade is always whining about the discounts they are forced to give, but even they only give them to actual purchasers. You may be reading this book to try to discover how to gain some kind of competitive advantage. Well, take it from me, price is probably the least reliable way of doing it. All right, then, you can have my million-producing magic marker for a fiver. Send it to me now, and the marker's in the return mail. See, you still won't do it. Price is not the key. Low price doesn't mean low risk. In fact, in most cases the lower the price, the greater the suspicion of *high* risk.

Imagine that, to your horror, your doctor tells you you need a major abdominal operation. You'll have to visit the surgeon privately, and he quotes you twenty-five thousand to do the job, take it or leave it. In shock and gloom you go to the local bar to drown your sorrows. Meeting a group of friends, you've just started to tell your tale to them when a strange little man sidles up to you.

"Oh, good evening," he says, peering at you through his huge Coke-bottle spectacles. "I'm sorry to interrupt your conversation but I couldn't help overhearing. My name is Arthur Scraggins and I'm chairman of the Amateur Surgery Club. I'm a tax clerk by trade, but in the evening I like to try my hand at a little bowel resectioning. My colleagues and I meet in a room above the Nag's Head on Tuesdays at seven. We'd love to have a poke round inside—bring your own pajamas, there'll be quiche afterwards if you survive and there's absolutely no charge."

Well, what an opportunity. This will save you twenty-five grand. You're not going to turn this down, too, are you? You are? Why? The answer isn't as obvious as you might think. I know you wouldn't let him touch you, but put into words why you wouldn't. Someone I pressed on this recently said he would want to see evidence of competence. I bet he wouldn't say to a surgeon, "Look here mate, you're not touching me with that scalpel until I see your last patient walk out of here." It must be the complete overall picture that forms the impression. Myself, I hate flying and I am very cautious about who gets me whizzing about at 50,000 feet. I look at the age of the plane, the cost of the ticket (not too cheap), the appearance of all the staff, the airline's previous record and its reputation for safety and good service. Basically the same point was made to me during one seminar I was conducting with a group to whom I put my magic marker offer. Like you, they demurred.

"Well, what would convince you?" I asked.

A young girl replied: "I would believe it if you were a ten-foot-tall green demon who had just shot up through a hole in the floor."

Of course, she was absolutely right. If you are going to buy a magic spell, you would be far more likely to believe in a huge green demon who had materialized in a cloud of smoke than a business guru. If you are going to have your innards recrafted, you are more likely to believe in the head surgeon at the General Hospital than Mr. Scraggins of the Nag's Head—regardless of whatever fantastic discounts are offered by guru and Scraggins. Perhaps this is why we don't buy our sophisticated office computer from the office supply store, even though we would save hundreds on the price the specialist dealer quotes us— because the juvenile who serves us in between selling a ghetto-blaster to his mate and two blank video tapes to Mrs. Molony doesn't inspire confidence and the situation has RISK written all over it.

So what exactly do you have to do to qualify as a risk-free zone? You may know that your target's current supplier has set fire to their customer's factory twice, that it overcharges them, and that its products are shoddy. Sadly, all this proves to your potential customer is that suppliers are a dangerous, greedy, duplicitous race; and he will still tell you that he is happy with the people he uses, because who is to say that you will be any different? Well, you do, of course; but that's what you would say, isn't it? When you talk to this person, you must find out carefully where the risks are that he perceives, and actually ask what would reduce those risks in his mind. What about an agreement whereby you share the supply contract with the current supplier? That way, the element of risk attached to making a change is offset by your company's acting as a kind of benign free insurance of continuity of supply if the current supplier goes bust or sets fire to the factory again; and he gets a chance to try you out without severing the existing connection.

Perhaps you may have to reassure your workforce that they can return to their old working practices if they don't feel happy with the new system once they have given it a try. Perhaps I should offer a money-back guarantee with my magic markers; but if I do, I should expect to make far more money from them— remember the 80 to 1 ratio that you offered to avoid risk?

The demo: if it ain't broke, don't fix it

That might be broadly called the negotiation route to overcoming the risk objection. Perhaps a more obvious way of proving yourself or your product to potential customers is the presentation or demonstration. These are two activities that actually invite disaster if carried out without understanding of why they are being performed. "The demo," as photocopier salespeople will have it, can be a classic example of counterproductive effort. I often get asked to travel with salespeople on a one-to-one basis so that I can try to iron out any problems that might be occurring. One day, a client who markets very sophisticated vending machines called me to say that he had a problem with one of his staff, and asked me to come over and help. When I arrived, the directors were discussing this particular young man.

"The shame of it is, Martin's got such a lovely demo."

"Oh yes, a lovely demo."

"One of the nicest I've seen."

"So what's the problem, then?" I asked.

"Well, he never sells anything."

". . . But he's got a lovely demo."

"Yes, a *lovely* demo."

Off I went with the hapless Martin. The omens were bad from the start, for if there is one thing I hate, it is salespeople who drive like maniacs, especially when I'm in the passenger seat. Through gritted teeth and in between frantic lunges at the invisible brake

pedal on my side of the van, I asked this callow youth where we were going and why. Over the sound of squealing tires, he explained that he had had a hot lead from the sales department.

"I'm going to see the customer and give him a demo."

"I hear you've got a lovely demo," I ventured.

He beamed. "Oh yes, it's a *lovely* demo."

We arrived at a glittering office block more or less intact, and our hero hoisted the demonstration machine out of the back of the van. He staggered under the weight.

"I suppose there's no chance of a hand?" he said.

"You suppose right," I replied.

He was horrified to see that his potential customer was on the sixth floor.

"Is there an elevator?" he asked.

The experience of this trip so far had made me vindictive. "Don't think so," I said, standing in front of the sign that said UP.

Martin set off up the stairs in high dudgeon, his only friend in the world a little three-pin plug that clip-clapped up the flight a respectful five feet behind him on the end of the power cord. When we finally arrived at the sixth floor he was panting with exhaustion and I was smiling a vengeful smile.

Enter the customer, in a very agitated state, explaining that he had forgotten we were coming and that he had an important meeting in two minutes, so could we make it snappy. He spotted the machine.

"Is that it?"

"Yes," came Martin's muffled and breathless voice from behind it.

"Oh, it looks okay. I'm a bit pressed for time. It'll do. Plug it in and send me an invoice."

Martin's head and neck shot up, giraffe-like, above the machine, for all the world as if someone had shoved a red-hot poker up his bottom.

"We can't do that, sir! You'll have to have the demo."

Customer sighs. "Oh, Lord. All right then, only make it quick."

Off went Martin, ploughing on with complete disregard for all the customer's protestations, fidgetings, tuttings, sighings, foot-tapping, and increasingly pointed glances at his wristwatch. He made coffee with, coffee without, coffee with more of this and less of that; he made seventeen varieties of leaf tea, garnished with a touching electronic version of the Japanese tea ceremony; he produced French onion soup with a freshly sealed pack of personalized croutons and conjured up a refreshing combination of orange juice and chilled borscht.

"And now," he announced, as the customer and I stood limply by with loosened ties and slack jaws, "the simple task of routine servicing."

With a flourish he depressed two hidden catches and the machine opened like some huge metal flower to reveal its gently throbbing innards. He then produced a pair of vast asbestos gauntlets, an apron of similar material, and a face visor. I was rendered speechless. The customer was not similarly afflicted.

"What the bloody hell is all this for?"

"Ah," said Martin with an air of superior wisdom, "you see, the natural flavors created by this mechanical marvel are the result of using only superheated water and live steam, the downside of which is that it does make servicing a little hazardous. Well, to be truthful, pretty dangerous."

"Out!" yelled the customer. "Out, out, out!"

Seconds later we were wending our way back down six flights of stairs, the faithful little plug once more plip-plopping uncomplainingly behind us. Back in the van, I informed my protégé that he was an idiot. He protested vehemently. He had to do the demo, he said; it wasn't his fault the customer had been difficult. As patiently as I could, I pointed out that the customer had in fact agreed to buy within thirty seconds of our arrival, and that it had taken the best part of an hour to find a feature of the machine that resulted in losing the sale and getting us kicked out.

Once again, a little gentle investigation would have found out the customer's particular problem or requirement, and we could have demonstrated just the relevant aspect of the product. We might have got away with something as simple as:

"No wish to hold you up on your way to the meeting, sir. What's your favorite drink?"

"Black coffee."

"Press that blue button. There, isn't that good?"

As it was, the customer was ready to buy with no persuasion at all. Why risk persuading someone who is already convinced? If it ain't broke, don't fix it. This won't be the last time in the course of this book that we shall see how a lot of recognized "persuasion" techniques can actually have the opposite effect.

Don't go fishing with strawberries

What else can go wrong with "the demo"? Well, beware tunnel vision. I bet there is some aspect of your idea, product, or service that you think is just brilliant, totally cool, no argument. So you'd concentrate on that, wouldn't you, reckoning that your enthusiasm will communicate itself to the customer? Wouldn't you?

A sales trainer I once watched asked his audience if they liked strawberries. Yes, they all said, delicious. Then he suggested that they went fishing and used strawberries as bait.

"But fish don't like strawberries."

"But you do."

"But I want to catch fish."

"What do fish like, then?"

"Worms."

"Do you like worms?"

"No."

"Then don't sell what you like, sell what they like."

A company we know makes security mirrors, the main feature of which is that they are made of unbreakable plastic. At a recent exhibition the managing director of this company decided to appear in person demonstrating his pet product with a fantastic wheeze he had thought up himself. He had constructed an Olympic winner's podium, on to which he would climb and then off which he would hurl himself on top of one of his unsuspecting and unbreakable mirrors. He would then leap up, purple-faced and breathless, to show his audience that the mirror was completely unscathed. He did this every two minutes, while people walking past either stepped around him and continued on their way or crossed over to the other side of the aisle to avoid this bouncing madman. At the end of the day he told us that he had had no response and that exhibitions were a waste of time.

"What are the mirrors for?" I asked.

"Shop and office security," he replied, clearly thinking: stupid question.

"And how do they work?" I persisted.

"People screw them to the ceiling, and..."

"How many people do you get jumping on your ceiling? You could have hidden bottles of champagne around the place and invited people to try to pinch them without being seen."

"But they are unbreakable!" he wailed.

"So what?" I said.

We parted bad friends. To this day, perhaps, his sales force are leaping from desks, chairs, and other high places onto indestructible mirrors.

Beware graffiti artists

So what *will* make you buy my magic marker? (I have just one or two left....) What about a demonstration? I will appear in front of you in a sulphurous cloud and proceed to show you it working.

"Look at this lovely pen! A robust satin-finished aluminum barrel, filled with indelible spirit-based ink dispensed through a chisel-tipped cut felt nib. The freshness is sealed in by an unbreakable polythene top. This means that, as you can see, it will write on any surface—never again will you be stuck for something with which to write abuse on the toilet wall of your choice—while its shape makes it a very handy pocket rolling pin for rolling out emergency petits fours."

Convinced, now it's been demonstrated? No? Why not? Perhaps it was because, like the mirror man, I demonstrated things that were irrelevant. You want the million, don't you? That's what anyone would want, and that is what I should demonstrate to convince you. But:

"Hey, Geoff, how much are the magic markers?"

"Only ten thousand, and look, it will conjure up a million."

"Mmm, price is fair; but I really wanted to write abuse on toilet walls."

I assumed. Never assume. Find out. What seems obvious to you may be wide of the mark, and if you don't ask what your target customer is really after, your anticipated glory can swiftly turn to ashes. It can be deeply frustrating when our customers agree to give us great wads of money for what we consider the wrong reasons. But this brings us back to the philosophy of the martial art: we need detachment, the ability to stand back and watch. A great card player who holds all the aces does not grumble if he wins without playing them. The important thing is to make that win inevitable.

Before we leave the question of demonstrations, we should consider how you demonstrate the intangible. Leaving aside Martin's worst excesses with the servicing routine and my assumptions about what you want to do with my magic markers, both these cases had the advantage that they involved a physical product, the relevant aspects of which could be demonstrated once we had established what they were. Now, I am a consultant, one of that nebulous breed viewed variously (by clients) as people who steal their watches and then charge huge fees to tell them the time, and (by ourselves) as people who are called in at the last minute to share the blame. How on earth do you demonstrate consultancy? Or, indeed, many other services, or ideas, or negotiations?

I used to feel that they were in effect undemonstrable, that the only thing that worked was track records—telling people about previous clients who are now multimillionaires thanks to our magic markers, mentioning the big names that use us and drawing to their attention books and broadcasts we have published that have been gobbled up. Then I had the luck to attend someone else's training seminar, at which I was confronted by a smartly dressed gentleman who showed how, by logic and organization, abstract services can be demonstrated. At first I was a bit dismissive; organization is not my strong suit and I was skeptical of the worth of what I was hearing, but on reflection I decided to give it a try—and it worked.

In retrospect, I should not have been surprised, because though this man's attitude and temperament were very different from mine, we both focused on the same central principle of creating a predictable outcome. This is how the system works. Instead of random name-dropping, you prepare a three-part presentation. In the first stage, you mention a well-known firm or organization and show in black-and-white and color pictures, charts, diagrams, and so forth, what a huge problem it had. You show how this problem was dragging them down and how they had failed to solve it. By the end of this phase, your potential customer is stifling sobs and gulping anxiously at the seemingly inevitable demise of a corporate giant. You sympathetically agree that it does, indeed, look hopeless.

Then it is time for part two. Here you present your solution, again lavishly illustrated with photographs, graphs, charts, tables. Wide-eyed and with desperation in his voice, your auditor lays an urgent hand on your arm.

"Did it work?" he begs.

Part three, of course, is the happy ending: how you applied your solution not only to eradicate the original problem but to generate all sorts of other unforeseen benefits as mere incidental flourishes.

And the catch to all this? Information. If you are going to make this kind of presentation work, it has to be just as relevant as if you were demoing a vending machine or a security mirror. In this kind of context, that means amassing a great deal of information about your potential client through some very thorough investigation. The key to eliciting information is the art of asking questions—to which we now turn.

4

The Gift of the Earhole

I have been known to talk a bit myself, and sometimes people will say to me, "I bet you can't half sell."

"Why?" I ask.

"Well, you've got the gift of the gab."

Here is one of the commonest misconceptions about persuasion. The fact is, I often talk too much, and have resorted to carrying with me a clipboard which looks like a sheet of questions or key points but in fact bears little reminders on the lines of: "Geoff, shut up." When I go out with salespeople I carry a concealed tape recorder and later on I play it back. It usually starts with an exchange of pleasantries, followed by the customer saying:

"Right, the floor is yours, tell me why you have come to see me."

"Well, my company was founded in 1896 and..."

The dam has been breached and the flood let loose. From that moment on, no matter where the tape is stopped, the salesperson is still droning on.

"Well, you see, my Aunt Florrie, well, she's still a martyr to her arthritis, so..."

In the later stages of the tape there is often a sort of rhythmic rattling noise. This is the customer snoring.

Knowledge is power

It's not the gift of the gab you need, it's the gift of the earhole. Machiavelli said that knowledge is power, and power is what we are after—the power to change the future, to bring about our desired outcome without fail. If you're talking, you're giving information and therefore giving away power; if you're listening and asking questions, you're gaining information, the raw material of knowledge, and therefore gaining power.

It's not surprising, then, that most sales and management trainers give some prominence to questioning techniques. The problem is that thinking on questions, as on so many aspects of our subject, has become fossilized, with the result that techniques based on what were originally sound ideas have become not only useless but counterproductive.

I'm well aware that I'm treading on dangerous ground here as I approach the sacred cows with my carving knife. The particular beast I have in my sights is the "open question." Now, "open questions"—those questions using the words who, what, why, where, when, how, which cannot be met with the answer "no"— are the holy grail of nearly all interpersonal transaction gurus. I have attended police interview technique sessions, social workers' training sessions, seminars for negotiators, personnel managers and salespeople, and the key topic at all of these was: open questions. Everyone says they are the key, so they must be, mustn't they?

Well, no; *not necessarily.* What we have here is the same kind of muddled thinking, the same tendency to slap labels on things that work and then try to bottle the replica, instead of asking what precisely is being done, as we had when we were talking Genghis Khan through the attractions of our tank.

I got my first inkling of trouble in this area when, in my early days of giving training seminars, I had a group of high-performance salespeople to teach. One in particular, immaculately groomed and very polite, was head and shoulders above the rest as regards performance. I asked him if he could recount to the group what he felt was the essence of sales success and was truly gratified when he repeated word for word the textbook response which pontificated about identifying the need and satisfying that need and emphasized the special discipline of asking open questions. It really seemed that this paragon's close adherence to the rule-book was the secret of his success. This lovely dream was shattered when I accompanied him on some calls to see the wisdom in action.

Our first appointment was with the senior buyer of a major conglomerate. We were ushered into this man's office and our chap started.

"Hello, Charlie, going to give me an order today?"

The buyer replied, "Forget it, you sold me too much last month."

"Never did; anyway, you were too drunk to notice."

"Wouldn't be able to get drunk when you're buying. Oh well, if I don't buy off you no one will. Here you are."

"Forty cases? Is that all? Come on, make it eighty, I'd be embarrassed to hand this miserable article in."

"Oh, all right, eighty then."

"Ta ta, Charlie."

"See you later."

The next call was at a very stuffy, old-fashioned establishment. Our man's demeanor was the very height of reserve and good manners and again he came away with a fat order—but I had seen little sign of identified needs, open questions, or anything else out of the textbook. To my horror, I realized that the guy was a complete natural, a human chameleon, and that was why he was a success. Somehow I had to try to pinpoint the root of his skill, what it was that made him so effective. I started to study successful persuaders, from Goebbels to Kissinger, and sure enough they all tended to ask more questions than other people—but not necessarily open ones.

So where did this fashion for open questions come from, and what real value do questions have?

How to catch chickenpox

The problem started, I believe, with the tendency of business, particularly the retail business, to be imitative. Now, it makes good commercial sense to rip off good ideas—as long as you are sure you know what it is you are copying.

At the head office of a huge national retailer, a shadowy figure sneaks quietly into the boss's office. He is the company spy and he is returning from a mission to find out why certain other organizations have been enjoying certain levels of success.

"Well, Higgins, what gives Consolidated Retail the edge?"

"It's very simple, sir. The entire staff have got chickenpox, sir."

"Chickenpox, Higgins? What are chickenpox?"

"Well, sir, they are sort of little red spots all over the staff, sir."

"Is that all, Higgins? Well, we can do that. Line the staff up and I will use my felt tip pen to cover them in little red spots."

We must now ask ourselves: If someone paints little red spots all over us, do we have chickenpox? If you have replied No, tell me why. What's the difference? You will look as though you have got it. So what *is* chickenpox? Well, of course, chickenpox is a disease, an internal infection that kicks up little red spots as a symptom. It is also highly contagious. Now, if you can infect your team with your commitment and enthusiasm by giving them good conditions, sharing your dreams and goals, and treating them like human beings, they will erupt into the symptoms of good, profitable, caring service. Your people are your biggest asset and as long as you gently and caringly explain, encourage, and reward the behavior that you need from them, success is guaranteed. The exciting thing about this benign infection is that, like chickenpox, it spreads, and new members of your team will soon catch the enthusiasm bug and be working as well as the rest. (The flip side, of course, is that if you have by mismanagement created a bunch of demoralized, moaning mutineers, they will be equally contagious.)

Greedy, thoughtless people who have watched your successful eruptions with envy try to copy them by imitating the symptoms rather than creating the infection, and the result is there for all of us to see—the verbal equivalent of little red spots painted on with felt tip pen, with such classics as: "I'mMartinyourwaitressfortonightisJanetsoupofthedayisOxtailpleaseenjoyyourmeal," all delivered in a monotone and accompanied by a look of distinct contempt. It is just the thinnest of veneers. I will have more to say on this theme when we move on to look at what has come to be known as "customer care" in Chapter 6, but for now let's concentrate on where the idea of open questions came from and how it has been fostered by this kind of imitative behavior.

A good place to start would be at the beginnings of what is now a major retail chain: say, a shoe shop. The two partners would stand attentive and alert, waiting to attend to any customer who came in. A lady would be greeted with joyous recognition and her every whim gratified.

"Oh, good morning, Mrs. Scraggins."

"Hello Mr. Smith, Mr. Jones."

"What can we show you today, Mrs. Scraggins?"

"I need something rather special. You see, it's my boy's wedding on Saturday."

"Not little Martin? Oh, Mr. Smith, it seems just like yesterday we fitted his first pair of school shoes."

"It does indeed, Mr. Jones..."

"...Oh, Mrs. Scraggins, these look lovely on you. What a good choice, a glove leather kid skin court shoe."

"Mmm, they are nice."

"Will you wear them now or shall I wrap them up for you? By the way, can I give you just a little tip on taking care of them?"

"Oh yes please, Mr. Smith."

"Well, don't polish them because it hardens them. Just use a dab of aniline cream. Do you have any aniline cream?"

"No, I don't think I do."

"Oh well, I'll just pop a jar of that in."

That last stroke, by the way, is known as hawking the polish, and in the heyday of shoe retailing represented a hefty part of their turnover. Now, sadly, it has degenerated into a lout shouting "Do you need any polish?" from the store room, to which you of course reply in the negative. This little plum has withered so badly that one large shoe chain suggested to their staff that the polish should be concealed in the shoebox so that customers could be presented with a fait accompli at the moment of purchase. So: "Are these the shoes you wanted, madam?" "Yes, but you can take the stupid polish out."

Anyway, Mr. Smith and Mr. Jones do so well that they decide to open a second shop; and this is where the trouble starts. The new shop, which should have been so profitable, does absolutely nothing. The anxious partners run around to see what can have gone wrong and discover that what they have put in place is a character who has over the subsequent years become part of our retailing tradition. This is, of course, the dolt: the person with its finger rammed firmly up its nose, gazing vacantly into space. We have became used to it; but to Mr. Smith and Mr. Jones it is an unwelcome revelation. With horror they realize that their carefully cultivated, lovingly tended customers are being ignored. Their most valuable asset is being allowed to seep away— because, as Messrs. Smith and Jones are outraged to discover, their new recruit does not share their enthusiasm for selling shoes.

"It doesn't even go near the customers!" wails Mr. Smith.

"Well, it will have to," snarled Mr. Jones. "Now listen, you: you must approach the customers."

"Ooh, I don't like to..."

"Why not?"

"I'm shy."

"Shy or not, you approach the customers or you're fired. Do I make myself clear?"

The result of this tirade is something with which we are familiar to this day. We enter a shop and after a few moments become aware of a presence. It is the descendant of the original dolt, and generations of careful breeding have changed nothing. Its jaw is slack, the eyes blank. It speaks:

"Can I 'elp you?" and we inevitably reply:

"No thank you, I'm just looking." It moves on:

"Can I 'elp you?"

"No thanks, I'm just looking."

Of course, after some years it becomes, with experience, a little more sophisticated, branching out to:

"Can I 'elp you or are you just looking?"

Why a hammer won't cure boils

Businesses began to realize that if their first contact with the customer produced the response "no," they were in trouble. They had to make their sales forces more effective, and with this in mind they called in the experts. Probably the same firm that manufactures new suits for kings.

"It couldn't be simpler," smiled the expert as he pocketed his check. "The problem, you see, is that the customer tends to say 'no.'"

"Yes," said Business nervously, with something of that I've-been-had feeling.

"Well," laughed the expert, with a twinkle in his eye and another large bill in his pocket, "all you need to do is ask the customer a question they can't say no to."

"Like what?" asked Business, still nervous, smelling the distinct aroma of three-part invoices. The expert went on to explain the old children's game where one child bets another he can ask a question the other can't say no to. When the odds are secured, the first child says: "Okay, what's your name?" There it is: a question you can't say no to. And what is this? Of course: it is the Open Question. Our royal tailors would have us believe that success is assured if our question is based on one of the following words: who, what, why, where, when, how. If you phrase a question using one of these, it cannot be answered with a simple "no."

It is because of this, if you have ever wondered, that in place of the old-style dolt you now come across people on the telephone or in shops who put on a sickly high-pitched voice and say, "How may I help you?" working on the theory that if you can't say "no" they will be getting somewhere.

You will already have seen that there is a huge problem here. Some questioning techniques, including some using the so-called open question words, have massive power to change opinions; but only if they are used correctly. We are back to treating symptoms instead of diseases. When Mr. Smith and Mr. Jones discovered that the dolt's customers were saying "no," all they had identified was a symptom. If you have some horrid disease that throws up boils, you won't cure it by whacking the boils with a hammer. All you've attacked is the symptom and by attacking it inappropriately you might well have made the disease itself worse. The disease in the case of the shoe shop is that the manner of the salesperson is failing to interest the customer, and teaching them to repeat words and phrases parrot-fashion, however respectably backed up by the most revered training manuals, is no cure. Think back to the glory days of Mr. Smith and

Mr. Jones in their first shop: they were using open questions, sure—but as an expression of their commitment to and enthusiasm for their business. The difference is immense.

What we are identifying here is the way a potentially valuable tool in the persuader's armoury is completely wasted by being applied with insufficient understanding and at a superficial level. We had a memorable example of this phenomenon recently. The chairman of a major housebuilder arrived on our doorstep sobbing uncontrollably. Once we had wiped away his tears and given him a nice cup of tea, we asked what was upsetting him.

"I've trained my staff," he wailed.

"Now, now," we soothed, "that shouldn't be anything to get upset about."

"Oh, but it's awful," he insisted, the tears starting to flow again.

We asked what had happened. He explained that he had visited the California and had seen a girl selling houses. He gazed at us in rapture.

"She was wonderful," he said in hushed tones. "She was everything I want my staff to be."

"What was she doing that was so wonderful?" we inquired.

"Well," he said, "You would walk into one of these houses and this bubbly, vivacious creature would rush up to you with a smile like sunshine itself and she would say, 'Hi, my name is Janet. You sure have picked a lovely day to choose your new home. Now, how may I help you?'"

"Sounds good," we said.

"Yes, yes," he replied. "It was good, so wonderfully good that I brought the training package home. That's where the trouble started."

"You shouldn't have had any trouble. What's the problem?"

Before we go any further, let's just establish why the approach he had seen in action was technically so good; then we will be able to see more clearly where the potential for disaster lay.

"Hi"—a nice big smile and a cheery greeting. Many businesspeople think that it is somehow inappropriate, irrelevant, even weak to smile. Not so. Smiling has huge persuasive value, as we will see in a later chapter on psychology; for now just see how it alters the tone of your voice. Put a huge smile on your face and say, "My dog's just been run over. Would you like your dog run over?" People smile back, and almost agree. Smiling has a warming power that can melt the hardest resolve and is a very undervalued tool.

"My name is Janet." She volunteers her name. It is important to know who you are talking to. I often ring companies and get: "Hello. Stores." Or: "Accounts." Or, even worse: "256."

I make an effort: "Oh, good morning. Who am I speaking to?"

It crashes. "Why do you want to know?"

One company, in fact, believed so strongly that the customer should know to whom they were speaking that they set it down as a customer's right. But beware of the one-sided contract; if your customer has a right to know who you are then maybe you have a right to know who they are too. "Who am I speaking to, please?" is a simple line which might just help to stem the hemorrhage of business lost because of lack of customer awareness (according to one estimate, a horrifying proportion—four-fifths—of new custom slips through businesses' fingers in this way)

"You sure have picked a lovely day…" Not only does this statement set the scene and create a little empathy with the customer, it is also congratulatory. If the other party makes a certain choice or decision and you attempt to criticize it or sneer at it—and you can do this just as noticeably with tone of voice and attitude as by explicit verbal sniping—conflict has to be the result. Remember, whether you like it or not is irrelevant; if it is a decision that is making you money, then you may as well congratulate them on it. As our consultancy is a training outfit our video players are constantly being lobbed into the back of cars and getting broken, so we buy the cheapest machines we can lay hands on. Looking for replacements once, I went to a big electrical retailer and found a recorder at an incredibly low price. On seeing an eager young assistant, I asked, "Why are these so cheap?"

"Because they're crap," came the merry rejoinder. I still bought it; but I watch it with deep suspicion. What's more, I wonder to this day whether this large national company buys in "crap" because they are stupid, or because in their cynical quest for profit they think I and others like me are stupid. Whichever is true, it is a very damaging impression to give. That assistant could have congratulated me on rooting out the best bargain his company had to offer and, while understanding that it hadn't got all the bells and whistles of a more expensive machine, have reassured me that it was ideal for my specific purpose—not, of course, that he had even bothered to find out what that was.

"...to choose your new home." These words have been selected very carefully. The precise words we use have a very profound effect on the person we are addressing. Like so many basically sound principles, this one has been overblown to the point of lunacy. I love to watch the showman trainers, especially the really over-the-top ones. They have stocks of phrases that act as verbal emetics, literally making you heave as they trot them out. I collect them, because—especially if accompanied by the right sort of oily smile—they can stop a mugger in his tracks. A couple of my favorites are: "Geoff, if you want to soar with the eagles, don't hang around with the turkeys" and "Don't talk about the past; let's discuss the future because that's where I intend to spend the rest of my life." These people are also masters of the euphemism: one man who has made himself rich from sales claims that he has never sold anything in his life; oh no, he says, all he does is help people towards happy decisions. Now, this may well make you want to throw up, as it does me; but once your stomach has settled down again, think about it and you will see that he isn't all that far wide of the mark. Using words that express only your own point of view, such as "sell," "sold," or "win," can be like a fox saying "lunch" to a chicken; it does tend to bring out the victim in people, and victims get defensive. Try instead expressing yourself in terms that attract rather than repulse. When someone says, "I called you because you sold my friend Mr. Smith one," you might say: "Oh yes, I remember helping

Mr. Smith." Our Californian lady doesn't want to sell you a house; she knows that you are not prepared to buy one, but she does believe that you would love to "choose a new home."

"Now, how may I help you?" There you are: the classic "how" to avoid the simple answer "no." Are you getting nervous yet? Is all this getting a bit like one of those spooky films where everyone around you is starting to change horribly? Perhaps you hear those words "how may I help you?" just a little too often, and with nothing Californian about them. Which leads us back to our client. We explained all this to him in some detail and he seemed to take it all in, so we gave him our consultancy bill and went to fetch his coat. Then he stopped in his tracks.

"Hang on," he said, "I'm pleased to see why it should be working; but it just isn't. It's a disaster!"

"In what way?" we asked.

"Come with me and I'll show you."

I climbed into his Rolls-Royce and we set off. The sky darkened and lightning flashed as we ploughed down the motorway through an extended cloudburst. Eventually we swung off, turned down a smaller road, then a smaller road still, then down a muddy track, and finally parked in a two-acre mud puddle. I climbed out of the car and immediately sank up to my knees. As I extracted myself, a kamikaze dump truck driver did his best to take me with him. Through the sweeping rain I could see a wet rag slapping against a pole; the words "Show Home" were just visible. I squelched up the path, down the hallway and into the drawing room—and there it was: a sort of terrified, wrinkled sumo wrestler in an ill-fitting stewardess costume. She stared at me, wide-eyed in horror. Then an invisible key seemed to revolve on the side of her head and her voice emerged, constricted with fear:

"Hi, I'm Doris you sure have picked a lovely day to choose your new home, now how may help you?"

"You can't!" I cried, and galloped back out into the rain a lot faster than I had gone in. My guide was waiting.

"Well?" he asked smugly. "What's going wrong?"

"Are you nuts?" I responded, thus causing a little friction between us. More calmly, I explained that it was not the words that were magic but their meaning; if people were to be effective, they had to understand the reasoning behind statements, the real content of what they were saying, not just learn a set order of words. Once they have gained that understanding, they can use language like an artist uses a palette of colors, selecting the tone and shades appropriate to the subject and the mood of the piece. So, I pointed out, that speech he had dinned into his unfortunate staff was excellent for a sun-bronzed beauty selling homes in California but less than effective in the west of England in the pouring rain.

"What should she have said, then?" he asked. I explained that he was still missing the point. When he had told me what he had seen in California, I had approved of the meaning of the message, not the words themselves. Yes, the Californian words were inappropriate here; but Doris needed to understand the concepts behind what she was being asked to say before any set of words would "work."

Can you land a jumbo jet?

Suppose I hadn't turned tail on being confronted with the apparition in the storm-drenched building site, but had responded with another question. Would Doris have squeezed out another stock response? Which one? Or didn't her "training" go that far? It amazes me that embryonic persuaders, from shop staff to detectives, are taught a bit of the powerful art of asking questions—a miserable little bit, admittedly, but a bit none the less—and then none of them is told what to do with the answers or even why they are asking questions in the first place. It's like being instructed how to get a jumbo jet off the ground by someone who then calls after you, "We'll tell you about landing when you get back." Teaching staff to say "How may I help you?" does nothing unless they know what to do with the reply—*any* reply. It's all very comfortable, as long as the customer doesn't react positively.

However gentle and caring you are in your pursuit of perfect persuasion, human nature being what it is there will be days when you would really like to make someone suffer. So if you feel like being a bully one day, take our art out and use it to test the power of questions and to demonstrate what happens to staff trained by rote when the customer departs from the script.

"Can I help you?"

Smile, fix the sales assistant with a steely gaze, and reply:

"With what?"

"Pardon?"

"You have just offered me help. I wondered if it looked as though I needed help. With what, exactly, did you want to help me?"

The most common reaction is blind panic. The result in my own case has been that none of my family will go into shops with me any more.

The essence of persuasion is getting predictable outcomes from normally unpredictable situations; in other words, it is reactive. Therefore, scripts are the road to hell. There is an old classic in the sales world: "The salesmen have got a great script; it's just that the customers keep forgetting their lines." I love to see complacency shattered and I delight in that look of horror that comes over the smuggest of faces when the promised outcome spins out of control. I once saw a documentary about saving some huge crocodiles from a dam project. For once the crocodile was the victim—for its own good, of course. This huge brute had been shot with a powerful tranquilizer and was now being carried to its new home by a team of earnest zoologists. There were two men at the jaw end, two on each leg and two on the tail, and even so they were struggling. The man on the far end of the tail was the team leader, and he was calling out commands in a reasonable imitation of Bob Newhart.

When the creature reached its new lake home, the coolness of the water immediately revived it, and it awoke in a mood of some malice towards those who had messed about with it. The jaw men were the first to see the wicked eye snap open and without a moment's hesitation they were off, followed in short order by the leg men, all of them running in that peculiar high-stepping way one does in shallow water. At this point, of course, the chain of command had failed completely, but our man on the tail continued to shout: "Okay guys, I've got him!" The crocodile realized that it still had a tormentor on its tail. In fury it lashed wildly. Our hero, for his part, realized as he took off in a huge arc at about ninety miles an hour that his grip on said tail was now his only hope of survival. The monster found that by bending double he could almost reach the interloper with his teeth. His jaws would snap shut microns from the man's bum; in fury at missing, the croc would lash again. It was snap, scream, lash, snap, scream, lash, with the rest of the team (by now safe on the shore) shouting for him to let go and adding to the confusion by taking pot shots with the stun gun. Eventually the professor was thrown to the shore, having illustrated to perfection the danger of thinking you know in advance how any other intelligent life form—be it crocodile or customer—is going to behave.

My home-building client wasn't all that interested in natural history, and I didn't seem to be getting through to him. In defense against my tirade, he said that every big company was teaching their customer contact staff (which in my view should mean everybody) this sort of speech. I asked him why they bothered, as they don't even understand what they're saying.

"Well," he replied, "whether they understand it or not, you should have heard what they were saying before."

This was a bit like the tale of the old farmer who, whenever engaged in conversation, would talk endlessly about "dung, great steaming piles of dung." When people complained, his relatives pointed out that it had taken them five years to persuade him to call it dung. That is all these companies are achieving with their set speech programs; as long as they appreciate that this is all, I suppose they may have got something from it.

But what a waste of possibilities! I persisted with my builder, pointing out that if the ideas behind the original scheme were understood, Doris could have achieved the same impact by getting the same message across in her own attractive regional accent, and in doing so would have been able to release her own wonderfully warm personality.

"Hello, my name's Doris, it's lovely to see you. Come in out of the wet, my loves, it's warm and cozy in here. Now, what would you like me to show you first, my dears?"

Dismantle this yourself and you'll see that we have the same ingredients, even down to the sacred open question at the end. My client was ecstatic, and as we drove away he kept bouncing up and down on his seat repeating "Hello, my loves." But then his face clouded. I asked him what was bothering him.

"Trouble is," he said, "it's going to be hard to get our other staff to put on a country accent." Some people never learn.

Keeping your hedgehogs in the air

So how *do* we use questions, open or otherwise, to our best advantage? We come back to where we started. Don't talk; listen.

If you were playing cards with me and I told you that I had four aces, I would get no decent bet from you. If I told you that I had an assortment of rotten cards, and you bet merrily only to find that I had four aces, you would feel a little aggrieved. As we saw in the last chapter, this doesn't matter if I never want to play cards with you again; but if I do, you won't be so trusting next time, in fact you'll probably never believe me again. So, you lose if you are truthful, you lose if you lie. What can you do?

Keep your mouth shut. Pick up your cards and say: "Ho hum. What have you got?" It is much better to find out what the other party holds than to show what you have. I carry around with me (besides my clipboard) a character called Horace the Hedgehog. He reminds me that questions are like prickly little hedgehogs and should be tossed back straight away.

"Geoff, why do you always answer a question with a question?"

"Do I?"

Whenever we wish to persuade, we need information. This is the first fundamental purpose of questioning; I call it investigation, and we will see how it is used in later chapters. For now, remember: to persuade, don't give information, get it.

The second fundamental purpose of questions is to fix people's attention and establish your importance. Remember the Amateur Surgery Club and how crucial it is to present yourself as credible? Questions can do that. Just as an experiment, find a vacuous or distracted person, or even a group of people, and say: "Can I ask you a question?" Then just shut up. After a while you will find you have one hundred percent attention. This may be a primeval instinctual response based on our genetic programming, which teaches us that important people ask questions—parents, teachers, doctors, judges, captors, potential employers. Ask more questions and you gain in credibility. And, of course, there is the added benefit that while a person is answering a question they are responding to an agenda you have determined for their mind, while your own mind is free to think ahead.

"Here, you, how much are you going to charge me?"

"Well, before I answer that, may I just ask you something?"

"Er...Okay."

"What currently is the situation with these?"

Their mind becomes occupied with the response while you think out your next moves.

Even abuse is devastated by questions.

"You are an idiot."

Instead of thumping this boor, which may well be what he's expecting you to do, try:

"Mm, idiot. That's an interesting choice of word. Why do you choose the word 'idiot' in particular?"

Now, however, we are on perilous ground again, because these questions have hidden powers and can backfire quite dramatically. These open question words are not just information-getters but are also dangerously powerful opinion-changers. If you don't know what you are doing with them, you could all too easily find yourself clinging to the tail of a furious crocodile. These question words have the potential to change someone's heartfelt and long-held beliefs. If you don't believe me, find a friend who is truly politically committed and I will show you how to change their views. Be warned: it works.

Go up to your pal and say:

"Hello, friend, I am going to change your political view."

"Oh yeah? Go on then."

"What do you normally vote?"

"Flat Earth."

"Why on earth do you do that?"

He will tell you at some length. If he starts to slow down, prompt him:

"But why?" Or:

"What's so good about that?"

And after a little while longer you will have changed his political views—he is now *even more committed* to the Flat Earth Society. Now, perhaps I was a bit naughty not to have warned you *how* those beliefs were going to change; but like all true Machiavellians, I had a hidden agenda. To give this example maximum effect, it was important that while I knew what I wanted, the other party—you—didn't. Similarly, it is important that you go into your transactions knowing what effects you want to achieve, without giving away your stratagems to the other person. Let the questions work for you; your partner in conversation probably won't even realize what is happening.

The first prompt I suggested you use with your political friend was "why?" The effect of that word was to make the other party work out self-justification and in doing so strengthen his own attachment to his position. The word "why" is explosively dangerous in terms of persuasion. Try another game. Ask a friend to say exactly these words to you:

"I'm sorry, I won't buy any more toilet paper from you."

Then say: "Why?"

Almost every time, they will tell you:

"It's too expensive."

"It's not soft enough."

"It's not strong enough."

Well, now, here's a bizarre situation: you don't sell them toilet paper, and yet they are convinced they know why they won't buy from you. The word "why" has forced them to justify their position, even if they have to lie because it is a false position.

This line of thought becomes even more interesting if looked at in reverse. You can guess a person's reaction if another party expresses interest in what they have to offer.

"I was thinking of using you to supply our toilet paper."

"Hey, have you come to the right place."

Strange as it may sound, this eagerness to oblige can be destructive; whereas the word "why," which you would think would be the last thing to say in this situation, can—if used very carefully—really anchor the potential customer's resolve.

"I was thinking of using you to supply our toilet paper."

"Oh, that's wonderful. Why exactly did you choose us?"

The justification will come from them.

Another question can be brought into play if the other party gives you some bad news and "why" is now out of court.

"I'm sorry, we feel it is time to look elsewhere."

"I'm sorry, too; look, what do I need to do to retain my position as your supplier?"

When all seems to be lost and you are being dragged away by security guards, you can always try: "Look, I really want to work with you. You name it; what have I got to do to get this business?" It often works.

At this point I am starting to get nervous again. I'm imagining the nightmare outcome if this book should really take off among the likes of my Somerset housebuilder. In every shop or restaurant you enter, you will be greeted with: "I'mMichaelsoupofthe-dayisOxtailandwhyareyoueatinghere?" Please, please: drink in the ideas, but understand the concepts on which they rest and use them to build your own style for your own circumstances.

What you have been reading here might be making you think that I favor the use of open questions. Well, do you want your dreams to come true? There you are; your answer was positive, and that was a so-called closed question. Different types of question do different jobs; but thinking about it too much is a waste of time and just cramps your style. I call open questions "thinkers" and closed questions "checkers," just for the sake of something to write down and to remind me of their functions, but I don't care if you call them liver and bacon. Terminology itself has no magic.

Near the end of the transaction, the "checkers" become more prevalent; the "thinkers" are most helpful during the investigation phase which should be completed earlier.

"You do want this one, then?"

Or: "Now, are you sure you are happy with this arrangement?"

Or: "So, it's the blue one after all?"

This won't be the last you'll see of questions in this book, because they are the currency of persuasion; but for now, whenever you interact with someone else, monitor your ratio of mouth open to questions asked. The closer you get to one to one, the more successful you will be.

5

Mimicking Sheepdogs

If you have stayed with me through the preceding chapters, it will have become clear to you by now that persuasion is a dangerous business. This should not surprise you: can you think of any powerful tool that isn't dangerous? In the last chapter we saw the power questions can exercise, even to the extent of entrenching a person's beliefs. Persuasion being all about change, it's obviously vital to any would-be successful persuader to be able to control the effect of these magical implements. The story of the sorcerer's apprentice makes a very nice fairy tale, but I bet the sorcerer's profit balance didn't look too good afterwards.

When addressing this crucial question of control we need to start at the end. What is it you want to happen? We've already established that successful persuasion can make normally unpredictable outcomes predictable—an ability that is about as much use as a mountain bike to a sea trout unless you have your outcome firmly in your sights.

No one runs out of gas by accident

At this point I want to draw on the arguments of a new branch of psychology called "neurolinguistic programming." We will leave aside for the moment the fact that, as far as I can make out, much of neurolinguistic programming is completely crazy, and concentrate on the way its exponents talk of outcomes. For these psychologists, any life event—what you or I would call a death, say, or a wedding, or an accident, or a sale—is not an event, something that happens at a particular point in time, but an outcome. In other words, it has a history of factors that can subsequently be seen to have been leading up to it. Sometimes these factors are complex and interwoven. Take a train crash, for example, in which a Mr. James Smith was seriously injured. Maybe the day the signal failed was the same day that a new driver had been put on that route, the day when that locomotive had been due for its annual brake service, and the day James Smith decided to go by train because his car wouldn't start.

It's hard to see on the face of it, of course, how poor old James Smith could have avoided this outcome, not being party to the railway system, its maintenance arrangements, and so forth. We all know that a favorite response of politicians and other authority figures when pressed by smug interviewers as to whether some event could and should have been avoided is to say that hindsight is the only exact science. Well, I'm not so sure about that. I think that they are probably wrong, and that it is possible to make foresight an exact science. Something is going to happen to you, dear reader; it might be something good or it might not, but it is going to happen and it will be the outcome of elements of which you are aware now. Perhaps you can't see them; maybe you can see them, but there is no pattern forming for you; or perhaps you don't want to see them. The great psychologist Eric Berne said that no one ever runs out of gas by accident (assuming, of course, that the fuel gauge is correct). Have you ever run out of gas? Go on, have you? Well, what on earth were you thinking of?

"Oh well, should just get me there."

"I want the gas with gifts."

"I'm sure there's another station near here."

From the moment you drove off after filling the tank the previous time, the gauge was moving downwards, showing an inexorable trend which, unless interfered with, could have only one outcome. You ran out of gas because you had for one reason or another chosen to ignore that trend.

A lack of awareness of the present elements contributing to a future outcome can lead to disaster; by the same token, if we can identify and understand the trend implicit in these elements, we should be able to take out those that will lead to disaster and thereby change the outcome—in other words, control the future.

If you have a clear idea of the outcome you want, you can feed in the right elements over any period of time to achieve that outcome. I appeal to women readers of this book to imagine such an outcome in the form of a man—a man you see standing at a bus stop every day as you drive home. You decide that you want this man. So what do you do? Acting on accepted sales practice, next time you pass him you slam your car brakes on, leap out, rush up to this fellow and shout:

"Hello, big boy! How about it then?"

Now, if he is real quality produce, it is more than likely that he will run a mile, and you won't be in control of his speed, let alone your progress towards your desired outcome—but according to the textbook you have made the initial approach just as you should have, with a dramatic and insistent opening. So what went wrong? According to the people who write these textbooks, you shouldn't worry; in this "prospecting," as they call it, a ten percent success rate is quite acceptable, so the fact that nine out of ten men make for the hills when tackled in this manner is just par for the course. I shall have a bit more to say about so-called acceptable success rates later on in this chapter; what concerns me at the moment (apart from the fact that this soothing response is no use at all if it is *that* one, not the other nine, that you want) is that you have to be a certain type of woman to shout "Hello, big boy" at complete strangers. Therefore, it's more than likely that if you take this approach you will be doing it against your natural instinct; it will be apparent that you aren't comfortable doing it and your success rate will be hampered by your lack of conviction as well as the reaction of the target. Does this mean that people who can't happily shout blatant propositions at ten potential partners for the sake of getting one are doomed to failure in relationships with the opposite sex? Obviously not.

Now ask the question another way. Does this mean that no one except the caricature of a "natural born salesman" with the hide of a rhinoceros and the persistence of a wasp can ever sell

Your answer to this question might not be so rapid; but it ought to be. It is the prevalence of this image of the salesperson as a cross between a circus performer and a reptile, and really not at all respectable, which gives continuing life to that bête noire of mine, the belief that only "salespeople" have anything to do with selling. It takes a certain type of personality to use the bold, insistent, up-front techniques, let alone make them work; but as I see it, if we can find a method of persuasion that feels comfortable, anyone can use it. And if anyone can use it, everyone in your company can—as they should—be involved with the promotion of the firm and whatever goods or services it produces. Everyone will sell if they feel happy with the product and the process.

Back to the bus stop, then. We've agreed that "Hello, big boy" terrifies both ninety percent of targets and yourself; but you still desire the object. It doesn't help to drive past each day in a red haze of lust, so what *do* you do? Why are you asking? You know. Unless you are pure and unsullied, you know. With that exception, everyone reading this has succeeded in getting someone to make one of the biggest decisions they are ever likely to make. After that, all other persuasions you undertake should be a piece of cake.

Let's analyze the situation and work out how you can take it step by step, staying in control all the time. There is the desirable hunk, and you want him. You have a goal in mind and a clearly defined event which will be your end point. You also realize how far you are from achieving it. (You haven't even spoken to the poor guy yet.) It is the firmness of this objective—not the volume or directness of your appeal—that will lend effectiveness to your first approach. As long as the objective is cast in iron, an initial approach may be never so tentative and yet work.

I have just been talking about objectives, and in a minute I am going to bring in strategy and tactics. At this point, you may have a sinking feeling and think: Oh no, not another boring business book about objectives, strategy and tactics. Or you may already have recognized bits of classic business techniques here and there in what I have been saying and be less surprised. So far I have put more energy into pulling some of the received wisdom to pieces than into reinforcing it; but it must be said that aspects of it are sound and just need using intelligently. You might think that I have used a lot of it and left bits out; but then, a key is just a piece of metal with bits left out—and it's only because those particular bits are left out that it opens doors.

So, for once, a golden rule with which I have no quarrel. You must enter the situation with a clear and fixed objective. A football team's objective is to score more touchdowns than the other side. Yours is to get this man away from the bus stop and into your arms.

Once the objective is set, the strategy for its achievement can be adopted. Strategy is a forward plan of campaign, based on the knowledge and experience in your possession at the outset. The football team may choose specific players and plan a style best suited to the known strengths and weaknesses of the opposing team. You may plan what to wear, what to say, and where you will lure your man for the grand finale. Strategy can be changed; but this is tricky because you will usually have adopted certain techniques and styles in advance of events and altering these midstream can cause chaos. Tactics, on the other hand, are changeable by their very nature. It is with tactics that you respond to the moves of the other party as they happen. Remember the awakening crocodile and the party of zoologists? Their objective was clear, their strategy was quite strong, but they fell dangerously apart on tactics. The paradox with tactics is that they are a reactive, moment-by-moment thing, and yet you need to be able to anticipate to use them effectively. Firing from the hip won't get you far if your aim is poor. I'm good at tactics: if I smell flowers, I look for the funeral, and I live by the code of "What If." If that had been my crocodile, I would have said: "What if it wakes up?" I sit by fire exits. If there is a fire, that precaution will color my tactics and make them effective. Tactics, used with good anticipation, are the lifeblood of persuasion.

The pleasures of seduction

Let us return to this poor man still waiting for his number eleven bus and plot his seduction. Now there's a key word: seduction.

Back in Chapter 1 we saw that persuasion could be a middle way between rape and celibacy in the business world; what better image for the way this works than seduction, a smooth, gradual process that winds inexorably towards the desired outcome and leaves both parties looking forward to their future dealings with pleasurable anticipation? So let's think about seducing the other party to our point of view; and when we have been through this process with the man at the bus stop, I would like you to take each step of his seduction and apply it in principle to any persuasion situation in which you find yourself.

The first thing you need to do is approach the target. Maybe you should start by flashing him a modest smile as you whizz past for a few days, in due course perhaps expanding this into a coy little wave. Then a day will come when it is pouring with rain. Adapting your tactics rapidly, you stop and ask:

"I hope you don't think this is too forward, but I see you waiting there every day and you look so wet; can I drop you somewhere?"

At this point we hit a problem. It is quite clearly laid down as an article of faith in every business book, assertiveness seminar, and negotiating skills program that an agenda should be set and the other party be made clearly aware of your intentions. This has never come easily to me, and when I was a little chap and less experienced, my reluctance to lay my cards on the table in the prescribed fashion was described as slyness. Well now, if we go by the book in the situation we are developing at the moment, you should now say:

"I should let you know that the purpose of this meeting is to establish whether at some time in the future you would be prepared to sleep with me."

I may be wrong, but I have an awful feeling that this takes us straight back to "Hello, big boy." Those of you who have been made anxious by my apparent adherence to the received wisdom in terms of objectives, strategy, and tactics will therefore be relieved to know that at this point I strike off once more into my own path. After all, if you always inform the other party explicitly of your objective, you allow them to fix their defenses and entrench their resistance to you before you have really got your persuasive campaign into full flight.

Let's assume, then, that you don't at this point blurt out your intention; also that the weather being what it is, and your smiling invitation being what it is, you have the object of your desire in the car. When you move away from the curb you might accidentally brush his knee as you change gear. If he bounces off the roof you give him a gentle little smile and say, "Sorry." A conversation would take place, apparently of the desultory type favored by strangers thrown together: but beneath the idle chit-chat you always have your goal in view.

"Yes, I hate going to the cinema on my own, which is a shame because there are some great films on at the moment."

"Yes, there are."

"I tell you what, if you're not too busy, we could go together. What about tomorrow?"

(If you think I am coming on a bit strong, remember I have to compress the process a bit for the sake of brevity.)

"No, I can't, I'm playing cricket tomorrow." (Cricket? In this weather? Don't let yourself be sidetracked.)

"Oh, that's a shame; when are you free?"

"Well, I'm around on Thursday."

"That would be lovely; what time shall we meet?"

Now, consider what you have done here without informing the quarry of your objective (though he may well have an inkling by now): you have taken events as far as possible on this occasion, and although at one point you met with a negative response, you were able to adjust your tactical response so as to regain control. The result is that by the time you parted, some positive and irrevocable progress had been made. Contrast this with the accepted technique, according to which you should have attempted to close the deal, or at least used one or more of the standard range of trial closes:

"How about it then, big boy?"

"Ever seen one of these?"

"If I could show you proof that fifty other people have enjoyed it with me, then would you?"

"Your place or mine?"

"Is it only catching something that worries you?"

"I can understand that you are happy with the wife you've got, but I sincerely believe that if given the opportunity I can show you a better time."

One of us has got it wrong. I hope it isn't me; but the people who still train sales staff this way don't think it's them either. I leave you to judge.

Of course, if you don't have the temperament of the fire-eating salesperson of popular legend, you might have said:

"Well, if you don't feel like it at the moment, have my vital statistics and a telephone number. Please feel free to ring at any time."

He says, "Oh yes, I'll do that, thank you," you write "V. Interested" in your little black book and that is the last you see of each other.

Our method, on the other hand, was good because while it was obviously too soon to attempt to reach the objective, by fixing a next meeting you kept control of the process and achieved a clear and measurable advance on your previous position. We move on.

"Wasn't that a great movie. Would you like to come back for a coffee?"

"Not tonight, I've got to get up early."

"Oh, Okay. When shall we meet again?"

"Well, I'm free on Sunday."

Again, the next step has been gained. In your experience, when an intended partner says "I'll give you a ring sometime," what do you take that to mean? So when a potential customer says it, who are you fooling when you write "V. Interested" in your little black book? They are obviously not V. Interested.

We will draw a veil of modesty over the remaining stages of the campaign from the first kiss onwards, having already shown how you make progress on each occasion by pushing as far ahead as you can without losing control of the process. Do you know how far you can go? Going too far is often more damaging than not going far enough. The key is to make inexorable progress while staying in control: not making risky leaps into the dark, but not sinking into inertia and self-deception either.

The long-term benefits of the seduction-style approach are quite fascinating. First, there is the potential to reap success from an apparently unpromising start. Look at your partner: did you find each other attractive at first sight? We often hear the tale that a couple repelled each other on their first meeting and now are inseparable. This suggests that with patience, persistence, and control the goal can be reached however poor the initial impression. Second, there are huge future benefits. When the seduction is complete, both parties are eager to repeat the experience, and each time the goal is easier to achieve—to the point where, after a few years of happy marriage, "How about it, big boy?" is quite enough. That is why it can be so easy to sell to customers you already have, an area of business that is often neglected. We come back to the point we reached at the end of Chapter 2: if your techniques encourage and foster the development of a continuing relationship with your client, you can derive benefit from that relationship in direct proportion to the effort you put into maintaining it, and the relationship will become self-regulating.

The benefits of bad news

In my seminars I illustrate the idea of control in achieving success by talking about a frozen pond. On an island in the center of this pond is our objective, usually a potential customer. I take three very different types of persuaders down to the shore and explain that the simple task ahead of them is to cross the ice and secure the customer.

The first to try is an eager young salesman. He scampers down to the edge of the pond with unbounded enthusiasm and puts his foot on the ice, whereupon there is a cracking and a squirting and his shoe fills with water. Moments later he's back, bouncing around and grinning all over his face.

"Well," I ask, "how did you get on?"

"Oh, Geoff, it was great! Thanks for all your advice! The earth really moved for me!" This effusion is accompanied by a few gyrations and air punches. "Hey, I feel good!"

"So you got the customer, then?" I persist, gently.

"Well, as good as..."

"What do you mean, as good as?" Slightly less gently.

He then goes on to explain that he has got the situation entirely under control and that having put his foot on the ice he has made a strategic decision that the time was not quite right for crossing. He tells me that, assessing the facts as he saw them, he has got the business in the bag; while the current condition of the ice is dangerously thin, the customer is in his sights and all he has to do is wait for the frost he knows is coming, when he can be sure of an easy crossing over the safely thickened ice. What is more likely to happen, in fact, is that either he arrives at the edge of the thickened ice to find that his competitor has been a bit quicker off the mark and has beaten him to the island, or there has been a thaw and the ice has disappeared altogether. To be fair, of course, there is the chance that the freeze does arrive and he does beat the competition across it to the customer; but chance is not control.

Before we go on to examine the approaches of persuaders number two and three, let's just take a closer look at this first person and analyze why he behaves as he does. He is the salesperson who, when asked to fill out a customer contact report, makes lavish use in the comment column of my pet hate phrase: "V. Interested." Or, for brevity: "V. Int." It may not be these exact words; it might be "Likes it, will call us soon," or "Will order when he gets OK from Board." I know, and you know, that he is wrong in all three cases. Sadly, he knows it too. He will tell you quite candidly over a pint in the pub that a very small percentage of V. Ints ever become Int. enough to buy anything. This is because these people are "time-wasters," "tire-kickers," or "price quote fishers."

Before you start dancing about indignantly at the thought that anyone might describe you as a time-waster or tire-kicker, just ask yourself what the last thing you said to a salesperson was. If you wanted to pass a little time and decided to go and look at the latest Ford, did you say to the salesman, "Go away, you little worm, I haven't come to buy anything, I've come to pass a little time, and in any event I wouldn't buy from you"? If you did, at least they knew where they stood. But I bet you didn't. I expect you said something like, "Yes, very nice; I could quite see myself in this. Do you have a brochure? Think I'll take this, give it a good read, and I might arrange a test drive." You make your escape; he writes down "V. Int." You know you're not; he knows you're not. If he knows that, why does he do it?

Quite often, in my view, management is to blame. More often than not, "V. Int." is a coded message, designed to gloss over either the salesperson's knowledge that the customer is not interested, or the manager's reluctance to address the reasons why potential customers are not interested. This kind of deception, of self or others, is a real barrier to gaining control of the situation. You can't deal with the elements producing or hindering your outcome unless you face up to them. Yet many firms bring out this kind of defensiveness in their employees. I have been in monthly sales meetings that make the Spanish Inquisition seem positively motivational. Praise and approbation are given not only for success, but for a promise of success: and as the victim sees the irons being heated in the corner of the conference room, he is of course convinced that he will land the deal next week. The hard time is reserved for those who come to the meeting and speak heresy. Lesson: don't come to a sales meeting with bad news.

I will have more to say about conditioning in chapter 8, but there is a tale that is apposite at this point about a trainer who insisted that any behavior could be modified through conditioning. A friend challenged him to put his theory into practice on a huge dog he had that was beyond all control. The trainer took the dog to his home, where the first thing it did was to rush past him into the drawing room and produce a huge turd on the pale pink lambswool carpeting. The trainer leapt on the animal, thrashed it, rubbed its face in the mess and threw it out of the window. The next day the same thing happened, and the response was the same: a thrashing followed by being chucked out of the window. Day after day the pattern was identical until one day a breakthrough occurred: The dog was let into the house, rushed into the drawing room, crapped on the carpet and immediately jumped out of the window.

It always surprises me that people continue to fail to see the message in this tale. I have had bosses tell me proudly that since they introduced their draconian new system of punishments, no member of staff has been caught stealing.

"Oh, good," I say. "Has the pilfering stopped, then?"

"Well, no," comes the reply. "But we haven't caught anyone." They have not taught people to resist temptation, or to see that they are harming their own interests by stealing, but to avoid getting caught. And yet I nearly got my throat cut at one management conference where I suggested that staff should be made to feel happy about discussing their mistakes and should in fact be rewarded, not punished, for bringing them to the attention of management. I escaped with my life, feeling considerably aggrieved; only the week before, I had witnessed a situation where this philosophy of mine, however cockeyed it might sound, would have paid dividends. I had been called in by a parcel delivery firm to do some customer relations work. One of the key features of customer care, in my view, is that the company should do its basic job as promised (more on this vexed topic in the next chapter). If you're a bus company, your first customer care task is to see that the buses run on time. If you're a parcel delivery firm, it is to deliver parcels when and where you say you will. One of the many problems from which my client company was suffering was the failure of certain parcels to reach their destinations. A customer whose package had not turned up rang to expostulate in very high dudgeon indeed, and the manager swept on to the despatch floor. I watched him with interest.

"That's done it!" he screamed. "Mr. Smith's parcel hasn't arrived! Whoever is responsible for this is fired!"

Out of the corner of my eye I saw a dispatch clerk quietly push a package under a bench with his foot. The boss happened to choose this very man as his next target.

"What happened to it? I've just had him on the phone and he's livid."

"Dunno boss, I certainly put it on the truck."

When the driver of that truck returned he said that he had never seen the parcel.

That parcel, in fact, was not seen by anyone ever again. If the manager had been a bit more level-headed, he could have calmly encouraged his staff to explain how things might go astray—perhaps each truck is expected to take too many parcels, and some get left off from sheer lack of space; perhaps urgent parcels are sometimes left by messengers without being properly logged into the system in such a way that the cause of the problem could be identified and remedied. Instead, by putting them in fear of their lives (or, at least, their working lives, which in these times comes to much the same thing), he lost any chance of learning the reality behind the problem—or, to return to the terminology with which we started, the factors that are contributing to the wrong outcome. Knowledge is power, that we already know; it's really only putting this another way to say that there can be no control without accurate information.

Beware the blunt instrument

Now, this is not to say that I am always and immovably opposed to the use of threats as a tool of persuasion; but they are very big, heavy tools and prone to do more damage than good in inexpert hands. My view is that they should only ever be brought out of the box on very specific occasions and only when the person using them has a very clear view of the likely outcome they will create. A cautionary tale may be in order. I was once in the office of a friend who ran a refrigerated transport business. A driver who had been causing him one or two difficulties and was at this moment in charge of a consignment of herring phoned in. My friend started to shout.

"What do you mean, you haven't delivered them?!...That's it: you're fired. Get back to the office!"

I was there again the next day when the driver appeared. He picked up his money and papers and my friend asked for the key of the truck. It was duly handed over.

"And where have you parked it?"

The driver smiled. "Ohio. You find it." And left.

When the vehicle was finally found, the twenty tons of fish inside were just a little past their sell-by date—in fact, it was their pungent condition that guided the searchers to their whereabouts. My friend had forgotten that to stay in control, you need always to secure the next step ahead; and to do this you need to coax people into giving you the information you need, not blast them back into their defensive shells—or worse, as he had just done, into blatant noncooperation. You need the detachment to keep your ultimate goal in sight and to deal tactically with problems as they present themselves.

The intimidatory sales meeting breaks all these rules with one yell. I sat in on one such meeting chaired by the company owner, an unspeakable bully of a man, before whom each salesperson trembled in their boots awaiting their turn to report. The star among them had elevated "V. Int." into an art form.

"And how are Consolidated Engineering, Mike?"

"Well, their people are talking to our people and I think we are on course for some pretty exciting news regarding the Sudan job."

"Well done, Mike. Terry, how have you got on?"

"Not very well, as a matter of fact. People think our prices are too high."

"How dare you creep in here whining about our prices! Laziness, that's your problem. Sell the price, and don't bother coming here again until you've got some good news!"

Terry's nose having been comprehensively rubbed in it, he is thrown out of the window.

If you are a sales manager, try to think of your team not just as salespeople but as navigators and lookouts. "V. Int." is not much use to a ship's captain: you need to know where the sandbanks are as well as the open channels, and you wouldn't think much of a lookout who told you the way was all clear because he thought that was what you wanted to hear if the ship ran aground the next minute. Or imagine yourself on a long car journey. You ask your passenger what that sign said that you just passed, and Mr. V. Int.

says "Oh, it said Glasgow five miles." Three hours later, still no sign of Glasgow. You pass another sign.

"What did that one say?"

"That one really did say Glasgow five miles."

How can you be sure of ever arriving if you don't know where you are now? How can you be sure of achieving your outcome if you aren't properly informed about progress towards it?

Imagine a scene in sales heaven.

"Well, Terry, how did you get on?"

"Actually, it's a tough one. We are a bit adrift on price and they don't like the color. I think we're a long way off selling to them."

"Okay. How can I help to put things right, and what do you think should be the next step to bring them closer?"

If you take this line, you will see the rocks and can steer round them; safe arrival is no longer a matter of chance. Just imagine if road maps were made optimistic so as not to depress you about the real distance to your destination. It would drive you nuts: but somehow when mapping out our path to commercial success we only want to hear good news.

Some while ago we left persuaders two and three shivering on the bank of a frozen pond. Let us now return to them. The next to attempt the crossing is a huge, greasy tub of lard whose attitude to persuasion is one of pure aggression. This is the man who will boldly tell you that he has spent years in the home improvement or financial services industry and that the customer needs a bit of arm-twisting now and then. You think these tubby monsters are things of the past, commercial dinosaurs? Think again. There are still sales operators—and, much worse, training outfits— who advocate these unpleasant techniques. Not long ago I attended a training session at quite a respectable company. The speaker recommended about five books he had written, all with words like with TOUGH, WIN, and GET in the titles, and then went on to show a video that kept cutting to scenes of people physically fighting and arm-twisting to illustrate what a slippery, devious creature The Customer could be, and how it needed Firm Handling. Many widely publicized seminars put across the same message, reinforced by lots of fist-waving and finger-pointing. The atmosphere is blatantly confrontational and almost violent in its attitude to persuasion.

It doesn't convince me at all. The aggressive types who use and teach these techniques will display their own wealth as evidence of the effectiveness of their methods, and say that the large percentage of the people who go to their seminars and subsequently fail do so because they don't use the techniques they are taught. Well, even supposing this to be the case, doesn't this just beg a rather large question? I suppose a sawed-off shotgun is a great solution to the problem of a noisy neighbor, but to most people it is not morally acceptable. Most companies consist of kind, warm, reasonable human beings, and this should not exclude them from contributing to the increased profitability to be gained through successful persuasion. Quite the contrary. Bullying one set of perfectly normal people into bullying another set of perfectly normal people is in my view no way to go about business.

We have one of these louts by our pond at present. The way this creature attempts to cross to the island is to climb to the highest part of the bank and then hurl his massive bulk as far out on to the ice as possible. Sometimes, to my amazement, he will actually reach the customer in a series of huge bounces; but more often than not, the leap is followed by a sickening cracking noise as two large butterfly wings of ice rise either side of him and he sinks beneath the chilly waters.

Almost more depressing than the fact that he takes this approach in the first place is that, once pumped out and dried off, he will tell you that such setbacks are to be taken in your stride, and then proceed to drivel on about conversion rates. Now, some time ago, when I was almost tempted to believe in the arguments about acceptable success rates, I was approached by a major financial institution to help with the conversion rates achieved by their counter staff in selling investments to the public. I was told that at present they were getting a rate of around 20 percent; this daunted me a little, because the best insurance sales people rarely do much better than that. Who are the potential customers? I asked, knowing that some of the top performers in this game pounce on people in the street. I wasn't prepared for the answer.

"Oh," I was told, "mostly people who walk into the branch and say, 'I've just been left $50,000. What do you think I should do with it?'"

From that day onwards the conversion rate I have aimed for is 100 percent. You think this is unrealistic, even perhaps unfair? You probably also think that a medical student who gets 90 percent in an exam is pretty clever. You do? A mere 10 percent hole in his ability is nothing to worry about? So, when he becomes a brain surgeon, you wouldn't mind being the one in ten that is his potential kill rate? I'm not saying that I achieve 100 percent of what I set out to do, just that I aim to; and then I analyze the misses rather than accepting them as natural wastage. Dismissing failures and setbacks as unimportant or irrelevant does your prospects of success no more good than losing your temper and making people clam up about them: in both cases vital information gets swept under the carpet when it should be examined and fed back into your campaign.

The last of our trio is about to attempt the crossing of the icy pond. She puts her foot on the ice. There is a cracking and a squirting and her shoe fills with freezing water. After a moment's thought, she sets off carefully across the ice. The key is that she has assessed the potential dangers of the crossing and has a plank, a ladder, a coil of rope, and a rubber dinghy with her, and a helicopter following behind her. She encounters hazards—for example, a large hole labeled "I'm sorry, but I don't think I'll change my mind": here she uses the plank labeled "I can understand how you feel, but perhaps if you could explain why you made this decision, I could help you to improve the situation." In brief, her preparation and equipment make her success inevitable.

One dog and his sheep

People often ask me to name great salespeople I have seen, and I can very rarely call one to mind to order; but the other day I was sure I had seen the world's best performer. It was on the BBC television program *One Man and his Dog,* in a competition for sheepdogs. Each dog has to move a group of very unruly sheep from high ground, through bogs, bushes, and gateways and around all sorts of obstacles, until they are safely penned up some considerable distance from where they began. The sheep, gathered together in their starting position, quite clearly believe that they are boss, but they are also nervous and easily spooked, and mill around bleating half in arrogance, half in fear. Imagine what would happen if the dog rushed at them barking. You would have sheep scattered in all directions, the competition lost before it had begun. Most people, apart from our high-pressure friends, would accept that this is the case; but often the alternative is seen as just hanging loose by the gate and saying, "Oh, hi, sheep, it's really cool to see you. Please feel free to graze about. There's a pen at the bottom of the field if you want to shut yourself in it. I've got some brochures somewhere…anyway, if you want any help I'll be over there in the corner. Just give me a bleat if you need me."

This method tends to show a distinct lack of success as well.

What the dog does is weigh up the overall position without emotion and with a clear and realistic assessment of the job in hand. He then moves off carefully round the edge of the field so as not to startle the sheep or even make his intention clear to them. As he begins to move in from behind, the sheep, still quite confident that they are in control, move away from the dog, but towards the dog's objective. If they are slow, he moves close and they speed up; if they become skittish he will lay back and let them relax. The dog undertakes the whole task with cheerful enthusiasm and makes no noise as he moves this way and that. When the objective is achieved and the sheep are penned, no one is more surprised than they are; they had, after all, been convinced throughout that it was they who were in control.

Even if things go wrong in mid-roundup and the sheep scatter, while the shepherd may panic the dog just carries on inexorably collecting them up again, pulling them together and resuming the drive towards the pen. At the end of a difficult run, he does not slink back demoralized to his master:

"Oh, I'm really depressed. Those sheep were out to get me. I don't think I could face another lot."

No: his tongue is lolling out in a huge doggy grin, and he can hardly keep his legs still until he is given another opportunity to demonstrate his skill.

This dog gives the clearest demonstration I have ever seen of how an unpredictable group can be put through a sequence of alarming variables and still arrive at the predicted goal every time by the use of complete control.

Pin yourself down

All this will probably have given you the impression that I above all others remain in constant control of my own destiny; but, sadly, to recall a Buddhist saying from my hippie days, "He teaches that which he most needs to know himself." I am one of the most disorganized people I know; I have always been able to persuade, but usually to achieve outcomes that have just popped into my head the moment before. The reason why I am so strongly attracted to the idea of control is that chaos can sometimes become rather trying. If organization is applied to ability, the effect can be devastating. There must be surgeons who are temperamentally as shambolic as I am; so why, when they make that first incision, don't you hear them say:

"Um, now, what's actually wrong with this guy...hang on, let's have a look. Ooh, by the way, anyone got a clean scalpel on them? I've forgotten mine...."

It doesn't happen, regardless of the personality of the doctor, because it mustn't happen. Systems are put in place to prevent death by lack of organization. When I learned this, it was like learning the secret of fire. You want to get somewhere? Get a map, and you will. Motion for its own sake is like the old joke about the new motorway system: now you can drive all day and get absolutely nowhere.

I was travelling with a representative not long ago, and by way of friendly conversation asked where we were going. He looked at the road ahead and saw we were approaching a fork. One road went to Boston, the other to New York.

"Oh," he said, "Bos or New um er Boston or New York..." and with a howling of tires we took the Boston turn, pulling up a bit later outside a large factory.

"This'll do," he said, with rare decision. "We do a lot with these people."

"Why are we here?" I asked.

"Oh, courtesy call, um, you know; building bridges, keeping in touch and that."

This random scattering of ill-directed endeavor is a close cousin of the single-minded pursuit of high "call rate." This idiotic measure is supposed to indicate salespeople's work level. I was once sitting in a client's reception area when a representative came whizzing in past me, slid to a halt by the receptionist and said:

"Give me a comp slip, honey." As he left, he gave me a broad wink and waved a sheaf of similar slips at me.

"Eight today! I can go home now."

It was eleven o'clock in the morning and he had got eight V. Ints already.

My own quest for a better-regulated existence took a great leap forward when a very successful and well-organized company chairman who used my services a lot but considered me a bit of a loose cannon sat me down one day and gave me a few tips. One of these in particular has been so successful for me since that it makes me furious to think I didn't know about it earlier. Now, when I visit a client, as soon as I leave I pull out a very well-used and grubby bit of paper on which is written a series of questions I must answer.

First, did I achieve what I set out to achieve at this meeting? That might seem straightforward; but it's not so simple as it sounds, because if I am to answer Yes I have to have gone in with a clear objective in the first place. If I have to say to myself: "I don't know, I don't remember what I went there for," I give myself a sharp clip on the ear so I won't be so vague next time.

Second, have I made definite, measurable progress? In other words, have I got a second appointment, have I got agreement to do a presentation: is there a date in my diary?

Third, have I learned anything to my advantage? Well, I won't have if I haven't asked any questions. I should be asking: "So who is in charge of that?"/"When is he in?"/"Where do you get these from?"/ "How much did you say these cost?" The information gathered doesn't have to be confined to the client company, so long as it is about areas of interest to me: "So who is X [the company next door] using?" I have discovered, too, that it does no harm at all to slow the pace enough to write all this valuable stuff down. Quite the reverse, in fact: it makes one look very professional.

Fourth, how did it go overall and where could I have improved on the results I got? If I were to start again, would I do anything differently? Obviously, if I didn't get what I wanted, the answer will be yes, and I will do it differently next time.

People in my seminars ask me whether I know everything that is going to happen, whether I know what they are thinking, whether I can make them do things against their will, and thankfully the answer is no. To be over-organized all the time would be terribly boring. But the world and its people drift and bump around each other in an almost completely random way, and if you bolt a rudder on your life's boat, the effect is instantaneous and almost frightening. And when you don't need it, of course, you can take it off, stow it away, and just lie back and enjoy the trip.

6

Keeping Promises, Keeping Customers

It's boom time in the customer care industry. Everybody has jumped on to the bandwagon; even my consultancy now offers a range of stimulating customer care programs. And yet I remain very uneasy about this accelerating snowball of activity. Where did it come from, and why? Before the Second World War customer care—or "good service," as it was called—was taken for granted as an essential and integral part of successful commercial activity. Now it seems to have become an optional extra, a distinct and separate gloss to be added like an extra coat of paint. And, like an extra coat of paint, it is often applied with blithe disregard to the unattended rust corroding away underneath.

The very idea of "customer care" as a separate compartment makes me deeply suspicious, and by now it should raise your hackles too. What have we been doing so far in this book if not showing how getting customers and keeping them should be parts of the same enterprise? Is this not at the very heart of the idea of seduction we have been exploring? It seems to me that to understand why the business world is participating in a lemminglike rush into customer care programs, we need to look back at an earlier approach to achieving our ends, be they finding customers or persuading colleagues or unions to fall in with our plans.

Weasel words and parrot phrases

A large building society recently called me in to consult with them on a customer care program—not necessarily because they had any hard evidence to show that they needed one, but because everyone else had one. I had come to them recommended by one of their sister companies and the presentation to the board could have been a simple formality before getting the program under way; but I felt impelled to do my yucca-watering routine and expressed some ideas that seemed to conflict with what they believed should be a fairly simple, if also fairly expensive, project. This put them in a quandary. On the one hand, I had come with impeccable credentials, and on the other I contradicted what they thought they wanted. They did their best to get me into line, telling me that their largest competitor seemed to be getting the sorts of results they needed. How did they judge this? I inquired. By the behavior of the staff, they said; they liked the behavior that was being achieved. How did they know, I persisted, that this behavior was valuable to the business? Well, they said, it was just the sort of behavior that other "successful" customer care programs had produced. Thus I was faced with a kind of Mad Hatter's Tea Party in which the campaign's success would be measured by seeing how it compared in appearance with other companies' campaigns.

We had reached an impasse. The company then asked me to see how their competitor went about this process. To my surprise, this competitor was more than eager to show off its fabulous customer care program. This was a large company, employing more than ten thousand people nationwide. The training program had been put together by a high-profile international consultancy organization whose size of operation was exceeded only by the size of its invoices. The core of its program was to gather the client's employees in theaters, about a thousand at a time, and make them learn their lines. This would be followed up by distributing a propaganda book and posters, stickers, and badges to hammer home key phrases.

I tacked myself on to one of the mass group sessions. As I and the other thousand were ushered to our seats, I could already hear mutinous mutterings; it was clear that many of the staff felt the whole business to be an imposition. Then silence fell as the lights went down and the show began. First the chairman and the head of personnel came out to do their bit.

"Hello, everybody. I'm so glad that you have been able to manage to spare us so much of your valuable time today."

Weasel words. From what I'd heard on my way in, far from choosing to spare their valuable time for this circus, many of the staff were there because they were well aware of an underlying threat: you'd better turn up because if you don't you won't have a job to turn up to afterwards. The latest hip thinking about empowerment does work—but only if responsibility and rewards are genuinely shared, with a sincere commitment to teamwork. Thanking staff for coming to disguise the fact that you have coerced them into doing so is a piece of disingenuousness that will only increase their resentment; and that in turn is hardly conducive to their learning anything of value.

The chairman went on.

"Well, you have a treat in store today, because presenting our exciting new program of customer care is Ms. Crystal Boggins of Grabbit and Split International—so without further ado, I hand you into her care."

Lights off, followed by a burst of stirring martial music and the glare of a spotlight that picked out the figure of a woman. Power dressing is a mild way to describe the outfit of someone with shoulder pads like a football player. Her auburn hair was styled so firmly that if she moved her head quickly, the hair stood still for a moment before catching up. The whole ensemble was topped off by a silk cravat, a lot of expensive dentistry, and a high, piercing voice that was obviously the role model for every receptionist from New York to Paris.

"Hi, everyone! Oh dear, what a lot of worried faces. I can see you're all scratching your heads and saying, 'Customer care, what does customer care mean to me?' Well, boys and girls, it means a lot. The customer is the most important person in the world to us, boys and girls, because without customers we wouldn't have our jobs, would we, boys and girls, but don't look so worried, being nice to customers can be fun and perhaps we'll have just a few little giggles today."

Disregarding sounds of retching from some seats, including mine, she launched into the business.

"So, what's the first thing we want to say to our friend the customer? Anybody?"

There was a long, embarrassed silence.

"No? Aren't we forgetting our manners, boys and girls? What have we been taught to say when someone gives us something? Something as important as our very job?"

A voice from the back: "Thank you."

She went for it like an alligator for a swimming fawn, with a flurry and a flash of teeth.

"Thank you! Yes, that's right. We say, 'Thank you.' Let's hear you all say it."

A mumbled, discordant sound came from the assembled masses: "Thnkyu."

"Oh dear, I think some of us have left our voices at home today. I'm sure we can do better. Come on now—"

This exhortation is reinforced by savage glares towards the audience from the table containing the Board. The reply is still ragged, but louder: "Thank you."

"That's better—but what are we thanking them for?"

Silence.

"We're thanking them for calling the All Atlantic Building Society, boys and girls, aren't we? So we say: 'Thank you for calling the All Atlantic Building Society,' don't we? Let's hear you." The response came back in a medley of tones and volumes.

"Thank you for calling the All Atlantic Building Society."

"That's good, boys and girls, but our customers are still a little bewildered because they don't know who we are. You can't be someone's friend unless you know their name, can you, boys and girls, and we want the customer to be our friend, so let's tell them our name and say thank you for calling the All Atlantic Building Society, my name's Crystal. Now come on, it's your turn, boys and girls, nice and loud now—"

"Thank you for calling the All Atlantic Building Society, my name's Crystal."

"Oh gosh, that was nice and loud, but I think you ought to use

your own names—unless we have a lot of Crystals here today!"
The chairman flashes a "laugh, you bastards" look at the audience and dredges up some nervous tittering and a few attempts
at an ingratiating guffaw from middle management.

"Okay, let's try again."

"Thank you for calling the All Atlantic Building Society, my
name is Brian/Kevin/Sue/Doreen/Steve/Colin..." The noise degen-
erates into a mishmash of names.

"There we are; we're getting the hang of it, aren't we, boys and
girls? Now, what are we all here for? We are here to help our
customers, aren't we? But do you know what they need help with?
Well then, we need to ask them by saying, 'How may I help you?'
Can we all say, 'How may I help you?'"

We are indeed all getting the hang of this awful charade by
now and sing out: "How may I help you?" This puts Ms. Boggins
into a paroxysm of ecstasy.

"Ooh, that's lovely! Now, boys and girls, let's see if we can put
it all together: 'Thank you for calling the All Atlantic Building
Society, my name's Crystal, how may I help you?'"

We shriek back again and again until it is like some kind of
revivalist chant. All of us have very sore throats and most of us
have a headache.

If the recipients of this performance are allowed to take it or
leave it, it's fair to bet that "leave it" will be the preferred option.
Even with the best training, "leave it" is often the choice, because
people find it hard to change their established way of doing
things. A friend was watching me playing pitch and putt golf with
my kids one day—a fairly hazardous business because I have lots
of fun with a slash and hack technique that has the ball flying in
all directions. A keen golfer, this friend couldn't bear to watch
such sacrilege and attempted to show me the correct way to hit
the ball. Under his tuition I addressed the ball, bent this arm,
straightened that leg and adjusted my grip *so.* By the time this
series of contortions was complete, I could feel every inch of
elastic in my foundation garments straining beyond endurance,
and when I hit the ball, all hell broke loose. Everything that could

be strained or dislocated was, and the ball shot vertically up into the air, something even I hadn't achieved before. Grimacing with pain, I thanked my friend profusely for his advice and waited till he was out of sight, when I resumed my old style.

Anyone who is trained in anything has a tendency to go back

to the old style unless there is a strong incentive not to; and that takes us straight back to carrot and stick. In this case, the Board had already made a large investment in the wisdom and performance art of Grabbit and Split International and had decided that leaving it was not an option. The chairman walked onto the stage clapping.

"Well, I'm sure we have all learned something of value today, and I'm sure that you will go back to your branches full of enthusiasm for this program. I and other members of my team will be ringing round you all next week, and woe betide any of you who aren't using the words you have learned today."

So there is the bind. If they are given the choice, they will choose not to do it, so they aren't given the choice and do it under duress, which makes the effect even worse. Next time you go into your friendly little local branch of the All Atlantic Building Society, instead of getting:

"Hello, my dear, got a bit more to pay in? How lovely, soon be able to afford that vacation then. Little Mickey over his measles yet?" you will get:

"Thank you for visiting the All Atlantic Building Society, my name's Doreen, how may I help you?"

Who'll warn Caligula?

The situation begins to resemble *Invasion of the Body Snatchers* or *The Stepford Wives,* with all the normal people being taken over one by one. And yet the powers that be seem to be incapable of seeing how destructive this artificial "customer care" can be. Well, who's going to tell them? It comes back down to the management attitudes we looked at in the last chapter. However much lip service is paid to trendy concepts like empowerment and participation, if employees know that their reward for calling management decisions into question is going to be a boot up the backside, managers will never be told what they need to know. As I said earlier, I'm pretty sure that the little kid who cast doubt on the glamour of the king's new clothes fell foul of the tailor's heavies.

This is a real problem, because very few people indeed will listen to criticism that threatens their own security. Some years ago I was asked to test a major insurance company's procedure for recruiting senior staff. I was introduced as a candidate for a senior planning role and went through a preliminary sifting stage conducted by a member of the personnel department. He asked me the usual questions, which included: "What's the first thing you would do if you joined us, Mr. Burch?"

I replied: "I would fire you." His jaw dropped and he asked why.

"Because you don't do your job well."

Anger replaced surprise. How dare I say that when I didn't even know him? I told him that now he knew that I would fire him he would be most unlikely to offer me the job, thereby proving that his interests came before those of the company in selecting new staff.

The point is that no one wants to undermine their own position. This is a constant problem for consultants, who must always resist the temptation to tell clients what they want to hear. When we hear the news of the downfall of another world dictator, we wonder that no one told him it was coming; but no matter what my day rate was, I wouldn't dare tell Hitler that the Eastern Front was a disaster, nor would I tell Caligula that his sexual excesses and irrational behavior might be his undoing. In fact, I do tell more than most, and have earned a degree of undesirable notoriety as a result. In the next chapter we will see how complaints from customers can be a real help in getting around this difficulty, because if you can bring yourself to listen to them properly, customers will often tell you the real truth that no one else will dare point out to you.

It's a big "if." There is a large national travel organization that I won't name which insists that it has customer care down to a fine art. I travelled with them one day and saw a young girl lying in a pool of her own vomit and a man trying to claim his reserved seat being threatened with violence by the huge lout who was occupying it. When I complained about the fact that I was put in a smoking area, I was told to write to the company. Eventually a member of staff was found and shown this hellish scene; he said he would fetch a colleague. We never saw him again. Now, about this time the chairman of this company gave an interview in which he said how proud he was of his customer care program, on which he had spent millions. He had a pile of survey reports a mile high to support his claims of success. The interviewer had another point of view to put.

"But your customers say your service is a disgrace."

The reply was a classic: "Well, they must be mistaken. I have firm evidence here to prove our customer care is second to none."

My response to this is: If the customer says it's bad service, it *is* bad service. Is this man a fool, or has the truth been kept from him so faithfully he just can't see it? Marie Antoinette may have sincerely wanted to understand the peasants when she started her farm at Versailles, but the courtiers gave her washed and perfumed sheep. Tom Peters famously suggested management by wandering around to keep directly in touch with what is going on; but some readers of his book have obviously twisted this into having an extra layer of Wandering Managers who are no more likely than anyone else to tell the top brass what is actually going on. The senior management of one train company decided to wander around to get in touch with their customers (no longer "passengers"). They bravely went in person among the people waiting for delayed trains, offering mobile phones to businesspeople who were going to be late for their meetings and picture books to unhappy children, all in the name of customer care—when what they should really have been doing was making sure the trains ran on time and therefore rendering these stratagems unnecessary.

So how do we cut through all this obfuscation and misdirected charging around and get to the heart of what customer care really means? I think we need to have a look at what our business is actually about, and accept that its first priority is to be commercially successful, or, in other words, to make a profit. This is nothing to be ashamed of; go on, admit it, beat your chest with your fists and cry: "I want to make a monster profit!" Well, if you upset your customers, you won't. That is the best reason for customer care.

Boomerangs and banknotes

Often this means taking a long-term view, and some decisions which seem commercial folly eventually pay dividends because they keep the customers coming back. Conversely, an idea that seems a very good way to make a quick buck or two may well make the customer think twice about returning, once they realize they've been had. A very successful entrepreneur wrote a book in which he described the basic principle of customer care as the "boomerang effect." As a child, among the toy weapons I had was a boomerang that someone had given me. I spent hours practicing to get it to come back, refining my skill and trying new variants of my throw, all with that sole objective. Apply the same single-mindedness to your customers and the focus is dramatic. Charge for the carrier bag, will they come back? Stick on an unexpected service charge, will they come back? Put your small toys and sweets where little hands can reach them, will they come back? Let the computer sue them for a small invoice, will they come back? All sound commercial ideas, until you apply the boomerang principle.

I have another name for this guiding principle: I call it the village idiot effect. This is based on the story of a village idiot who, if offered two banknotes, one a fiver and the other a twenty-dollar bill, would always take the fiver. His reputation spread and busloads of people came to offer him money. Idiot? Far from it. If once he took the larger note, his career would be over. Likewise, we must be careful what we take out of our customers if we want them to come back for more. The central point is that your customer care policy must be based on gaining the desired response from the customer—more business. Yet again we come back to the same fundamentals: gather accurate information and keep your objective firmly in view. My client who sent me off for an afternoon's torment in the hands of Ms. Crystal Boggins was more concerned to match what his competitors were doing than to pursue his real objective: happy, satisfied, loyal customers and more of them.

In contrast to the robotic verbosity that passes for customer care in many companies now, another worrying trend that has recently become apparent is creeping inertia. Some people have clearly become concerned about the methods their sales forces were using and have decided to put a stop to them. The car trade is a case in point. Desperate to shake off its back-street car lot image and yet maintain profitability, retailers started indulging heavily in bizarre sales systems which relied on a lot of spurious science to bemuse and pressurize customers. What this produced was not only disgruntled, pressured customers but also pressured, disgruntled sales staff, and a lot of these systems were abandoned as discredited, to widespread relief. The problem then was that the sales staff seemed to be completely neutered and failed to do anything very much.

The great Sigmund Freud was giving a lecture one day when a tearful girl stood up in the audience and cried out:

"Professor Freud, you have robbed me of all my beliefs. What am I to believe in now?"

Freud replied: "One of the labors of Hercules was to clear out the Augean stables. He was not expected to refill them."

A more recent but equally plaintive cry was uttered by a correspondent of one of the national newspapers, who wrote to say that he missed the attention of the back-street car dealers. "I know they were out to rob me," he admitted, "but at least they paid me a little attention while they did it."

What had happened showed yet again the perils of seeing "selling" as something not very nice that is done by a small number of rather objectionable employees, chosen for their bumptious temperament, and ignored as far as possible by all respectable members of the organization—and of seeing "selling" as something quite separate from the continuing relationship between vendor and customer. It's neither fair nor sensible to stick a badge on someone and say, "Okay, Smith, you're Sales. The future of this company depends on your ability to sell the product." The "It's nothing to do with me, it's a sales problem" approach has been the downfall of many companies.

I recently conducted a secret survey of car dealers for a motoring magazine. The dealers did not come out of this very well, and their sales staff, misinterpreting the article, felt that I was having a go at them. Quite the contrary; their failure to sell me a car was not their fault but the fault of everyone else who worked with them. Some large dealers had just two or three salespeople on duty and when they were tied up I was ignored; no end of managers, cleaners, mechanics, and office staff walked past me without a second glance. In your business, everyone can sell and everyone should sell. This is where the power of true customer care lies.

Civility and servility

At this point we should address a cultural issue. I don't know where you are reading this book, but your attitude to service may be colored according to which side of the Atlantic you are on. If you are American, you may be surprised and even possibly slightly offended to learn that British audiences sometimes accuse me of putting forward a view that is "too American"— whatever they actually mean by that. In fact I believe that both cultures have a lot to offer each other and each has gaps which the other can help to fill. The United States is a nation whose whole history is based on personal freedom and individual rights; that is bound to create a different kind of attitude to service from that which prevails in Europe, where many of the best traditions of service are related to being *in* service within a much more formally hierarchical society.

Although what I call the Jeeves model is dying out in the UK's swiftly relaxing culture it can still be breathtakingly superb when applied. Recently I spoke at a conference attended by some of the principal captains of British industry, held at a premier hotel. I stayed on for the glittering entertainment of the evening's dinner, which by the small hours, lubricated by a few hundred bottles of fine wine, was getting rather wild in an impeccably public-school sort of way. After an inning or two of cricket with a sign board and some rather ripe grapefruit, a senior director of one of the major retail groups diverted us by swinging from a chandelier, which took its revenge by tearing from the ceiling in a shower of sparks and plaster. The acrobat was left sitting in the middle of the ballroom with a drunken smile on his face and an ornate Victorian chandelier cradled in his arms. A hush fell as the duty manager swept in, subtly resplendent in dark jacket, striped trousers, silver tie, and silver waistcoat. The crowd parted like the Red Sea as this apparition approached the reveler, in front of whom he stopped, paused, and gave a stiff little bow. Then he said:

"May I take that for you, sir?"

He left with the chandelier and no further comment.

The next morning at breakfast I saw the erstwhile Tarzan and remarked on the quality of service. He smiled wryly and showed me his little card of expenses. It read: "Teas £4.70; papers £3.49;

drinks £27.40; to repair and rehang chandelier £880.27; telephone calls £6.30." It was assumed that while if a gentleman wished to take his pleasure by swinging on the furnishings it was not for the management to demur, equally, said gentleman could have no objection to paying for said pleasures.

The trouble is that service on this model is too closely tied to traditional assumptions about social class. Since deference has gone out of fashion, we have become so wary of seeming to admit that another person is our social superior that we are often reluctant to show common civility lest it appear as servility. Americans, on the other hand, more often take the view that everyone, of whatever social position, can demand good service. The girl in the polyester jumper at the corner diner, who wishes you a nice day when she serves you, can change to go home and have her windshield washed and be wished a nice day herself by the guy at the gas station. There is no stigma, no shame in treating others well, for it is your right to be treated well.

It is also in your interests to contribute to the success of your company, as it preserves your job—something many of us English have still to learn. Not long ago I heard a member of the royal family criticize British industry and I wondered why, because quality control programs have given us a level of product reliability that is second to none. That night I fell into a fitful sleep and dreamed that a prince was being shown round a bearing factory somewhere in the north of England. He stopped to speak to a man on a bearing machine.

"Oh, hello, your Royal Highness."

"How do you do. What exactly do you do here, then?"

"Can't say I really know, your Highness. I think we make bearings an' that."

"And your managing director?"

"Mr. Fazakerly? Oh, 'e's a stupid old sod, but I keep out of 'is way, 'e keeps out o' mine and that's the way I like it."

"And what are these bearings used for?"

"I sure don't know. Tell you a funny story, though: railways bought six hundred of 'em for t'new high-speed trains. Four miles outside Halifax, all the bloody wheels fell off! Eh, me and the lads had a right laff over that!"

My dream swept me over the Atlantic to the Kowalsky Bearing Company of Ohio, where again I saw the prince talking to a man on a machine.

"Well, howdedo, your Highness, great to have you here!"

"Good morning. And what is it you do here?"

"What do we do? I tell you, sir, we make just about the finest damn bearings in the whole wide world."

"Really. And your managing director?"

"You mean our president, Mr. Kowalsky? D'you know, that guy came here in the last war with nothing but an iron bedstead and a ladies' nail file. That man was making bearings with his bare hands. I'm real proud to be working for him."

"And these bearings that you make, what are they used for?"

"Take a look here, your Highness, that's the state railroad and every one of them railcars is running on Kowalsky bearings. After one million miles we check 'em over, and there is no wear; and that is because they are the finest bearings in the world."

Now, the American approach may make us Europeans feel slightly nauseous, but ask yourself whose bearings you would buy. If every employee is saying what a great firm they work for, it tends to get believed; but the rule in Britain seems to be that if you work in a pie factory, there is one thing you would never eat.

"Don't eat that, lad, I work in that place and we had a rat in the other day. I'll swear it went in the chicken and mushroom."

Filthy Miguel's and the importance of expectations

Some of you reading this may be outraged at the broad sweep of my brush and the apparent arrogance of my judgments when I don't even know how hard you are working at the service side of your enterprise. In fact I am well aware that companies are making great efforts and are improving all the time; but there is even a snag here, because that improvement can itself cause problems. If you know your outfit is truly awful it may be that the best thing to do is just to revel in it (until you go bust, of course), because getting better contains a hidden threat.

I am a great fan of Spain and was in the middle of a very enjoyable stay there once when I needed to find a restaurant to feed my tribe. I'd left it a bit late, and the only place still open was Filthy Miguel's, which I'd been warned about: his paella had earned the affectionate nickname of Salmonella Pie. Hunger overcame resistance and in we went, to be greeted by a laughing man who looked startlingly like a Mexican bandit. There was no need to ask for a menu as the current specialities *à la maison* were liberally spread over his vest. His family joined us, the wine flowed, and when the huge paella appeared, complete with tentacles, I threw caution to the winds and plunged in with abandon. That night I slept like a baby and I have nothing but the fondest memories of Filthy Miguel's.

Why was it so wonderful? Because I was expecting much worse and the experience was superior to the expectation. Now, if you have any sort of a marketing department, or if you handle publicity yourself, I bet you wouldn't say:

"Eat with us, you might not get food poisoning," or:

"Never knowingly given a refund," or:

"You've tried the rest and we are pretty awful as well really, so…"

But if you don't say any of these things then your slogans are raising customers' expectations and one of my personal definitions of customer care is giving a customer 100 percent of what they have been led to expect. What exactly have you led your customers to expect? It is only natural for you to make your customers expect the best; but if things then fall apart, you have to ask whose fault it is. We will be going into complaints in more detail in the next chapter, but for the moment consider how many complaints are prompted by disappointment. I go on holiday and find that my hotel is sandwiched between the sewage works and the Jumping Gorilla disco. Who wrote the brochure? What would have happened if I had been warned?

A client of ours owns a large nursery that produces house

plants for the high street retailer. He employs a team of highly competent representatives, a bunch of people who are in fact some of the nicest, funniest, and most talented salespeople I know; and yet their colleagues have a bone to pick with them. When one of these representatives has a selling trip planned, he or she goes down into the nursery and selects a perfect specimen plant for a sales sample. I would do the same; but the nursery and despatch staff wish they wouldn't, because, they say, this quality of plant cannot be duplicated in every case and therefore the promise that the salesperson has made with his vegetable ace cannot always be kept.

A consultancy I recently visited expressed this idea in terms of a seesaw with expectation on one end and experience on the other. When experience sinks below expectation, the result is disappointment. Now, I wholeheartedly agree with this analysis; but they used this message in their customer care seminars as a whip-crack to encourage staff to fulfill the promise their employers have made, whereas seesaws should swing two ways. If one end is loaded too heavily, no amount of effort can restore the balance. If employers give their customers unreasonable expectations, there is no way their employees, on whom the burden of fulfilling these expectations is placed, can respond adequately.

A recent television advertising campaign shows a trendy young man driving a competitively priced hatchback at speed on a rough desert road. A beautiful young girl slumbers in the passenger seat, despite the speed, but all is not well: there is an annoying squeak in the otherwise quiet car. It becomes apparent in a roundabout and humorous way that the squeak comes not from the car but from the swinging of the sleeping beauty's huge pendant earrings. Very clever, and very funny, but are they suggesting that all you can ever hear in this car is your partner's earrings squeaking? That's some promise—and who is going to keep it? Not the advertising company, that's for sure, nor even the manufacturer's slick marketing executives. The recipient of your complaint is more likely to be a very surprised little mechanic in the boonies. Imagine him, sitting in the sun on an upturned bucket eating his cheese and onion sandwiches, when you screech to a halt inches from his toecaps and shout:

"Look here, I bought this thing a week ago and the level of noise would never allow me to hear my girlfriend's earrings squeaking!"

Machines don't keep promises

Here we meet another very important point about customer expectations. Whenever the machinery fails, the system always defaults to the human component. British Rail came up a while ago with the now notorious slogan "We're getting there"; when they didn't "get there"—or rather, when we didn't get there because their trains were late and we missed our connection—we would go and find a platform guard to shout at. Well, he hadn't made the promise; the Board of British Rail had approved that slogan; but they weren't there to shout at. I'm sure that British Rail were making every effort to "get there," but effort is not enough if the people who have to operate the machine cannot deliver on the promise. Nor is a layer of artificial "customer care" applied over the top of a disappointing service going to remedy matters. Teaching the guards to call passengers "customers" and to wish them a nice day is no use at all if the trains don't run on time.

In the case of the railways, mechanical improvements weren't keeping up with attempts to improve the human face presented to the public. More often, improvements in technology are not matched by improvements in the human element. When companies examine the areas in which they can improve, they very often concentrate on mechanical developments, especially in these days of rapid technological advance when firms naturally want to keep up with the state of the art. What they tend to forget or gloss over is that the more technology can do, the more humans have to be able to do if the technology breaks down. Computers can open doors, pay bills, plan your holiday, and prevent you having to stand in line—and they can replace many expensive staff. On the other hand, they say that to err is human but if you really want to foul things up you need a computer.

"Ladies and gentlemen, you are aboard the world's first fully automated aircraft. We are cruising at fifty thousand feet. There is no human hand involved in the flying of this vessel, and therefore nothing can go wrong...can go wrong...can go wrong..."

When I was a kid, a soda-pop machine was a dangerous and cantankerous brute. It was a large steel cabinet and it bore dire warnings about how it wanted your money presented: copper first, then silver. If you complied with these stipulations, and waited patiently for each coin to drop separately, you might just qualify for a pull at the drawer. This in itself was a challenge requiring strength and determination. Should you be tempted to rest in mid-pull, all would be lost: the ratchet would reset itself and your money was forfeit. If you were successful, a warm, chipped bottle of pop would be presented—useless, of course, because a frayed piece of string would stand testament to the stolen bottle opener.

Naturally, the mighty soft drinks companies could not tolerate their wonderful products being so abused and set their marketeers, engineers, and technocrats on to the problem. The result is there for all to see, in every sports center, club, and college in the land: a gleaming, illuminated structure that seems to have landed from the planet Zarg. As you approach, it invites you to drink a delicious nectar—don't worry whether you have the right coins, put in any money, it will give you change. Its panels light up and it entices you in seductive tones to make your selection, offering diet, decaffeinated, or sports-orientated cola, served at exactly five degrees Centigrade.

Faultless service, yes: but even in this utopian device there is a time bomb ticking away. The first clue to this is the tatty brown manila envelope stuck on by its gummy bits to the front panel among the illuminated plastic and stainless steel. Scrawled on it in felt tip pen is the message: "Catering staff can accept no responsibility for money lost in this machine." The second is a rather scratched gold sticker on the side of the machine which reads: "Supplied and maintained by Skoggits Automatics, New Jersey."

The fateful day comes; the machine fails and we lose our money. Obediently we ring Skoggits. The phone rings and rings and rings. Finally it is answered.

"Hello." This tone of voice could only be produced by someone wearing nothing but a vest and grubby trousers while chewing gum and scratching his belly at the same time.

"Oh, hello. Um, I'm afraid I have just lost some money in one of your machines."

"So?"

"Well, I rather wondered what to do."

Replies to this remark vary from the unhelpful to the unprintable. As technological capabilities and mechanical service improve, failure causes a sudden and rapid default to a human element which is completely out of touch and cannot cope. Some have tried to solve this problem by attempting to apply the principles of mechanical improvement to people. Why not? You can rewrite the marketing campaign, you can refit a shop, you can update literature; perhaps you can refit staff. How this idea gained credence is beyond me: if you have a poor football team that loses every match, it doesn't help to build a new stadium, or to buy new team strips, or, strangest of all, to change the names of the players.

"Your play is disgusting, Smith. You are no longer a quarterback, but we are pleased to tell you that you are now a counterattack strategic defense executive."

I worked a while ago with a chairman of a firm of fast food outlets, and they sent me to test the competition. I was served by a huge blob of a boy wearing a badge saying "My name is Kevin. I'm here to help" and clothed in a brightly colored boiler suit three sizes too small. The whole ensemble was topped off by a jaunty baseball cap. I took my burger to a table and had just taken a bite when a door nearby exploded open. Out of it backed an apparition with a huge rear end jammed into a dreadful parody of a business suit. In one hand she held a broom and in the other a

spray can of polish. She thundered around whacking people's
ankles with the broom and spraying their French fries. She was
too quick for me and had polished the remains of my lunch before
I could get them out of her way. Seconds later this dervish had
vanished back through another door like some nightmare version
of a Bavarian cuckoo clock. I rushed up to the counter.

"Who the hell was that, Kevin?"

"Oh, that was your hostess."

Calling the cleaner a hostess doesn't do any more for me than
dressing her in what look like a bank clerk's castoffs, and I
wondered where on earth the company's rulers had got their
ideas from. Actually, I had a pretty good idea. I could just imagine
the board of directors sitting in a darkened theater at the behest
of their very expensive marketing consultants and hearing a
voice ring out:

"Ladies and gentlemen, Grabbit and Split International have
pride in presenting the image that takes Hamburgers Universal
into the twenty-first century!"

Throbbing beat music emanates from myriad speakers, and
down from the ceiling in a cloud of dry ice descends a spaceship.
It lands, and out leap a group of young dancers...Didn't anyone
pause to think that a colored boiler suit might look a bit different
on a slim black male dancer from how it will look on poor old
Kevin in Brooklyn? Clearly not; so poor old Kevin stands there
serving half-pounders in a boiler suit so tight it's flossing his
bottom and desperately trying to understand his company's
promise, let alone deliver it.

Of course, your enterprise is nothing like this. You are
dedicated to bringing about real improvement in your products
and in the service you offer to your customers. But just how far
does this commitment go? Some years ago, when Tom Peters's *In
Search of Excellence* hit the business book bestseller list, everybody I spoke to was suddenly searching for excellence; but with
certain modifications for the sake of convenience. I remember
one client writing to us to say that the training program we were
developing for him must be shaped by his company's unstinting

and uncompromising dedication to Excellence. This was all fine; but he had then gone on to write:

"Of course, it must be understood that this excellence will be achieved within the boundaries of a tight budget and the constraints of good staff discipline."

I smell danger here. You may be sincerely dedicated to excellence—or, as I would prefer to put it, to constantly improving quality—but the temptation is always to concentrate on honing the mechanical aspects of service at the expense of the human aspects. Technology holds out the wonderful prospect of reducing staffing levels and costs while expanding and developing your operation. You run a tight ship, you say, your sails trimmed to perfection: but take this sailing analogy further for a moment and imagine this craft in more detail. Every rope is taut; the sails are humming and every inch of speed is being gained from the available rigging; the crew have been reduced to a minimum because all that is really needed is your firm hand on the wheel. This is maximum speed for minimum output achieved at the price of flexibility. When a squall breaks, all hell is let loose. That is when you need your crew. When mechanical service fails, you need the very best personnel to deal with the damage and put it right. The more sophisticated the technology, the more you are asking of your staff and the more you need to equip them to do.

The whole operation must be in balance, like the seesaw; and yet without stagnating. Expectations must not shoot ahead of experience; but good experiences lead people to expect as good *and better* next time. When you enjoy a meal at a restaurant and recommend it to your friends, it is awful if they then have a lousy meal; but even if they love it too, have you noticed how it so often doesn't appear quite so good the next time you go? Your expectations have been raised by the first good experience and you are now expecting even better. If you are trying to be the best, you will have to keep trying for ever. Unlike dear old Filthy Miguel's, you have made a promise and now you will have to keep it or risk disappointing your customers and thus losing them.

Caring for customers consists fundamentally of giving them at least 100 percent of what they have been led to expect, whether through advertising, sales efforts, or experience.

You know that you cannot stand still; but if you are going to go on making mechanical advancements, you must take your people with you. Your improvements may be computerized temperature control on your ovens, electric doors, automatic sales ordering, or a price list on floppy disk; whatever form they take, you must sell them to your staff before you ask the staff to sell them to your customers. You must enable your employees and colleagues to understand the promise you have made so that they will help you to keep it. This will not mean humiliating them in bizarre clothing or teaching them parrot phrases; it will mean undertaking a caring, gentle explanation of your dreams for the future. They must have a stake in this future, or neither you nor they will get there. Every member of your staff can and should promote the company's success; but if they aren't committed to your ideas, there is little chance of their taking the responsibility they need to assume if they are to play their part in your success.

7

Welcoming Complaints

I have very little desire to do anything unless there is a point to it or, in business-speak, an objective. I don't call my customer care program a customer care program but refer to it as a "profitable consumer handling course," because unless the customer handling practices taught result in improved profits there is no point in using them. Whenever I am asked to undertake a project, one of my first questions is: Why? What is it my client needs to achieve? The answer is very often: to improve service and reduce complaints. Very laudable, I'm sure, I say: but why do you want to reduce complaints?

"Well," with a laugh, "no one wants complaints, do they?"

Don't they? Maybe they should. This is another area in which it is very dangerous to make what seem obvious assumptions.

Various stances can be taken towards complaints. The first is to assert that we get no justified complaints, that people who do complain are troublemakers and that we are better off without them. This is in fact an excellent attitude for bringing about a reduction of complaints, because a very simple formula applies: zero customers = zero complaints. There may of course be one or two tiresome commercial ramifications associated with following this course, but who cares? No complaints. Marvelous.

Would you drive five miles with a rotten pineapple?

The next choice is to accept that we get occasional complaints—

111

but we are brilliant at handling them, and anyone who says we aren't is an idiot. These can be some of the saddest cases. Our local supermarket has instituted a superb complaints handling procedure by which customers can bring back goods if they are not satisfied with them and not only get a full refund, but get the goods replaced as well. This is very generous, and so I was rather surprised to see a new brand name appearing in our kitchen cupboards.

"Here," I said, "don't you shop at thingy's any more?'

"No, their stuff's rotten."

Apparently, it was a pineapple that broke the camel's back. When it was cut open, this expensive bit of fruit was found to be brown inside. It was then thrown in the bin with a cry of: "That's the last time I shop at that place!"

But we could have got a free pineapple and our money back. I asked why the offer had not been taken up.

"You must be kidding. If you think I'm driving five miles with a rotten sticky pineapple just to get a couple of dollars back, you're crazy."

The question here is this: is the supermarket using what they believe is a sophisticated complaints handling procedure as an automatic quality control technique? Because if they are, it's not working. If customers don't think it's worth going back with their defective goods, despite the apparent generosity of the scheme, the store will not get a true measure of the actual dissatisfaction of customers: there will be no perceptible increase in complaints, and if the volume of customers falls off, there will be no evidence to connect this with the quality of the merchandise. A complaint doesn't stop being a complaint because it doesn't get back to the ears of the vendor. "What the eye don't see, the heart don't grieve over" is a wonderful old saying, provided we are not talking about a falling piano, in which case if the eye don't see the heart is likely to get stopped.

The next possibility is to perfect our product or service to the point where there could be no possibility of any complaints. If the pineapple had been perfect, there would have been no problem.

Of course, we should be doing precisely this every minute of the day, striving for constant improvement towards the ideal: but apart from the little dark cloud hanging over this elevating thought, namely that you have to work pretty hard to be perfect, there lurks here another misunderstanding about what a complaint is. You might think you had achieved perfection; but if the customer says it is no good, then it is no good. You are in business, and if you have a perfect product the customer doesn't like, it isn't perfect. I know people who would complain in heaven: "It's boring here, I hate harp music, and sitting on this damp cloud in a nightshirt is doing my hemorrhoids no good at all."

The final option, and the one I prefer, is actually to encourage people to complain. Yet again, I must sound a warning about jumping to conclusions. I'm not talking about giving people reason to grumble; I'm talking about dragging out of people what it is that they really think. Now, I know that complaints contain the news that we don't want to hear. We don't enjoy hearing that our staff have been abusive, that our food tastes foul, that our prices are way ahead of the competition, that our quality has slipped. We don't want to hear these things; but we need to. We have to know, or we will never be able to put things right. We are back to the need for accurate information, without which we will never be able to get people to do what we want them to do.

If you are not president or chairman of your company, perhaps having read this you feel that your board does not have the right attitude. Are you going to rush off now and show them this passage? No? Nor would I. This may be part of the problem. The Bible says God knows of a single fallen sparrow; company presidents (many of whom think that they are God anyway) should know of a single fallen customer, and not just for pastoral reasons.

Complaints build business

The reason why I have something of a messianic zeal on this point is that I have discovered that complaints can actually build business. A complicated survey that I looked at confirmed my hunch that this was so; for the sake of sanity and clarity, I have simplified their mathematical calculations to sensible levels. It seems that out of a hundred people who buy a product and have absolutely no trouble with it at all, about forty say that they would buy again. If a hundred people buy a product and have a problem that is poorly dealt with, only five of these would buy again. (I can never understand those five; still, I suppose there's nothing so queer as folk.) Now the crunch: if a hundred people buy something that develops a fault that is dealt with well, *eighty* of them would buy again. In other words, if you do have complaints and handle them properly, you get more return business than if you had no complaints at all. (Don't confuse this with the pineapple story; we are talking here about no complaints at all, meaning no dissatisfaction, not just no complaints reaching the shop.)

If you find this hard to swallow, imagine another scene. A woman is driving along in a six-month-old car when all of a sudden it expires at the roadside in a cloud of steam. Before she can even start cursing it, a man on a parachute has landed just feet from her front bumper. He says:

"I'm so sorry this has happened to you, but if you glance over your shoulder you will see a transporter pulling in behind your car with our very latest model on board. Please use it as your own until we have repaired your car and returned it to you."

When the breakdown victim returns home that evening, her own car is back in her driveway, not only fixed but sparkling clean; and when she looks through its window, she sees on the front seat a huge bouquet and a note saying:

"Dear Mrs. Smith, we are so sorry to have let you down. Please accept these flowers and theater tickets as tokens of our respect and to assure you of our best service at all times."

If it ain't broke, you can't fix it

What this has shown Mrs. Smith is that this car, like all cars, is capable of breaking down. What it has also shown her is that this supplier will give her a standard of service she wouldn't bet on being matched elsewhere. Would you risk changing if you were her? If I have had a product that was unfailingly, even boringly reliable, I often fancy a change. If I have had no service, that proves no service is needed, so there's nothing to stop me roving.

I recently read about a customer who was so furious about being ripped off by a company that he said he would not complain. That's right: *not* complain. He said that complaining to a company did them a favor, allowing them to see where they could improve, and he had no desire to do this company any favors.

Strangely enough, complaints—audible complaints—are quite hard to get hold of, even from people who aren't hiding them for malicious reasons. Most people don't like to complain and much prefer to have a good grumble when they get home. This is what we must change, and it takes quite a lot of persistence. When the waiter sidles up to you and actually asks you, "Is everything all right, sir?" you say "Yes," and on the way home swear that you will never eat there again.

The waiter should have grabbed you by the throat, put his nose to yours and said:

"Now come on, there must be something, you can't tell me we are perfect in every detail."

"No, no," you croak, "it was lovely."

His fingers should tighten.

"Come on! What was wrong?"

"Oh, all right," gulping for air, "if you insist, the chips could have been hotter."

Before we get on to the best way of handling this lovingly extracted complaint, let's consider its value. First, we get to hear of the problem before anyone else does, and can deal with it swiftly. An untreated complaint is like an untreated wound: it festers and gets worse. Stories abound in all walks of life that bear this out. It is said that if a politician ignores the protests of one disgruntled voter, he can expect to lose 400 votes at the next election, which means that one person can infect another 399 with her germ of dissatisfaction. According to another version of the same formula, one unhappy customer will tell at least twenty other people what happened to him (with embellishments as he gathers steam), whereas we would be lucky if a happy one would tell even one other. In other words, if 95 percent of your customers are happy, that other 5 percent who aren't can create a hundred enemies for you who will outnumber the ninety-five friends you started off with.

Just numbers? You think I'm exaggerating again? Contemplate two little stories. One of our clients is a major furniture retailer. One day, some ten years ago, a young couple bought a three-piece suite which they put on the roof of their car and took home. Apparently the suite was very comfortable and they have enjoyed sitting on it for the last ten years. Now, I bet that's a story you'll be telling all round the party circuit. It isn't? Why not? All right, try this one instead. Another couple went to the same shop and picked out the most expensive leather suite. Their car roof rack wasn't big enough to take it, so the shop arranged for a carrier to deliver it. This carrier arrived at the couple's home late on the Friday evening and rang the doorbell: no reply. This suite was the driver's last delivery of the day and if he could get rid of it he would be free for the weekend. He decided to leave it around the back of the house on the lawn, where the couple would see it. Well, they would have seen it if they hadn't been in the middle of a three-week holiday at the time—the wettest three weeks since records began. When they got home, they didn't have a new suite, they had a new compost heap.

The second tale amuses you more? You are more likely to tell that at dinner parties? Yet while both are true, it is the first, the admittedly boring one, the "non-event," that represents the norm. This firm sells one million suites a year, and over ten years, the boring story represents 9,999,999 customers, the interesting story just one. It's that one you need to find out about before some clever dick writes about it in a business book.

Look for the other seven-eighths of the iceberg

The next wonderful thing a complaint will do for you is to give you a view of a possible trend. Let's go back to the restaurant. You have managed to squeeze out of one customer the admission that the chips weren't hot enough. Now, obviously that customer has to be looked after; but, working on the principle that most people don't like to complain, you might well suspect that he isn't the only one affected. You should suspect many plates of cold chips, many customers grumbling to each other on their way home. You need to find out the cause. Go to the kitchen.

"One of the customers' chips were cold. How did that happen?"

"Well, Billy discovered that nearly everyone is having chips, so he put out thirty plates of chips and I put the appropriate fish or whatever on when it's ordered."

If that one person hadn't uttered his complaint, you would have gone home that night happy in the illusion that your standards of service were impeccable.

High-powered negotiators reading this may be wondering what the concerns of a fish and chip shop owner have to do with them. Everything, is the answer. In any negotiation, face-to-face sale or other situation involving persuasion, either you succeed or the discussion is broken off before you get to your goal. If it's broken off, it's because the other party doesn't go along with something. This is called an objection by some salespeople; but it's also a concealed complaint about your proposition—that dangerous kind of complaint that will fester if left covered up. But we don't like to hear bad news, so you write "V. Int." and the customer drifts away mouthing polite nothings.

It isn't pleasant to hear negative comments, so it would seem to be a peculiar form of masochism actually to elicit them; and yet, as we have seen, in our martial art of persuasion it is essential to do so. What you need, remember, is detachment: the ability to stand back so that you can see the pianos raining down from the sky. This, of course, is easier said than done. Like all neurotic performers I am very sensitive to criticism and if I receive even the mildest amount I retreat into a dark cupboard and sulk for days. On reflection, however, I have to admit that every substantial improvement I have made has been in response to criticism, not praise. It's hard to take, but it's necessary if you are to get better. Of course, if you are famous for being good in the first place, a complaint against you is both harder to take and more damaging. You can't allow the first aspect to rule your reaction: think of the second, and deal with it.

By now we have drawn a picture of a complaint as a rare and delicate plant; poisonous, probably, but to be diligently sought and properly valued. Now what? We have this prize specimen in our hands; what do we do with it? Well, the first thing to ask when it comes to handling complaints is: *whose* hands, precisely? Complaints, like all plants, tend to breed; we've all had experience of the complaint that turns into a much worse complaint about the way the original complaint was dealt with. In other words, most complaints turn out to be about people, even if they weren't to start with. What tends to happen is that a grouse about a physical object or mechanical operation has ended up in the hands of a person. This stands to reason. You can shout at a late train or an unexpected invoice as much as you like, but if you want any response, let alone redress, you have to seek it from another human being. How well equipped is that human going to be to deal with it?

Fear is not the key

At this point it's worth taking another backwards glance and asking again how it was that some businesses were once so good at giving great service. If we look at the people who were on the receiving end of the customer's grumbles, we see that one of the explanations, sadly, was fear. I had a great-aunt, a huge dragon of a woman, who lived in Canada and every so often came over to England, where she took a part-time job to pay for her holiday. This involved a chain of very chic ladies' dress shops, in the window of each of which an outfit was displayed on a tailor's dummy. This outfit would be in one of the smaller sizes, and my aunt was elephantine; nevertheless, she was hired to go in and ask to try on the outfit in the window. She would try it and of course it didn't fit, so she would drop it on the floor and leave. She would then go and have a cup of tea somewhere and then, when the shop assistant had had time to press the outfit and rebuild the window display, she would return and ask to try it on again. If the saleswoman made any negative comment, she would hand over a small brown envelope with which her employers had provided her for the purpose and which contained a notice of instant dismissal. The staff knew of the existence of this ploy, but never knew where, when, or with whom it would be used, and in consequence were extra polite to difficult or complaining customers.

Judging by the looks that come over some faces when I tell this story at business dinners, there are those who wonder how that scheme might be reintroduced. Well, it can't, fortunately, so we have to find a better way of ensuring that staff are civil and helpful to customers, one that treats them as equals and both uses and appreciates their ability to earn us increased profits. You will see again why I put so much emphasis on the idea that everyone in a company can and must sell. If everyone is committed to your goal, they will contribute to its achievement. As I said at the beginning of this chapter, the sole point of good customer handling is to increase profits; if every member of your staff is committed to increasing profits, every one of them will look after your customers.

Remember, you have made a promise to your customers, and your first responsibility to them is to keep it. Now, take a look at your worst employee and ask yourself: Can this person keep my promise? If you have any doubts about this, ask yourself another question: have I defined his job in such a way that he *can't?*

Whose job is it anyway?

One of my clients runs a big theme park, and as part of my research into his business I went out visiting theme parks. This is a weird industry: you get paid up front, and then provide the goods in unlimited quantity. The more a customer enjoys the product, the more he will consume. Why not, you might think, just take the money and then on the other side of the turnstile set a large billboard saying EVER BEEN HAD? I hope the answer is obvious to you; it certainly wasn't to one park I visited. I had decided that if I arrived as myself on reconnaissance, the management might prevent me getting a true picture, so instead I turned up at the gate as a visitor, along with my wife, our two kids, and two more that I had borrowed (they had a free day out, and I'm sure they found their way home). It was a very wet weekend and the park was busy, which meant that I had to leave the car about fifty miles from the entrance in a parking lot about twice the size of New Jersey. We then all crammed on to a quaint little train that puffs its way to and fro between parking lot and entrance. At the end of this journey the train stopped and about two hundred of us fell off it and fought our way to the pay desk where an inert lump sat cozily sheltering from the teeming rain.

"Two adults, four children, please."

It didn't even look up from its manicuring. "Eighty dollars."

"How much?"

"Eighty dollars."

"Oh, all right." I pulled out my checkbook. This made her look up; with a deep sigh she turned to the 194 people behind me and mouthed: "He's got a checkbook," which had the effect of turning this dripping crowd into a howling lynch mob who saw me as the cause of their discomfort.

I finally got through the gate in a very ill humor to be greeted by a sign that said: WELCOME TO THE WORLD OF HAPPINESS AND MAGIC. This just about finished me off and I was in no mood for frolics when a large bear approached me, accompanied by a clown juggling balls, a man on a unicycle, and a fairy princess giving away balloons. The bear looked down at us.

"Ho, ho, ho, I'm Bongo the Bear, what's your name?"

I made an effort and smiled. "My name's Geoff."

"Not you, you idiot, the kid."

I persevered. "Oh, this is Simon."

By the time we had been given a balloon and a honk on the clown's hooter, we had cheered up a bit and were ready to try to enjoy the outing. Then the kids started whining about going on the monster roller-coaster, where we were greeted by a sign saying: THIS LINE IS TWO HOURS LONG. Well, one aspect of their organization at least must have been accurate, because one hour later I was standing beside a sign that said: THIS LINE IS ONE HOUR LONG. It's hard to imagine more human misery than that concentrated in a huge crowd of wet people desperate to enjoy themselves. There I stood, with one hour's worth of sad, steaming humanity ahead of me and one hour's worth behind. I've seen more optimism in a crowd of cattle outside an abattoir.

Then the trouble started. I don't know if you've ever been shopping in a supermarket when an old lady drops dead, but if you have you'll know that everyone seems to know about it instantly. She might have keeled over in frozen chickens and you might be in yogurts, but a sort of electric buzz runs through the building and everyone knows. I suppose it is the collective consciousness of the herd. Well, in much the same way an electric current of barely suppressed panic was coursing through this line. A hubbub of voices rose in volume; people were tense and frightened, but didn't know which way to run. Then in the distance I could make out another sound. It was a faint whooshing sound, punctuated with blasts on a horn and a tirade of profanities. It got louder and closer and the panic peaked, with children screaming and people trying to climb trees. Then the crowd parted to reveal a tatty, disheveled man astride a huge machine with whirling brushes on the front: as people stumbled into his path or were prevented by the throng from getting out of it, he would bang his fist on the horn button and gesticulate fiercely while shouting abuse at the obstacle and doing his best to sweep it out of the way. Eventually this juggernaut, having forced its way through the mass of people that had formerly been an orderly line, moved on; as it went away from us I could still hear in the distance the horn, the relentless swishing of the brushes, and the unstoppable torrent of obscenities.

Later on, when I had presented myself to the management and declared who I was, we had a meeting to discuss how the park was run. I asked what on earth the demented midget on the sweeper had to do with the World of Happiness and Magic.

"Nothing," they replied. "That's Charlie, the janitor."

"Yes, I can see that; but what about the World of Happiness and Magic?"

"Didn't you see Bongo the Bear?"

"Yes, I did."

"Well, that's *his* job."

I then looked at Charlie's job description and the recruitment ad. It read: "Wanted: janitor. Must be honest, good timekeeper essential."

I was tearing my hair out. "But how does that help to make your guests happy?"

"Oh, people like a clean park, and he is on a bonus scheme."

"Oh, I see. That sounds better. But how do you measure the level of guest happiness to calculate his bonus?"

"We don't have to. His bonus is based on circuits of the park."

So of course Charlie goes round the park like a crazy man, and on a busy day you prevent him from earning his living just by being there. Not only is Charlie's job seen as completely separate from the main business of the park—the promise made to the customer—but, even worse, its conditions are framed in such a way that he works *against* it. Whose fault is all this? It has to be laid at the door of the management. You can't blame Charlie for wanting his bonus; and if he had stopped to help guests or to comfort a lost child, he would no doubt have been told that it was not his job.

Does the mother who has lost sight of her child, or the grandfather who can't find the men's room, automatically know whose job it is to help them out? Hardly. Their first impulse is going to be to latch on to the first employee they see, especially if that person is one of the lowly ones. Disneyland discovered this very early on. Well, would you bother Mickey Mouse himself if you were lost? Surely you'd be far more likely to ask a hot-dog seller or a sweeper (if you could get near one). Disney realized this and made sure the whole "Cast," as they call them, was briefed to project the magic of Disneyland.

I get some peculiar jobs to do, and one of the weirder ones was at a college whose management team had decided to jump on the customer care bandwagon. They no longer had students, oh no; now they had customers. During my investigations, the student welfare/customer care officer remarked how surprised she was that the "customers" had a tendency to fling themselves under trains.

"Silly young people know my door is always open, but they just don't want to talk about their little troubles," she said, with a patronizing smile.

"They talk to me all right," said Aggy, who cleaned the students' (sorry, customers') bedrooms. "I always know when they're sad 'cause they won't go out into the sunshine. Then I have a bit of a chat with them."

There was outrage when I suggested that Aggy could usefully be given some training in counseling. The welfare officer more or less suggested that she was just a stupid maid and the head of college services decided that she was wasting time with the students and for this reason was slow at her job—her job, of course, as defined by the college with its best pair of blinkers on: cleaning.

And yet, as we have already noted, if you have a complaint or a worry, you are likely to take it to the first person you see. In my opinion, that person, whether it be the maid or the group chairman, should be able to accept the responsibility on behalf of the whole company: in other words, to use the latest fashion in terminology, they should be "empowered" to act as the spokesperson for the whole enterprise. All the techniques I recommend for actually handling a complaint are based on this assumption, which means at the very least two things: first, that no person's job is framed in such a way that it gives them disincentives to help customers; and second, that every person is committed to the enterprise and its success.

You therefore have a big selling job to do before you even contemplate dealing with a customer. You have to sell to everyone in your company, absolutely everyone, what it is that you hope to achieve. If you make the best jet turbines in the world then your office trainee has to believe that, and should stick down their envelopes with that in mind. I know that you and your sales force go out to tell the world how great your turbines are and that your marketing department is churning out slick ads that you hope the public will believe, but do your staff believe in them? Perhaps your marketing team might like to spend a little time selling in before selling out. Internal sales might not show up on the balance sheet but they can have a massive effect on your profitability when reflected in your employees' treatment of customers.

Beware the talking bottom

Take the sad case of the "talking bottom." I encounter talking bottoms wherever I go. Sometimes it is sticking out of a shop window display when I ask where I should pay for things. In this case it is often embellished with a waving finger emerging from somewhere to give a vague indication of the recommended direction. Sometimes I meet it when a piece of machinery breaks down. Anyone who has dealings with the machinery industry will be familiar with the phenomenon of the three-stage purchase. On the first day, a slick salesperson signs you into an agreement; the next day the machine is delivered; the next week it breaks down. You now have a complaint, one that has been generated by the fact that the expansive promise uttered by the salesperson has not been kept, and you scoot to the telephone in high dudgeon. I say carefully "the promise uttered by the salesperson," not "the salesperson's promise," because, of course, it's the company's promise. Everyone is involved in making it, everyone is involved in keeping it.

This principle clearly hasn't been explained to the person who turns up to deal with your grievance. You might think that whoever sets out to make good on the promise originally given would be even smarter and more deferential than the original salesperson; if you did, you are disappointed. It is a jerk with a cigarette dangling loosely from his lips and a greasy toolbox grasped in an even greasier fist. This paragon speaks:

"Who sold you this, then?"

"Oh, a very nice young man called Kevin."

"Kevin's an idiot. Do you know how many of these I've had to fix today? This is the fourth. They're made in Korea, you see. They're all cardboard inside; not safe. Last place I went to, the bloody thing caught fire and burned half the office down. Doubt there's anything I can do."

With this, he plunges head-first into the machine. You address his bottom, which is all that is left to you.

"But when will it be fixed?"

The bottom replies in the muffled way that bottoms do: "Ain't got the parts."

We shall see in the next chapter on psychology the importance of eye contact; but leaving psychology aside for a moment and thinking only in terms of simple civility, all he had to do was get up, turn around, address me face to face, and clearly explain what was to happen. He should also have reassured me as to the quality of his company, his products, and its sales staff. Kevin may not be a great friend of his, but they should be doing the same job. What do your fitters think of your sales people? Equally, what do your sales people think of your fitters?

It's no good sticking badges on people saying "sales" or "customer services" and turning your back on them. If your firm sells cutting-edge technology, you may still get a small broken cog-wheel thrust under your nose, or a carpet tile bearing the oily footprint of your service engineer waved in your face. Whether you are the company chairman, a high-level salesperson specializing in the sophisticated technological aspects of your products, or the cleaner, it is your problem. Noel Coward wrote a very clever play called *Blithe Spirit* in which the ghost of a man's dead wife comes back to haunt him. The joke is that only the husband can see her and talk to her. All the characters, including the dead woman, are played by live actors, and if it's skillfully performed the impression that none of them except the husband is aware of her can be very convincing. I think that a huge number of businesses train their staff by putting on this play. If I'm paying for something, the cashier can see me; but when the supervisor appears to check my credit card, I'm invisible. Before anything else can be done, I need to exist.

Next, whoever I have chosen to complain to has to accept responsibility for the problem. Salespeople are very often referred to as representatives. If you are a representative, then you are representing your company; when a customer comes to you, you *are* the company. Countless times I have seen salespeople in mid-sale being faced with a complaint and responding:

"I'm sorry, sir, that would be a service matter. I'll get them to ring you." Or:

"Oh no, not transport again! I tell you, they are killing this company." Or even:

"Oh well, there's no point trying to sell you another one."

If you buy a car and it is faulty, you go back to the salesman and he takes you to service. He should be the one to deal with it.

Whose mission?

Hang on a minute, though: just whose fault is this? Just how much power does an individual have to put things right? There has been a fashion for a while now for a thing called a mission statement, which is supposed to help the Board share their vision of the company with the staff. Some plums among these include "We Try Harder," "We Live By Our Quality," "Our Name Is Our Bond," "Your Happiness Is Our Reason For Living" and of course "We Have Ways Of Making You Talk." Each statement encapsulates and expresses to the staff the aims and unique skill of the company. Good idea; but as in all cases where a good idea becomes a fashion, it has come to be misunderstood and misused. If a delivery firm has a mission statement which says, "We Deliver On Time," then they shouldn't paint it on the outside of the vans. I don't need convincing; I'll be convinced if my parcel arrives on time. They should paint it on the inside of the van to remind the driver, and then let the driver have whatever is necessary to help him keep that promise.

A large engineering firm called in a group of renowned consultants because they wanted a bit of this newfangled mission thing. The outcome was dramatic. The logo was changed to represent a happy customer smiling. The chairman's photo was put up in each production area with the mission pledge and a statement of support for every employee who was dedicated to quality. Staff seminars were deafened by shouted messages about upside-down pyramids and the customer being king.

Then a forklift truck driver noticed that the paintwork wasn't quite right on a huge shipment of vehicles bound for the Far East. He stopped the loading, sent the trucks away, and proudly presented himself to the general manager. The shit duly hit the fan, the forklift driver was fired, the shipment was sent, and moustaches and spectacles mysteriously began to appear on the chairman's portraits. Have your staff got the power or the authorization to put things right? Have they got confidence in each other that they are all doing fundamentally the same thing?

A garage that sells a huge number of cars—or, to use the trade vernacular, "moves the metal"— would, you might think, have a very slick sales force, and so when I heard of one that seemed to sell more than most, I had to see it in action. I arrived at a medium-sized garage of average appearance just as a man was leaving, smiling, in a brand new Chevrolet. When I got inside, I found that the boss had called everyone together, including the cleaners, office staff, and mechanics.

"Well, can anyone guess what we've just done?"

They all chorused back: "We've sold a Chevy!" and with that started cheering and hugging each other. Seconds later they had all vanished, leaving me feeling just a little bit bewildered. A bit later still I saw a figure wandering about the used car area, obviously a bit lost. An old man who was doing a bit of sweeping up noticed him and walked across.

"Good morning, sir, you are looking a little lost. Can I help?"

"Er, yes, I'm looking for the sales office."

"And your name is, sir?"

"Peterson."

"Well, Mr. Peterson, my name's Joe, I keep things clean around here, and you need to speak to our sales manager Mike, so if you'd just like to follow me, I'll introduce you. Thinking of driving a Chevrolet, Mr. Peterson?"

"Yes."

"That's great. I've had a Bel-Air since 1958. It's done half a million miles and never even needed the cylinder head off. They sure are great cars...Hey, there's Mike. Hi, Mike; let me introduce you to Mr. Peterson, he wants to talk to us about Chevrolets."

"Hello there, Mr. Peterson. My name's Mike, I'm the sales manager here."

Joe leaves with a cheery wave and a smile. "Enjoy your new Chevy, Mr. Peterson, and have a great day."

Mike thanks Joe, and turns to Mr. Peterson. "Before we get down to business, Mr. Peterson, the folk out back would never forgive me if I didn't introduce you. May I take you to meet them?"

He forthwith takes this man into the workshop. Now, I don't know what your local garage is like, but in quite a lot I have visited no one would ever dare do that. They would all be playing frisbee with your hubcaps and would greet you with aggressive stares.

"Hey, everybody, here's Mr. Peterson come to see us about driving a Chevrolet."

"Oh, hi, Mr. Peterson, it's great to see you. When you get your new Chevy come down and see us get it ready for you. We'll give you coffee and doughnuts and show you our race car."

"Come on, Mr. Peterson, these people will keep you talking all day. Now, here's my office; take a seat and we'll talk about what you'd like."

I suddenly realized that the car had been sold, the deal was done, and the salesman had not been the one to do it. Nor had any other individual. Everyone had sold it. Everyone there knew that their future lay in promoting and keeping the promise of their company. When you show a prospective customer around, does everyone want you to succeed? Have you told them whom you are showing around and how important they are?

There may be some among you reading this who are fidgeting a bit at this and thinking, "Prospective customers? Why is he going on about *prospective* customers? This chapter is supposed to be about complaints!" To which my response would be: there is no gulf between the two. Just as in my view there is no hard-and-fast distinction between how you gain customers and how you keep them, so there is no strict division between how you treat a potential customer and how you treat an existing customer with a problem. Overcompartmentalization is a blight that has descended on a lot of business training: "Oh, selling, that's Chapter 3; complaints, that's Chapter 6, we haven't done that yet."

Whoever you are, the customer can sack you

Nor should you be getting complacent if you are the big cheese. You might be a magician at getting everyone else motivated, but do you consider yourself somewhat above the fray? Even if you would never utter the words out loud, do you have somewhere in your razor-sharp business brain the idea that it is not your job to deal directly with the public now that you have thousands of keen, bright, committed employees at your disposal? If so, let me point out one thing. Even if you are the chairman of the world's biggest international conglomerate, you still have a superior who can dismiss you from your job, and without all the fuss of a shareholders' meeting, either. That person is the customer. If the customer withdraws their business, even you will have no job. Nothing can, or should, protect you from direct contact with this all-powerful being. When ordinary people are disappointed with something they have bought, they often write to the company chairman; and if they are lucky, they get a standard letter back drafted by the public relations officer, peppered with an illegible scrawl. It's not good enough. All this does is lower the head of the firm to the position of a very bad ambassador.

Imagine this scene. Lord Dryberg of Dobersham, chairman of Super International Engineering, is at the launching of his new racing yacht. His burly bodyguards stand around preventing the huge crowd from pressing forward. A voice comes from the back:

"Here, my lord, I bought some of your cutlery and the teaspoons were useless!"

Lord Dryberg swings round in surprise and, to the crowd's amazement, beckons the man forward, signaling to his bodyguards to let him through. Over a glass of champagne the international super-businessman listens intently to the complaint. When the man gets home, there is a parcel waiting for him containing the new improved canteen of cutlery and a personal letter from the chairman apologizing and thanking him for bringing the defect of the previous model to his attention. From that day forward this man will tell anyone who gives him half a chance what a great firm Super International Engineering is.

Never belittle a fuchsia

Contrast this outcome with what is likely to result from some of the classic so-called complaints handling lines. I have been put off with statements that are highly provocative and likely to cause far more trouble than they solve, and all of them can be roughly translated as: "Your problem is not my problem." They include:

"Now what on earth have you been doing to this?"

"Well, look at that. That's the first one of these we've had back."

"We'll soon get you another one."

"Now that's nothing to get upset about."

Nothing to get upset about? Soon get you another one? After constant nagging from his wife a man puts his elderly mother in a home. He will never forget the day they drove her there, sobbing in the back seat: "Gerald, how could you do this to me?" His consuming guilt is intensified when his job moves him four hundred miles away from the home. Now he can only visit her rarely. His mother loves fuchsias, so before one of these rare visits he goes to his local garden center and buys the best one he can find; it still costs less than five dollars. He puts it in the back of his car and drives for ten hours. As he sweeps up to the home, he sees a thin, lonely figure standing on the veranda, staring hopefully down the drive. When he opens the back of his car, there is a stick in a pot, surrounded by fallen leaves and flowers.

"Oh Gerald, I thought you had forgotten me. What's that you've got behind your back?"

"...It's a stick in a pot."

"Oh Gerald..."

He returns to the shop with the stick in a pot. I for one wouldn't say, "Now that's nothing to get upset about." Quite the reverse, in fact; and I have reason to know that it works.

I'm not keen on flying at the best of times, so when after a fairly turgid holiday I found that there were problems with the journey home I was not best pleased. The holiday company hired a Spanish taxi driver to take us in search of a flight, and what with his English and my Spanish we whizzed over most of the Iberian peninsula trying to find a plane to England. I ended up in a bleak and empty terminal at three in the morning with fractious children and no foreseeable prospect of going anywhere. The place was deserted; we were stranded, alone, in the cold glare of the vending machines. Then in the distance I heard the click-clacking of high heels and into view came a representative of the holiday company. Oh boy, oh boy, I thought, with my first stirrings of energy for hours, is she going to cop it.

"Mr. Burch?"

"Yes," I replied, taking a deep breath with which to embark on the stream of invective I'd been preparing.

She lifted both her hands, palms open and facing me. "Mr. Burch, I am so sorry. I have spoiled your holiday. What can I do?"

I was completely nonplussed. As I told her my troubles, rather more calmly than I had intended, she listened with sympathy and understanding. She took full personal responsibility for the situation. The result was that I respected her and I forgave her company. She was able to get me to agree to a course of action that wasn't ideal but that was, I understood, the best that could be achieved in the circumstances. And yes, I would travel with them again. After all, we all make mistakes, don't we?

8

The Psychology of Persuasion

It always seems odd to me that businesses will happily spend fortunes on training in selling and negotiating skills, customer care and so on, without particular regard to the science of psychology. It's equally odd, if perhaps less surprising, that the academic psychologists in their ivory towers seem not to understand the huge power they have at their command. To get a flavor of this, let's try an experiment. I want you right now to send me all of the money you have in your purse or wallet. Have you done that? You haven't? Why not, what was stopping you? You weren't being physically restrained. What stopped you doing this thing, which would have been very much to my advantage, was your mind. You read that request, and all the complex little mechanisms in your head came up with the response: "I should what!" Now, if I could control those mental mechanisms completely, I would have a mailbag of banknotes every morning.

The whole essence of this book is to show how one individual can use their power to communicate to alter another individual's point of view. If after reading this book and understanding the principles set out in it you go away and put them into practice, you will be able literally to change someone's mind; to cause them to make decisions that you want them to make.

Remember that we are talking about how to affect the behavior of individuals. Look at the people round you: they are all different even to look at, in shape and size, in age, color, and sex;

and believe me, they are even more different inside their heads. It would obviously be foolhardy to imagine that the same methods will work with everyone. Just as it is completely ineffective to repeat parrot-style phrases learned out of a textbook without understanding why you are using them, so you won't get far by assuming that you can treat everyone's mind the same. It's essential to be flexible, to adapt in response to each individual's thought processes. So while in this chapter we will be looking at some of the general principles of psychology and how they relate to our art of persuasion, don't fall into the trap of thinking that the next person who walks into your shop to buy a pound of sausages is The Human Being. It's Mrs. Jones, and she has, quite literally, a mind of her own.

What has psychology to do with us, anyway? The most succinct answer to this question that I have heard came up during a television program on the problems that fringe therapists were causing by making their patients believe that they had multiple personalities. An eminent professor of psychology had been coaxed out of his ivory tower, dusted free of cobwebs, and wheeled into the studio to contribute his respected academic view to the debate. When the presenter invited him to comment, he creaked into life and quite matter-of-factly said:

"Of course, a good psychologist can make anybody believe anything." Having delivered this simple but mind-boggling pronouncement he slumped back in his chair and was wheeled away.

I was stunned. Come on, be honest, where would your business be if you could make anyone believe anything? Do you need any more convincing?

In this chapter, I will attempt to bring some of the knowledge psychologists have amassed to bear on the subject at hand. I have drawn this material from wherever I could; obviously, when Professor Dusty was writing his monograph on "The Higher Decision-Making Capacity of the Subjugated Organism" he wasn't thinking about selling ball bearings, and for that reason I would like to apologize before I go any further to any academic psychologists reading this who have already started tearing at their hair. My defense is that what I set out here is my interpretation, for my particular purposes, of a very complex and technical subject; I don't see why, just because most of us outside academia can't grapple with the finer complexities and technicalities, we shouldn't try to use what we can of the core principles.

From the opposite view, I also think that academic psychology might benefit from rather closer acquaintance with how things work in the real world, especially the harsh world of business where nothing is done without a reason, and a reason to do with profit at that. Often, psychologists seem to postulate for the sake of it, without consideration of the practical implications; this, I am sure, is the famed scientific curiosity without which the whole academic enterprise would grind to a halt, but all the same I can't help feeling that if some of them spent half an hour with a market trader they could learn more about human nature than years of research would tell them.

Even germs get hungry

I had cause to visit a university not long ago, and I was shown into the library to wait for the person I had gone to see. The first book I picked up was a huge tome on the psychology of learning, written in sentences so long you had to read each one about ten times before you could get any sense out of the words. One of the first things I noticed was that it kept referring to The Organism; after a while I realized that this could mean anything from you or me to a germ. What had fascinated the author of this erudite work was the ability of every organism to learn—even ones that had no brain whatsoever. Again, I suppose this includes you, me, and germs. Many complex experiments were cited, but one that particularly caught my attention seemed to consist of taking a bowl of water which was populated with bacteria and each day at the same time putting a few drops of sugar in the middle of the bowl. After a while, it was found that at the same time each day, the bacteria would gather in anticipation of the sugar. The learned author then went on for about seven hundred pages to say that it was not entirely understood why this should happen.

It is at this point that they should have thought of asking any experienced salesperson, who would have told them that no one (not even a germ) ever learns anything unless there is a clear benefit to them from doing so. This is obvious in material terms in the animal kingdom—the bacteria learn when their sugar ration comes, a dog learns where its biscuits are kept—but with humans the benefits can be abstract as well. I learned the date of the War of Jenkins' Ear to avoid a whacking—a negative and abstract benefit, perhaps, but perfectly clear to me at the time.

The first person really to get stuck into this idea was the good Professor Pavlov, the Russian scientist who noticed that when we sit on a pin we tend to leap into the air without thinking: "Ho hum, I seem to have sat on something fairly sharp. I do believe the best course of action to avoid what is turning out to be a painful situation would be to arise swiftly." If you sit a baby on a pin, the effect is the same. When Pavlov pointed this out to his pals, they dismissed it as something blindingly obvious that we are born with. Then Pavlov pointed out that if you threaten to whack an adult with a raised arm, they automatically duck. If you do this to a very young child, they don't (I have gotten some very strange looks around the supermarket trying to substantiate this claim). Why is this so, he asked?

"It's obvious," replied his fellow scientists. "The adult has been hit before. He has learned what a raised arm means."

"Ah ha!" replied Pavlov, "but they still duck without thinking."

If the pin response is a reflex action that we are born with and the ducking response is a reflex action that we acquire, then it seems that we can learn actions over which we then have little control. Pavlov called these "conditioned reflexes," and set out to prove his theory using an unfortunate dog. Now, even the most devoted animal lovers among you must accept for the moment that dogs don't think—not as we do, anyway, if only because they don't have our language. A dog is blissfully unaware of its own mortality. If we feel ill, we wander around whining that we may be dying and no one cares. A dog simply takes to its bed. If after two or three days it goes green, stiff, and bloated and the flies come buzzing round, it didn't make it; if on the other hand it recovers, it leaps up full of vim and vigor ready to enjoy doggy life again. As someone once said, a dog has two states of mind: it is either happy or waiting to be happy.

What Pavlov did to his chosen dog was first to feed it lots of tasty tidbits while the whole time he was ringing a small tinkly bell. Then after a while the feeding and the bell would stop, and a bit later on he would bang a gong and at the same time whack the dog over the head with a stick. The effect of this was fascinating. Three major things happened. First, and unsurprisingly, the dog got a headache. Second, and much more interesting to everyone except the dog, when the bell was rung the dog's mouth would water—even though Pavlov had previously quite clearly proved that the dog's brain could not produce a thought process on the lines of "Yum, here's that bell, I'm going to get fed." Third, and equally interesting, when the gong was banged, the dog did a disappearing act, despite its having been scientifically proven that it was incapable of thinking in the abstract terms of anticipating a whack on the head. The dog, through reward and punishment, was being conditioned to exhibit some quite irrational behavior.

Here I would like to repeat my theory, which is that the essence of learning is that a person will only learn, or be conditioned, if there is a benefit to them in doing so. This is not Pavlov's explanation of what he found, and I have been challenged by people who ask me where the benefit is in being whacked on the head. To explain, I would ask you to think back to the Gulf War, to the point where the Americans had surrounded the Iraqi forces with missile launchers, aircraft, and other weapons of awesome power before the fighting had actually begun. At a press conference, a US general explained that the idea was carrot and stick persuasion. A reporter said that he could see the stick but not the carrot. The general replied:

"The carrot, gentlemen, is that we may not have to use the stick."

Or, if you prefer something a little more domestic, think of what I was telling you a moment ago about my history lessons: I learned, like Pavlov's dog, to avoid a whacking; he did it by clearing off when he heard a gong, I did it by learning the date of the War of Jenkins' Ear.

How can a speedometer get the wrong answer?

Of course, if you, knowing nothing of Pavlov's experiments, were given a dog that had been through the bell-and-gong procedure you would find its behavior very weird indeed and it would take

you a very long time to work out the reasoning behind what it did—if indeed you ever got the hang of it. If you accept that humans are subject to the same conditioning process, it should no longer surprise you that people's behavior in later life appears irrational and inexplicable to those who don't know how they learned it—particularly when the punishments meted out in the early years are themselves irrational and based on misconceptions and prejudice.

I have grave doubts about attaching the word "Fail" to exam performance. After all, an exam is only a crude measuring device; you don't accuse your speedometer of failing to point to 70 when it points to 60. All an exam tells you is where you are, so that you know where you are going. And yet exam results set off the most extreme reactions, with correspondingly extreme effects. A boy fails a school exam and his parents shout at him that if he hadn't hung around the park with the local hooligans he would have had the same success as his brothers and sisters. This punishing response—which may well have had nothing to do with the real reasons for the boy's perceived poor performance—will have its effect. Perhaps the boy grows up with an obsessive desire to succeed at all costs, or with an extreme reluctance to discuss his worries so that he will go to any lengths to avoid admitting even the possibility that something might be amiss.

How many of us were encouraged to clear our plates at every meal when we were small and praised when we did so?

"Ooh, look, daddy, he's not going to eat all that big man's dinner. Oh, he has! Well done! Mommy loves her big strong boy."

Of course, when mommy and daddy are long dead and the boy grows into a lonely 280-pound loser, he creeps back into his dismal room every night and shovels more food into his head. The long-forgotten image of his loving mom telling him what a good boy he is has become twisted into the association of comfort with food, now the only source of reassurance in his life; so he gets fatter and suffers more rejection and eats even more.

Perhaps your parents were poor, and one Christmas when everyone seems to be giving their children bicycles, they buy a cheap second-hand bike and do it up with a splash of pink paint. Of course, when you see this on Christmas morning you think it's the best thing ever; dear old mom and dad, they'd never let you down. You take it for its first spin, proud parents waving you off and smiling to see you so pleased. Then you meet up with your friends down the road; they've all had sparkling new bikes for Christmas and greet your souped-up castoff with sneers of derision. You go home feeling beaten and betrayed—and probably grow up determined to get rich and never have second best of anything ever again. Perhaps you buy the latest sports car and return to the old housing estate, "just to show 'em." Naturally, "they" have long gone, and the drive to "show 'em" is never satisfied.

The early Viennese psychoanalysts started to notice how these early experiences could alter the adult personality by producing these drives, these compulsions to behave in certain ways—and once they'd started there was no stopping them. One of them analyzed as many as 50,000 drives embedded in the subconscious. I'd love to run through these with you, but obviously only a relatively small number are going to be of direct concern to us here. The key point is that we are all striving for something, only most of us don't know what; and in situations where you wish to persuade, it is most valuable to understand the predominant drives in the other person. It will be obvious to you now, even if it wasn't before, why I stressed earlier in this chapter that you should remember you are dealing with individuals. Everyone's experiences are unique to them, though obviously there are features common to many; and the way each person acts tends to reflect the mixture of drives within that person resulting from their own experiences.

Go for the feelings

Not all drives, as I said, are relevant to us here. There is one group that goes under the heading of "biological drives," which basically means satisfying bodily demands such as those for sex, food, drink, and sleep. Now, I know that we can persuade by offering or threatening to withdraw sex, food, drink, and sleep, but these options are not really morally available to us in any normal commercial interaction, so we won't dwell on them. At the very minimum, all we really need is gruel, clean water, and a dry box to sleep in; but while this may have provided some inspiration for government housing policy, it doesn't really give us much scope. It's when we start moving above this level that feelings and emotions as well as simple physical needs start to enter the picture, and that is where we come in.

Feelings and emotions are the currency of persuasion; whenever we persuade we will generate feelings. When we sell products, we don't sell objects, we sell feelings. What was the last thing you bought? Whatever it was, a country manor or a toilet roll, you will have been left with some feeling: it might be pride, guilt, or relief, but there will be feelings. If you can understand these feelings and how they arise, you can play them like a musical instrument to achieve the outcome you want, generating positive emotions and avoiding negative ones, always leaving the other party feeling happy and willing to repeat the experience, not feeling resentful and cheated and determined never to go through that again. With this end in view, let's go through some of the drives and emotional desires that the psychology textbooks list and see how we can benefit from understanding them.

Yet again I find myself taking issue with accepted business training practice—particularly, this time, with those trainers who have single-track systems. How on earth can you hope to succeed if you use the same methods with a highly dependent person as with a very aggressive person? You just end up in the numbers game again, bashing up against the stone wall that says that you will succeed with one in ten and should be satisfied with that. How can these people not see that a different approach will succeed with a different one in the ten, and so on, until if you are flexible enough you can succeed with all ten?

Dependency is a good place to start. This refers to the need we feel for protection and reassurance from figures of authority and the disappointment we feel if they let us down. It is dependency that explains the outrage that flares up whenever authority figures—the police, the government, for instance—are found with their hands in the cookie jar. It's lurking around in most of us, but in some people it dominates, probably as a result of reward and punishment by parents. This early conditioning takes various forms. Perhaps when we were three we let go of the parental hand and toddled on ahead. Mother watched us trip and fall, and when we returned, wailing and with hands and knees bleeding, said, "There you are, that serves you right. If you'd held on to mommy's hand, that wouldn't have happened."

Or perhaps we got lost in a shop where all the counters seemed twenty feet tall; panic set in and soon we were scampering about crying for our parents. A whack on the ear like a pistol shot tells us we have been found.

"Don't you ever wander off like that again! It's lucky I found you. They would have shut up the shop with you in it, and then the boogey man that lives under the counter would have come out and torn you up and eaten your heart."

These little traumas can be quite effective at personality forming. The person who has a very strong dependency drive is always looking for reassurance from authority—and if you play your cards right, of course, that should be you. They will be nervous, undecided, and dithery, because they are crying out for guidance.

"Oh, I'm not sure, I can't decide. What do you think?"

The great thing is, if they trust you, you can tell them what you think. You can, in fact, tell them what to do.

"Well, I'd go ahead if I were you."

All you need to do then is pile on the reassurance; but stay alert and be a bit firm if they start to wobble.

"Yes, of course you are doing the right thing. I can't see anything but profit for you if you do this."

They love guarantees and other assurances.

"Look. Take it, try it, and bring it back if you're not happy."

If all else fails, try being honest

There is one particularly powerful trick that always succeeds with these people. When you find a dependency-led person, be kind, understanding, patient—and, above all, absolutely honest. There is a very good reason for this. These people will give you one chance to rip them off. If you do, you will never see them again. If, on the other hand, you put yourself in their place and prove yourself to be entirely trustworthy, you will have a friend and customer for life. This revolutionary recommendation will no doubt get me into trouble once again with the sales traditionalists, many of whom think that being honest isn't playing the game; but it's led me to great fortune, in fact it's one of the most powerful tools I know.

After dependency we have affiliation—the drive that represents our need to belong. To show it at its starkest, I will have to be a little sexist and say that small girls seem to me to be the most brutal at manipulating this need. One angelic little mite will throw her arm around another's shoulders and say: "Come along Susan, we don't want to play with Miss Smellypants," leaving a lonely figure standing in the playground. Why is that such a hurtful thing to do? The need to belong, to identify with a group, is a very powerful one, probably related to our most basic survival instincts and nurtured by very many experiences. Again, it is stronger in some people than in others. In some tribes it is so powerful that if a member is banished and physically put outside the settlement, they simply curl up and die.

The advertising industry has cottoned on to the need to belong in a big way, as is evident particularly from all the beer commercials that show laughing, singing, happy groups of bonded men all having a ripping time in a manly sort of way. I suppose our lonely loser sitting in his rotting attic, staring at a flickering black and white television, will pull the ring on his can of lager and be transported to a heaven of acceptance and belonging.

For us the message is quite clear: we can get positive action from our subjects by affiliating them to groups they wish to belong to.

"That's a decision I didn't want to make."

"I don't blame you, it would scare me; and yet it's funny, you know, it's something that serious professionals are committing themselves to wholeheartedly."

Can I remind you again here that I give you these examples just to illustrate the point. Some of them look so greasy in black and white that they make me cringe when they're written down; but I sincerely hope that no one who has read this far will even be tempted to use them verbatim. No art can be learned from a phrase book, especially not one that requires adapting to every single individual situation. So read, and then adapt.

Perhaps even more important than manipulating the need to belong is avoiding conflict with it. Being made to feel you don't belong arouses very strong emotions. Imagine being greeted by a supercilious head waiter who presents you with a *fruits de mer* that is all in its shell, gives you a pair of nutcrackers and stands back to watch the fun. Not only do you start to feel excluded, but this feeling brings with it great waves of anxiety, causing an even greater need for affiliation. The waiter starts by provoking the anxiety and then makes things worse by refusing the increasingly desired affiliation. If you make someone feel like this, you are going to have a real job on your hands to calm them down and open them up to whatever it is you want them to do; so rather than create work for yourself, you need to make a huge effort to get people to feel that they belong from the start.

You might just be noticing the catch in all that I have been saying about the power of psychology. If you are—as, of course, you should be—in control of the situation, your subject will most probably not be aware of what is happening, so all the adjustments need to be made by you. All the effort of working out the dominant drives in the other party and conducting the conversation appropriately has to be made by you. Yes, all right, it's hard work. Your ability to choose an appropriate strategy and adjust your tactics suitably as the interaction progresses is probably going to be tested to the limit. But just think: would you rather get one result in ten with your assembly-line training, or ten in ten from being aware of what you are doing and with whom?

Tell me how wonderful I am

Next in this catalogue of key psychological factors comes self-belief. Oh, how fragile our self-images can be. When I look at myself in the mirror first thing in the morning, smiling back at me is a bronzed Adonis, muscles rippling, a barely disguised, powerful yet humorous intelligence gleaming from the needle-sharp eyes. I skip down the stairs, ready to take on the world and right its wrongs, and my wife greets me.

"Your breath smells. Pull your stomach in, it's disgusting the way it hangs over your trousers, and don't hunch like that, it shows how much your hair is thinning."

I limp from the house, a paunchy, balding hunchback.

We need other people to reflect the reality of our situation; but we all like to dream, and you can sometimes make people very happy by cooperating with their dreams rather than being too harsh a mirror. I have a friend of much the same age as myself; we were hooligans together as kids. Both of us are keen on motorbikes, and in an aberration brought on by a mid-life crisis my friend bought a huge Harley Davidson. Admiring this gleaming brute, I noticed that it had no mirrors. I inquired about this.

"I took them off," said my friend. "They were faulty."

"How can a mirror be faulty?" I asked, insensitively.

"Well, I know I'm still nineteen," he replied, "but whenever I got on the bike and looked in the mirrors, there was this boring old fart looking back at me. So I took them off. He's gone now."

As I said, we all need to dream. It is our relationships with other people that tell us where we are; if you help people to be where they want to be, they are yours for life. I think it is called flattery.

For some people acceptance as part of the group or support

of their self-image is not enough: they have to be top dog. A few of these driven types claw, scramble, and fight their way to the top of the heap and then present themselves as difficult subjects because of the fragility of their position and the attitudes that situation creates. I call this the cesspool principle, according to which in life, as in the cesspools, the big lumps tend to float to the top. For every one of these there is a frustrated leader: the one who has quite clearly sunk to the bottom of life's septic tank but knows in his heart that he could do better. Perhaps he dresses as Napoleon in the privacy of his bedroom.

The problem for these people is that the psychological measure of leadership is acceptance. You can call yourself Napoleon all you like, you can even get on the horse and wear the hat, but if all your troops are busy walking in the opposite direction you can't carry conviction. Do others accept the small turd as the leader? Is he allowed to do all the talking, make all the decisions? More likely he is hated by his wife, despised by his children, jostled in pubs and abused on trains. Then you come up against him, and get:

"Hey, you! Fetch me one of those," or "This is completely hopeless. I think you'll find I'm right; I'm seldom wrong."

You reply: "Are you talking to me?" There is a huge temptation to take this moron apart, either verbally or even physically. To give way to it is a terrible mistake. This persuasion business may be a martial art, but it is a controlled, gentle martial art, and this kind of bombast is in fact very susceptible to flattery and manipulation.

One of my favorite fairy stories as a kid was about a gnome who had ideas above his station. He also had a hoard of potatoes at a time of famine. The other gnomes crowned him king and sat on his piles of potatoes as he, in his element at last, regaled them with sage advice. After the audience, they would leave, bowing low and backing out as the dignity of the king demanded. What the poor dupe with the crown didn't realize was that they had glue on the seat of their pants and were removing huge amounts of potatoes. So don't turn your nose up at people who are desperate to be treated with the respect they are convinced is their due; if you can bring yourself to be nice to them, they will love you for it and eat out of your hand.

Then there is the downright aggressive type. Again, it will do you no good to respond in kind. Remember, persuasion is the martial art of the mind; we use the opponent's violence to bring about their own downfall. Violence and aggression are signs not of control but of its absence, so bite your tongue and lie in that puddle and you will get what you want in the end.

We may not all want to be king of the castle, but most of us nurture a need for some kind of recognition or status. We cry out silently for others to acknowledge the statement we make with our home, our style, our car, or whatever. Have you ever wondered what the prat in the old Ford is thinking of when he drives past with his 100W stereo at full blast and his bare arm tapping the rhythm on the roof? When we cast glances of derision and annoyance at this spotty apparition in his reflective shades, he thinks they are looks of admiration and that we think he is a rock star or a hit man for the Mafia. What a sad little moron; but haven't we all done just a bit of the same thing? It's those dreams again, dreams that we are appreciated, admired, envied. Again, while playing to the desire can smooth your path it is even more important not to conflict with it—unless, of course you want to cause trouble, and I'm not saying that can't be fun, as long as you are prepared to accept the consequences. Referring to his turbo megablaster off-road four-wheel-drive RV as a "dear little van thing" or his home as "quite nice for such a poor area" is the sort of thing that can really get the sparks flying. Fine, if you get your exercise from this sort of thing; but don't do it by accident, because you will need all your agility when the reaction comes, and if you don't want that reaction you're going to use up an awful lot of time and energy deflecting it.

Mind the gap

The psychologists' name for this can of worms is the "ego ideal," and it has been so thoroughly poked and prodded by now that they have produced ways of quantifying it and measuring its effects. One of the most popular of these tests is based on a scale, numbered from one to ten, at the lower end of which is the least desirable state for a quality or feature, with the most desirable or ideal state at the higher end. Take "intelligence" as the quality to be measured. The scale is drawn up with "stupid" under 1 and "brilliant" under 10. The subject is then asked first to mark on the scale how intelligent they would like to be in the best of all possible worlds. Usually, of course, they put a mark somewhere near the "brilliant" end. Then they are asked to make a second mark indicating how clever they think they really are. The tendency is to place this mark a bit nearer the "stupid" end. You end up with something like this:

1	2	3	4	5	6	7	8	9	10
Stupid									Brilliant
					x				x
					(real)				(ideal)

The psychologists measure the gap and calculate the state of your mental health.

For example, a middle-aged woman who has been nursing her aged mother for years is finally set free by the elderly lady's death. Does she go out and party? No, she develops agoraphobia. So she is given this test to do.

"Agnes, would you like people to think you are kind?"
"Oh, yes!"

1	2	3	4	5	6	7	8	9	10
Cruel									Kind
									x
									(ideal)

"How kind are you?"
"I'm not kind at all, I let Mommy die."

1	2	3	4	5	6	7	8	9	10
Cruel									Kind

x
(real)

So there you are: the bigger the gap, the more of a problem you have. Well, up to a point; but this isn't the whole story, because when you go to the Happydale Home for the Criminally Insane and meet Slasher Higgins the mad axeman, after you ask him, "Slasher, would you like to be like Hitler?" and he says, "Oh, yes please," and you mark him down:

1	2	3	4	5	6	7	8	9	10
Ordinary man									Hitler

x
(ideal)

you then ask him:
"And how much like Hitler are you, Slasher?" and he replies: "I am Hitler! *Sieg Heil!*" which gives you:

1	2	3	4	5	6	7	8	9	10
Ordinary man									Hitler

x
(real)

So, no gap at all is truly preposterous. There has to be some gap, to show that a person is aware of the difference between fantasy and reality and can constantly strive towards their ideal; but if the gap is too big, the perceived size of that task can lead to neurotic behavior.

What I think the psychologists might have failed to notice is how flexible this gap is; and of course it is this area of flexibility that will interest us as persuaders. With any normal person, the gap can be widened to the point where their unease is bordering on the neurotic. This used to happen all the time in schools.

"Spratt, who won the Battle of Waterloo?"

"Er, was it Nelson, sir?"

"Nelson? You stupid boy! Stand on your chair, Spratt, so we can all see what a stupid boy looks like. Now who was it, Spratt?"

"Er, Napoleon, sir?"

"It was WELLINGTON, you ridiculous child. Who was it?"

"Wellington, sir."

"You stupid boy. What are you?"

"Stupid, sir."

A quick measurement of Spratt's gap here would show it to be huge. So whose ego benefited? It certainly wasn't Spratt's, who will hate history for evermore and hate his teacher with a particular ferocity. It was the teacher's ego that benefited; but what use is that to him? The thoroughly alienated Spratt is unlikely to turn out a star pupil and bathe him in reflected glory. And yet when I point out to salespeople how damaging contradiction is, and tell this story to show how no one benefits from it in the long run, I often get the uncompromising reply:

"But Spratt was wrong. He needed putting straight. When our customers get it wrong, they need putting straight."

And they do it. I was out once with a sales engineer on a visit to an important customer. The customer asked if the product vibrated.

"No, no, of course it doesn't," the engineer admonished, waving his pen at the man like a club. As we were brushing the dust off ourselves after being hurled into the car park by security, he said: "I think that went very well."

Prying my fingers from his throat, he went on: "Well, I had to tell him. I couldn't let him believe our product vibrates."

Ironically, I'm sure that this is where the great white elephants of sales, the statements "The customer is always right" and "Never knock the competition" come from. If correcting an error can only be done by contradiction, thus challenging the customer's judgment, attacking their ego, and making them uncomfortable and consequently uncooperative, better not even try to correct it. Where's the control in this? What our engineer could have said was:

"Yes, you are absolutely right. Vibration was always a problem with miniaturized powerpacks. That's why, if you would just look here, you will see that we have fitted shock absorbers to solve exactly the problem you were worried about."

Back in school:

"Good try, Spratt; Nelson was actually our sea commander, who defeated the French at Trafalgar, and Wellington was our land commander at Waterloo, but that was a very good effort. Thank you very much."

You can "put people straight" and still preserve their dignity and self-respect. If you can make people feel good about themselves, the gap narrows, and although they most probably won't know why, they notice that they always seem to feel "right" when they are with you. This, of course, puts you in a very powerful position.

We have ways of ruining your day

Discussion of this ability to change the way people feel just by being with them leads us on to consider the sometimes sinister technique of behavior modification—a practice used and abused by torturers, brainwashers, cult-religionists and, probably most chilling of all, checkout girls.

How do you know how to behave, anyway? It may be that once you have sunk sufficient amounts of alcohol, you will be sick all over the barman's cat and then rush up and down the main street with your pants on your head. It is quite likely that you will be rewarded for this behavior by your friends in the form of their laughter and willingness to introduce you to others as a great person to spend an evening with down the pub. So how do you explain that when you go to your mom's for Sunday lunch, you don't repeat the performance?

"Did you have a nice evening, dear?"

"Yes, thank you, Mom."

"Pass the potatoes, dear, would you? I do hope you didn't have too much to drink."

"No, Mom."

You aren't being sick all over her cat and you aren't scampering round with your pants on your head. Why not? That is behavior you are often encouraged in, so why aren't you doing it now? I bet there aren't any signs up in your mother's sitting room saying: NO PUKING ON THE PETS and PLEASE REMAIN FULLY CLOTHED AT ALL TIMES. When asked this, people usually reply:

"Well, you just wouldn't do that at your mother's."

"Why not?"

"Well, you just wouldn't."

"How do you know how to behave?"

"Well, you just know, don't you."

It may be blindingly obvious to you that your mom would disapprove of the throwing up/scampering around undressed, but I bet you haven't tried it. She might find it amazingly diverting.

What is actually happening is that the surroundings and behavior of your mother are somehow changing or modifying your behavior. Now let's see how checkout girls manage this with even less apparent effort than your mom.

I wake up one morning and the birds are singing, the sun is shining, I have a day off, and all is right with the world. Whistling a cheerful little tune, I decide that it might be a lark to while away a few hours putting up my new bookshelves. I am almost happy when I discover that I have no screws, because this will mean a gentle little stroll into town to buy some. As I leave the house, a little bluebird settles on my shoulder.

"Hi, Geoff," it tweets, "have a nice day."

"Thanks, Mr. Bluebird."

The crossing light changes to green just for me.

"Thanks, little light."

"That's okay, Geoff; enjoy your day."

The electric doors on the store glide open especially smoothly to welcome me and the hardware counter has exactly the kind of screws I need. I take them to the cashier.

The girl has her back to me, her arms are folded and she is deep in conversation with an accomplice at the next register.

"Excuse me...Excuse me, can I pay for these?"

"Do what?"

"I want to pay for these screws."

"You what?"

"Pay. These screws."

"Not here, I'm closed now."

"What do you mean, closed?"

"I'm on my break."

As my hand flies to her windpipe I marvel at the change that she has wrought in my personality in just a few seconds.

I'm sure most of you reading this think you are psychologically quite stable, but don't count on it. It's quite scary to realize how much your behavior, even your personality, changes in response to your environment and other people. Especially other people. Everything we do seems to be in response to others or to get a response from them. Ask yourself: if you had been stranded as a baby on a desert island, isolated from human contact, would you have developed the day-glo paisley fish tie? No. We only come up with these aberrations to make an impression on others. If it weren't for the different people involved, you might run around the sitting room with your pants on your head and pass the potatoes politely in the pub. As persuaders, what we have to learn is how to elicit the reactions we want and rule out those we don't want. Once you know why people tend to react in particular ways you have a head start.

Having taken quite a detailed look at the psychological factors that make people behave as they do, we can now go back to that old chestnut of reward and punishment and refine our style somewhat. In its most basic form there may be drawbacks in commercial applications:

"Well, Mr. Jones, do you like the contract terms?"

If he says no, you give him a smart clip on the ear and repeat the question. If he then replies positively, a nice toffee apple might be in order. For myself, I have found introducing this style of persuasion into high-level negotiations to be somewhat counterproductive, and in fact the only people I can think of who seem able to make it work are the Mafia.

A psychologist who was studying slightly less blatant styles of reward and punishment asked his students a series of questions, the hidden objective of which was to get them to use more plurals. He therefore rewarded plurals and punished singulars.

"Well, Jim, what do we see with?"

"Um, eyes."

"Oh yes! Eyes is exactly right, that's great, you're getting the hang of this really quickly!" he would say, smiling straight at the student with lots of eye contact. "And these wiggly things on the end of my hand here?"

"Fingers?"

"Yes, yes, that's wonderful! And you breathe through...?"

"My nose?"

"Oh. Nose. Well, I suppose nose is sort of all right." Here he would frown, look down, sigh, withholding eye contact. Later the same question would produce "Nostrils"; eventually he even had them saying "I'd like to go homes now." The rewards and punishments alike were expressed solely by the behavior of the questioner towards the subject.

How a frown can do as much harm as a smack on the ear

This experiment makes a couple of points that are highly relevant to us persuaders. First, the punishment consisted of some very simple signals: no eye contact, looking down, frowns, and a complete absence of any positively encouraging behavior. If this is the case, I get punished for visiting a lot of shops, hotels, offices, and other businesses. How can we expect to succeed with behaviors that have been proven psychologically to be as violent in their deterrent effect as a smack on the ear?

The second interesting point was that the reward/punishment behaviors were less effective when the experiment was tried with two students, rather than with one psychologist and one student. It seems that we are less interested in winning approval from a person we consider equal or possibly inferior to us. What effect does a wrecked, bored, smelly lump have on you? Do you want to win their approval and be their friend for life? This has obvious implications for your preparation and presentation when you go out to persuade someone—and I'm not talking about slick power dressing wherever you go. Think of the effect you want to achieve. I personally find that the role of ingenuous idiot can put people well off guard and pay dividends. Think of the power that court jesters could wield despite their officially insignificant status.

"Ah, fiddle me ree...my lord Coltman doth pay most kind attention to your Majesty's pretty young wife...Ha ha!" and with a whack of a pig's bladder he consigns someone to the gallows.

Earlier in the chapter I warned against meeting aggression with aggression. I have also described how I was brought to the edge of committing grievous bodily harm by the manner of a checkout girl in a hardware store. If we put these two things together we can see the nightmare downward spiral that threatens.

A man is driving home after a very rough day. It is pouring with rain, he has just had his rear light knocked out by a skidding taxi, and he's rushing to get home before dark, but he knows he's forgotten to buy something. Suddenly he remembers, does a U-turn in the road and in a frenzy of spinning wheels and blaring horns screeches to a halt outside your doors. In he runs.

"Hey, you, fetch me one of those and take it out to my car."

"Are you speaking to me?"

"Can't see anyone else, stupid."

"Now you listen to me..."

This customer is not pathologically violent, he's just had a bad day. His behavior has been modified by his experiences up to the moment of his entering your shop. Now his miserable and aggressive behavior has made you miserable and aggressive, and when after he has snarled his way out of the shop a dear little old lady taps you on the shoulder you spin round and scream, "What do you want, you old bat?" thus making her more miserable than either of you. A chain reaction has been set off, and you are getting stuck in a vicious circle. The surlier you get, the less likely you are to do any good business and the more likely you are to fly off the handle even more quickly next time you feel provoked by someone else.

The way round this seems clear enough on paper, given all that I have been saying so far in this chapter. If you are faced with a miserable or aggressive person, you can choose to adopt a behavior that will defuse the situation and make them happy and therefore well disposed towards you.

"Oh, I'm sorry you're upset, have you had a rough trip? Certainly I'll fetch one for you. Would you like to take a seat while I carry it to your car?"

The other party usually cools down, often even apologizes.

Effective, yes; and it will make you feel good, thus setting off an upward spiral instead of a downward one. But it's not easy, especially not when you're rushed off your feet on a wet Saturday afternoon with hordes of mistreated, misunderstood, and miserable customers lining up to make your life a misery and no one, but no one, being nice to you or encouraging you. To perform well in these kind of conditions is down to professionalism and confidence. I have a relative who is a doctor and his self-confidence verges on arrogance. He reminds me of the old joke about doctors, which I repeat here in case it has passed you by:

Question: What's the difference between God and a doctor?

Answer: God doesn't think he's a doctor.

Now, when I dream of being a doctor I imagine driving my powerful sports car through a raging storm to save a child's life and receive the everlasting gratitude of its beautiful young mother. In sober reality, my relative's Thursdays are probably more typical of his life. This day is devoted to his hemorrhoid clinic, where the rubber gloves don't leave his hands from dawn till dusk. When some huge, smelly patient shambles in and says piteously, "I've got a real sore bottom, Doctor," he doesn't say, "Urrgh, I'm not touching that" and start poking at the patient with a long stick; he gives him the same care and help that he gave to the first patient of the day and that he will give to the last. And he can do this day after day without the experience reducing him in any way. The only explanation I can come up with for this resilience is the professionalism, commitment, and status that go with the job.

If you manage a business where your staff are constantly asked to deal with difficult or unappealing customers and you want them to handle these situations in the way I have recommended, then your only hope is to make sure that they receive sufficient genuine support and encouragement. When you and your people are empowered with the knowledge that what you are doing will in the long run produce the outcome you all want, then you can and will feel good about eating a little humble pie when the situation demands it.

Some people call this business of behavior modification button-pushing, harking back to the old experiment with rats, buttons, peanuts, and electric shocks. Briefly, it went like this. The rat was confronted with a series of colored buttons. Most buttons, when pressed with the rat's nose, produced an electric shock, except one, say the red one, which produced a peanut. The rat's button-pushing would start as a random process and fairly swiftly turn into concentrated attention on the red button. We, then, push our metaphorical buttons to achieve certain behaviors.

What this useful if simplistic image reminds us is that it is perfectly possible to push the wrong buttons, however metaphorical they may be. Take, for example, the case of a neighbor who comes up your garden path in tears just as you are leaving the house.

"Oh, hello. What's up?"

"It doesn't matter. You're just going out."

"Don't worry, it was nothing important. Come in, have a drink and tell me all about it."

The tale of woe emerges. You listen, smiling and nodding sympathetically. The next day the same person returns; you ask what the matter is, and they say:

"Nothing, actually, but I enjoyed our chat so much that I

thought I'd pop round again." At this you tell them to clear off because you are busy. The upshot is that from that day on they always have something tragic to share with you, and every time you see them plodding up to the front door you think:

"Oh no. Not again. Why whenever I see X does he try to depress me?"

The answer is simple: because you rewarded the moaning and wailing and rejected a straightforward offer of friendship. You pressed all the wrong buttons.

Playing poker without cards

This whole book is dedicated to investigating persuasive communication, and a lot of it has been about words—to say nothing of the fact that it has so far consisted entirely of words. This is the way that I have chosen to communicate with you in this instance. However, it is accepted psychological wisdom that only a relatively small proportion of all the communication that goes on among us takes the form of words; the rest is achieved through vocal intonation and nonverbal communication (or NVC). This being the case, I would be leaving a yawning gap in the subject if I did not touch on these aspects. However, this puts me in something of a dilemma. To do the subject justice I would need to write another whole book that would devote space to the interrelationship of psychological disciplines and the art of persuasion; to examine in some detail body language, transactional analysis, psychometric testing, neurolinguistic programming, and many other areas, each of them complex in itself. Obviously all this has to be simplified and distilled down considerably for present purposes. On the other hand, I view with profound skepticism the negotiating skills and customer care training packages that chuck in a bit of body language for good measure. These trivial summaries owe more to tabloid journalism than useful information and do no more than cause delegates to spend their coffee breaks giggling and saying to each other, "I know what you're thinking," or "Cross your legs, Beryl, you're sending signals." Most normal, balanced people do not go careering out of these courses and apply this kind of idiocy in real life, but there are always the few halfwits who henceforth spend their meetings watching every move the other party makes and coming to wildly inappropriate conclusions.

Of course, having given you this health warning I must now touch on these topics, but I ask you to remember throughout a key word: congruence. In other words, look at the whole picture, don't take any "clue" in isolation and preserve your detachment. If someone scratches their head, they may have fleas, not an attack of galloping indecision. If you are really interested in body language, there are scores of books you could read, many of them entertaining as well as interesting, but do remember that all you get is clues, and clues that should be taken with a pinch of salt.

The first nonverbal communicator that we use is the face. It may seem obvious that our faces can express all our emotions— fear, sadness, anger, interest, happiness—but it also holds a few surprises, and the ability not only to read other people's faces but to control your own is very valuable. There is an interesting test based on purely diagrammatic illustrations of the human face as in Figure 1.

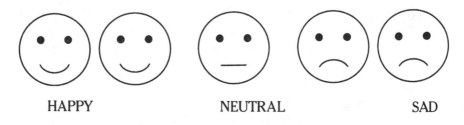

HAPPY   NEUTRAL   SAD

Figure 1

Considering that these are only simple lines on a page, it is amazing that already they convey emotion. The test involves asking people which of these faces they find the most and the least appealing. It seems fairly predictable that the happy smiling faces are the most popular; but the least popular is more surprising, for while people are upset by angry or sad expressions, what they find most disturbing is the completely neutral face. It is the lack of response, the deadness, that causes trouble. I heard it explained the other day by someone who said, "Love me, even hate me, but please don't ignore me." If a child is rude or cheeky and you pursue it shouting, it often laughs; but face it with a neutral, unmoving stare and it is usually crushed.

It stands to reason, then, that the first thing you do with your face to get positive reactions from other people is to put a smile on it. We are, of course, talking about generous, rewarding smiles here; flippant or supercilious smiles will drive people nuts and though this can be fun if you are feeling malicious it can also be very counterproductive.

If you look at the diagrams in Figure 1 again, you will see that there are two identical-seeming happy faces and two identical-seeming sad faces. Now, it so happens that one of these happy faces in fact belongs to a homicidal maniac, but the pair of them have disguised this by both shaving off their eyebrows. The sad pair have done the same to hide the fact that one of them is furious, the other upset. Any idea which is which? No? Then try them with their eyebrows replaced, as in Figure 2.

Figure 2

If even these tiny lines give a strong impression of feeling, just imagine what your face is doing to the person opposite you.

Clearly, then, you can tell a great deal by watching someone else's face, and body language books make a lot out of this; but I'm convinced that most of the time we read body language unconsciously, and if this is so we will be in a much more powerful position if we can manipulate our own body language to send the signals we want the other person to pick up without their even being aware they are doing it.

Sales and customer care gurus make great play of the idea of eye contact. Psychologists call it "the gaze" and time it to the split second. This is indeed a very important point, as we have already seen (remember the case of the talking bottom?). People who are being less than honest, or who are less than accomplished communicators, tend to give too little eye contact, or not maintain it; hence the expression "shifty." Perhaps I don't want to reveal all; can I manipulate my gaze? Yes, indeed. Let's call back the little diagrammatic face to illustrate how.

Draw an imaginary triangle connecting the pupils of the other person's eyes and a point below their chin, as in Figure 3.

Figure 3

Gaze into this; it is called the "intimate triangle," and if the person is of the opposite sex and responds, you can make whoopee for the rest of the day and forget about business. If, on the other hand, it is business you're after, try Figure 4.

Figure 4

A triangle again connecting the pupils, but this time with a point at the top of the forehead, is known as the "sincerity triangle," even sometimes as the "business sincerity triangle." If you incline your head slightly, smile gently, present open, upturned palms and gaze into this area, you are set to tell huge porkies without fear of detection. But there are dangers. The first one, particularly important in our case remembering the absolute importance of staying in control, is that you can be so convincing that your own feedback loop convinces you that you are in fact being honest. Politicians seem to have trouble avoiding this pitfall. Second, it is a physiological fact that a person who sees something or someone that genuinely attracts them cannot stop their pupils from dilating even if they are trying to sustain a poker face. This can in fact be very useful, especially if you play poker (actual or metaphorical).

We move on down from the face to the rest of our bodies. The first controversial area here is that of touch. Most customer care programs that I have attended recently make a great song and dance about the importance of touch. They tell checkout staff to touch the customer's hand when giving change; they tell transport clerks to hold tickets in such a way that touch is inevitable. They say it works; I say I hate being touched. Perhaps I'm just a miserable anal-retentive Englishman, but even if I am I'm certainly not the only one; which all goes to show yet again that you can't bank on getting the reaction you want without preparing for it—it all depends on the individual.

What can a wet fish teach you?

There is a thriving mythology all about handshakes, too, from the manly grasp all the way down the scale to the wet fish. There may be something in all this; but the only clue that I find valuable in practical terms is how the hand is presented to me. If it is palm down, it does tend to show confidence, even arrogance, and I tend to watch my step. If you're not out to gain anything and you don't mind making an enemy for life, it's great fun to grasp the back of this hand so that the clasping fingers wriggle impotently like a stranded beetle. Crushing, but it won't win you a friend.

It's all very fascinating, this body language business, but we must drag ourselves back to the core of what we are about and ask: What are we going to do with these clues? Many gestures adults make can be traced back to the much larger gestures of children. A child who doesn't want to see something will clasp her hands in front of her eyes; the adult will gently rub one eye. The young hand clasped over the ear to block out frightening sounds becomes ear-pulling or rubbing. Both hands across the mouth to hide a childish lie becomes the finger rubbing the top lip to hide the mouth. What are you going to do when you see this? You can hardly say, "Ooh, you little liar," to a valued client; but you might try "I'm sorry, I'm gabbling away. What is it you're not sure of?" Often you will get in response a smile of relief and an explanation—which is all you need.

Really useful information can sometimes be gleaned from the unspoken language between people, which can often give you the quickest way of identifying who is the moving force. Take a husband and wife. The husband asks,

"Can we go in this shop, light of my life?"

"You can go in, Charlie Scroggins, but if you buy anything you're dead meat."

Later the wife tells you: "Speak to my hubby, he makes all the decisions." Now watch: if this innocent scratches her nose or folds her arms and Charlie follows suit, it becomes quite clear who the boss is and you should consider routing your efforts in that direction. Similarly with the tyrannical old company chairman who sits in on your presentation and says, "Carry on! I shouldn't be here really, I'm more or less retired, my sons and the rest of the board make all the decisions now." Watch them, and be flexible.

You can use this gesture imitation as well as watch it; mirroring someone else's body movements often helps you to get emotionally closer to them.

I could go on and on with more examples; but the important thing here is to remember that these are clues, hints, possibilities: you can use them, but don't depend on them and don't over-interpret them. Maybe those tightly folded arms signify exclusion, but it might just be a bit cold in here. Leaning back may be a withdrawal, but he might have realized he went a bit heavy on the garlic sausage at lunch. Remember the principle of congruence and hang on to your detachment. I would certainly advise more reading on the whole subject of psychology; don't get bogged down or confused trying to remember it all, but do use its insights. When your aim is to have complete control over the situation without giving your own game away, they can be priceless.

9

Negotiating: Sympathize, and Trust No One

There is something about the very idea of a training seminar that puts me on my guard from the word go. Ostensibly, of course, these events are held to equip participants better for their work out in the real world; and yet so often they are held, and attended, and evaluated, for reasons that have nothing to do with the effectiveness of the training and even less to do with the real world. There is often a sort of implicit conspiracy between presenter and delegates, who for their own various ends need to say what a successful course it was. We once put on an executive course in partnership with another consultancy, choosing as the venue an exclusive country club. One of the leading national conglomerates sent a trio of upper middle management. During the event, none of the presenters caught sight of these three, and it was discovered that they had spent the entire time playing golf. In due course their employer sent a fat check and an assessment form which stated that their employees had found the course very valuable and would be eager to attend another.

The never-never-land atmosphere of the seminar room is reinforced by the awesome dominance of style over content that tends to prevail, with everyone adopting the "I'm on a course persona"—lots of nice sharp pencils, a clean collar and tie, but jacket off to show that we're really getting down to the nitty gritty. (If you think this is sexist, I concentrate on the male image because women usually have very little time for these kinds of boys' games.) In this sort of setting large quantities of so-called training are handed out in labeled packages by people who either don't see or don't care about the huge difference between the cozy world of the seminar room and phrase book and the real world of awkward people who haven't learned their lines.

I watched a video recently of a man training a group of classic middle management types in the art of negotiating. Within minutes his smug complacency had me baying and howling at the screen, slavering to tear his slimy heart out. The group were role-playing various scenarios, a dumb idea at the best of times, and obviously in some previous session the "tutor" had given certain actions catchy "hip" names, so that when a delegate messed things up, he could leap in and say, "What have you forgotten, Derek?"

Derek would smile an awful shit-eating smile and, to the uproarious laughter of his fellow delegates, he would say, "My dingley-do's?"

"Your dingley-do's, Derek! When you forget your dingley-do's, Derek, the other party moves in like a rat up a pipe."

As this is all happening on the video screen, none of the participants can hear me shouting abuse and grinding my teeth. I would love to be in there just for a moment, just long enough to tell this idiot what he can do with his dingley-do's. Now all his poor victims were busily writing notes with a kind of pitiable intensity, obviously feeling that they would go out of that seminar room able to negotiate for control of the universe; and yet they hadn't been given a single piece of equipment actually to deal with the real world.

A crucifix is no use with a Jewish vampire

A lot of what this man had been talking was complete gob-bledegook, even leaving out the excruciating catchphrases, but a good bit of it was accepted practice. And yet accepted practice can fall down in the most spectacular manner if you aren't prepared for departures from the script. In Polanski's film *Dance of the Vampires* a man is attacked by a Jewish vampire. He holds up the crucifix (as per accepted practice) to be greeted with the statement: "Boy, have you picked the wrong vampire!"

I did once attend a "dingley-do"-type seminar, not on negotiating as it happened, but on assertiveness. I made a contribution to the proceedings, and the resultant uproar was spectacular and terminal. The purpose of the session was supposed to be to teach project managers how to deal assertively with difficult workers. A role play was set up (naturally) with the presenter acting out the part of a fitter who was refusing to work overtime to finish an important project. A nervous young delegate was playing the part of his boss.

"Er, um, Jackson, I would like you to work late this week."

"No chance."

"Er, um, Jackson, it is rather important to us that we finish this project."

"No."

This went on and on until the youngster was humiliated, to the entertainment of his colleagues. Then the "right way" was shown, with two presenters playing the roles. It went something like this:

"Jackson, I would like you to work late this week."

"No."

"Okay Jackson, I think you know how important this is. I don't know if you are aware how your refusal will affect your appraisal, but," laying watch on table, "I am prepared to sit here quietly for four minutes while you consider your decision. If after that time you still refuse, you must accept the consequences."

This obvious success was greeted by applause. The delegates were then called upon one by one to try the same technique, and of course they succeeded too. I complained that it was a fix and offered to play the part of the fitter. A slightly less nervous and more confident delegate took the boss's role.

"Jackson, I would like you to work late this week."

"No."

"Okay Jackson, I think you know how important this is. I don't know if you are aware how your refusal will affect your appraisal, but…"

At this point I grabbed his shirt-front and hauled him up out of his seat. Buttons popped in all directions.

"You're asking for a punch in the mouth, sonny! Threaten me again and I'll shove my fist so far down your throat I'll grab your feet and rip you inside out."

There was silence for a moment or two, then bedlam.

"You can't use violence!" clamored the others, and the man with no shirt buttons said, "I would complain!"

So we role-played that. I was the chairman.

"Ah, young Smith, just the man I wanted to see."

"Sir, Jackson just…"

"Yes, Jackson. I understand that you have quite upset Jackson. Look. Good fitters are hard to come by, and I can get personnel clerks two for a penny, so take my advice and don't upset the fitters if you want a future here."

Seminars, especially ones based on role play, are a poor way of learning how to go about things because they fiddle the results. Intentionally or not, no trainer is going to set up a role play that fails; but the real world is a cruel and unpredictable place. That negotiating trainer with his cozy phrases and pat techniques was giving the false promise that everything is negotiable and that if you learn your code words, agreement is inevitable and predictable. His delegates leave with the impression that they have gained knowledge which will somehow give them power over the victims of their newfound talents.

A blazing monk can be difficult to negotiate with

Now, there are some very powerful negotiating techniques that we will shortly investigate, but first we have to consider the reasons why negotiations fail, sometimes quite spectacularly. It is not a foregone conclusion that agreement will be reached.

Perversely, in fact, it seems that the more powerful you are, the more likely the negotiation will collapse or explode. The reason for this is a factor that is rarely taken into consideration, namely the other party's feelings. During the Vietnam War, the mighty US army so upset some small and relatively powerless Buddhist monks that they set fire to themselves. It's rather difficult to talk to a blazing monk, which illustrates the dangers of assuming you can negotiate with anyone.

Most spouses have some favorite term of abuse for their partners. They may be unfaithful, or violent, or untrustworthy, or lazy, but there is always something and often it is pretty venomous. At the height of any row with my wife, she, pushed to the limit, describes me as "tricky." That may seem mild, but it isn't, and I confess that "tricky" is a state of mind that is near-impossible to deal with, because it means that irrational, even self-destructive decisions will be made, just to screw up the other party. The examples are there for all of us to see: the blazing monk; the union who will shut the factory even if it means the end of their own jobs; even the Charge of the Light Brigade. Can you imagine the Russians popping their heads up over the cannons and shouting, "Hey, lads, can't we talk about this? You're only hurting yourselves, you know."

Skillful negotiation can be very powerful and should get you what you want; but first you must deal with the blazing monk question, because no matter how powerful your position, if someone goes "tricky" on you, you've blown it.

We saw in the last chapter on psychology how deep-rooted and apparently irrational feelings can be, so it should come as no surprise to you that in negotiating you ignore the emotional side of the business at your peril. Nonetheless, this is precisely what so many of today's training hotshots do, with the consequence that their carefully produced little phrase books might as well be in Mandarin Chinese for all the use they are outside the seminar room.

Perhaps I should have said that you ignore *both* emotional sides of the business at your peril, because of course there are two lots of tangled feelings to be dealt with: yours as well as the other person's. Before any agreement can be achieved, or even much progress made towards one, you and your opposite number have to tackle, and then set aside, your own feelings. I don't know if any of you reading this know what it is like to write a book, and what bloodthirsty tyrants publishers can be, but for those of you who don't, what happens is that you start writing and then send bits off to the publisher to see if they like it. When I'd sent in a few chunks, my publisher said, "Ho hum, not too bad, but what's all this I, I, I, first-person business?"

"Oh," I replied, "I think it makes me appear as though I am personally involved and experienced in the subject areas I am discussing."

"Well, I think it makes you sound like a self-centered little jerk," he merrily rejoined, slipping his checkbook back into his pocket.

In personal negotiation, the "I" factor is in fact very important, particularly when it comes to expressing feelings in a controlled fashion. When someone displeases or insults you, the automatic impulse is usually to start your retort with "You..." instead of "I..." Many an impending explosion can be defused by your honestly revealing your feelings in this way. If your colleague says, "I'm sorry, your money has been trampled into oblivion by elephants," the temptation is to say, "You liar," or at the very least, "You clumsy oaf, why didn't you head them off?" All this does is to provoke self-justification. How do you actually feel? Concentrate on that instead.

"I understand how difficult that makes things, but I must say that I feel as though I am being deceived or even deliberately misled."

You can get across the fact that their action is causing trouble without prompting them into righteous indignation about a direct accusation. What this means is that you stand more chance of getting the real issue addressed without the conversation rushing off down side alleys. In other words, you are staying in control.

At the same time, you should be aware of the other person's feelings, and if you have sufficient time, prepare to consider them. Before a crucial meeting you could jot down how you feel, and how you think they feel, and why:

"I am worried, and they seem upset. What is it that I am worried about, and what has upset them?" Then, when the meeting takes place, you can say:

"I am worried that you seem so upset. Would you like to tell me about it?"

How to do nothing

When they do tell you about it, listen to them. This is neither as obvious nor as straightforward as it sounds. There is a powerful telephone sales technique which involves asking a question and then remaining silent until you get a response; people don't like silence, and feel pressured into replying. However, a sales engineer who had been on a course in which this technique featured said afterwards that he had enjoyed the course but that this telephone thing had him beat.

"I spoke to the client, put the question to him, and remained silent as I was taught, but after a while he said, 'Hello?' and then again, 'Hello? Hello-o?' and then he hung up."

When you listen, you allow the other party to speak while you absorb the information; but you have to remind the other person that you are there, mentally as well as physically, or the conversation will very soon dry up. Most of us know the frustrations of talking to the nincompoop whose simple mind is in another and perhaps happier place, or to the smooth operator at a cocktail party whose eyes are flicking right and left over our shoulders looking for someone more useful to talk to. Good listening is active, not passive, and requires concentration.

To illustrate the difference between the active listener and the passive idiot I can do no better than to refer you to my large ginger cat. Anyone who owns a cat will know that felines have at their disposal a range of ways of doing nothing. In the case of my cat, one of these occurs after he has eaten something particularly revolting discovered under a hedge or at the bottom of the garbage can, whereafter he will sit silently and happily digesting it underneath the radiator behind my favorite chair, unnoticed until he starts to fart. When the whiff of this obnoxious effluvia reaches me I leap out of my chair to look for the cause and see a motionless heap of contented ginger fur with a beatific smile on its face, like a large but gently bubbling soft toy. The cat is doing nothing. He is also doing nothing when he is sitting crouched for hours at a time under a particular tree waiting for the fledglings to fail their flying lessons; but in this case he is no longer a smelly blob but a coiled spring of muscle and bone, every sense attuned to his prey, ready to react in a split second.

When you listen, aim for crouching cat rather than farting cat. Nod, and smile, and grunt, and go, "mm, hm" at appropriate points in the conversation to encourage the other person to talk; be alert to the nuances of what they are saying up there in the tree and be ready to react.

When they have talked, and you have listened, you should have gathered plenty of material—some of it facts and figures, but a lot of it feelings and emotions. As we've already seen, these feelings need to be properly considered and taken into account if you want to avoid any nearby monks bursting into flames, but they must not be allowed to interfere with the achievement of your objective. Remember, you must keep your objective in clear and constant view; you have entered into this meeting in order to attain a particular goal, and no emotions can be allowed to get in the way. This great mass of information that you have extracted from the other party must therefore be panned to separate the gold nuggets from the dross; until you have done this you cannot go on to refine the gold. To take a simple example, if you see a traffic cop sticking a ticket on your car, your objective will be to get that ticket withdrawn; the minute you call the cop an officious busybody you have lost your chance. You mixed your feelings up with what you wanted to achieve. Again, it's all about detachment, separation, assessment of the situation, control.

It's not just negative emotions that can blow a negotiation off course. If you like the other person you will want to believe them and to conduct the discussion in such a way that it will please them. Here, separation of feelings and objectives is equally if not more crucial. You should acknowledge your feelings, but beware of letting them run you; this makes you very vulnerable. When I was a small child, my father picked me up and put me on the top of a very high old wardrobe. I felt frightened and alone, and started to cry. I saw my father far below me, and he smiled up at me in a kind and reassuring way.

"Jump into my arms," he said softly. I clung to the picture rail and cried out, "No, daddy, you'll drop me."

"Trust me, my darling, I love you. I won't let anything happen to you."

"No, daddy, you'll drop me."

"I won't drop you. Trust me, please."

Finally, trembling, I let go of the rail and stepped off the tall wardrobe. Plunging towards my father, I saw his smile and open arms rushing up to meet me. At the very last moment he stepped aside and I crashed onto the hard floor, bruised and winded.

"There you are, my darling son, that will teach you never to trust anyone." This memorable piece of advice has stood me in good stead throughout my life, and I commend it to you in negotiating. Never trust anyone.

Some people say that being untrusting can cause offense, but this need not be the case if you handle things properly. Again, be calm, be rational, relate everything to the task in hand without getting distracted into emotional byways. If you buy goods in a shop and you write a check, the salesperson will ask for your ID. Do you say, "Here, what's the matter? Don't you trust me?" No, because you know full well they don't, that's what these bits of plastic are for; you accept this without comment because that's the way things are.

"I know it's sad about that money of yours the elephants walked all over, but don't worry because we have got a courier to deliver you a new lot."

"Oh, that's great. Thank you so much. If I could just have the telephone number of the courier to check when he will be arriving."

"What's the matter, don't you trust me?"

"It's not a matter of trust, it's a matter of me getting my money correctly delivered."

If you preserve the calm demeanor of normality and avoid making accusations, you need not trust people to avoid offending them.

Bargaining is not negotiating

I don't know whether it's occurred to you before now that negotiating takes place after a sale, not before it. In other words, if someone has been convinced that they want something, if they realize that they need it and have worked out that they can afford it, *then* they will start to negotiate. All that is gained by even the perfect sale, achieved by the greatest salesperson in the world, is the chance to negotiate. Think of your own position. You and your partner want a new hi-fi. You've been wondering whether you can afford it for months, your old one's on its last legs, and at last the sums have worked out. You've been through all the brochures and magazines and pressed your noses up against a lot of windows and finally you've picked out the system you want. It is then that you go in and try for the best deal.

For the dealer, it is the most dangerous of times; he's not selling, he's negotiating, and the skills are often lacking. If you have a business and a powerful customer approaches you, getting their basic agreement to do business with you is only a very small part of the transaction. They will want you to extend ninety days' credit, to give a 30 percent discount and to deliver nationwide in small batches. You would like money up front, full catalogue price, and buyer to collect in bulk. Where you arrive between these two extreme points is critical: many busy companies go bust each year, simply by failing to make money. Powerful organizations can make the bulk of their money by screwing down suppliers, and if you're not careful you'll find you'd have been better off without this one.

The two views we have just outlined, the customer's and yours, are usually defined as "positions," and a negotiation is classically defined as the practice of finding a satisfactory compromise between these two positions (I will have more to say about the notion of compromise later in this chapter). I would rather call this bargaining—a respectable skill in itself but certainly not negotiation, which is far more powerful and correspondingly more intricate. The trouble with bargaining can best be illustrated by the story of two men walking home along a railway track. A train roars into view behind them. They start to run. Hearing the express thundering nearer, one runs up the embankment, while the other sticks to the track and doubles his speed. The train, of course, catches up to the second man and hits him. The first man kneels beside his broken and bleeding friend.

"Why the hell didn't you run up the bank with me?"

"Look, if I couldn't beat the bloody thing on the flat, I certainly wasn't going to get away from it uphill."

These are the short-sighted words of a bargainer who believes the issue has to be slugged out on a single track and fails to conceive of the idea of another route.

The first problem with bargaining is that to reach a compromise you need a common denominator. (What would be the compromise position between a tomato and Tuesday afternoon?) The next is that the very existence of that common denominator locks you into single-track confrontation. Take the situation of an employee who wants to be secure and happy, and a company chairman who needs to please the shareholders. If this combination is going to be dealt with by bargaining, the common denominator must be pay, and the two express trains are set on their collision course. The employee looks to satisfy his desire for happiness and security with high pay, the chairman looks to satisfy the shareholders with a tough wages policy. Neither side is going to be prepared to investigate nonfinancial side issues

Having said that, it's worth looking at the best way to bargain before we move on to see how true negotiating can be a better way to do things. The first golden rule is not to get caught out by an unexpected bargaining session. The essence of this discipline is preparation, because the success of duplicity on the part of the other side (never trust anyone) depends on your lack of knowledge. Remember that in an earlier chapter I warned you against being buttonholed into meetings or conversations at inappropriate times and places? Well, this is a perfect example of why. You need to know what you are going to be talking about and to arm yourself with the relevant information. If, despite preparing to the best of your ability, you find yourself getting out of your depth, or if you find yourself on the verge of agreeing to things on which you are not informed, be ready to stop and set the date for another meeting.

Imagine you're discussing a construction project of some kind, working out the various responsibilities and costs. If someone apparently falling over themselves to cooperate says, "Of course, if you just dig the holes," that probably means they know full well there is a six-inch water table and the one real expense of the whole business is digging the holes. If you don't know, don't agree. Before the meeting, check facts: prices, alternatives, precedents. Write it all down, and take it with you to the meeting.

The next point brings me slap up once more against accepted practice. The received wisdom is that before any dealing is done, a discussion takes place during which you attempt to find out the other party's demands and state your own. In other words, battle lines are drawn. My hackles rise even as I write this down, and I will tell you why. If you really want $100 for something, what will you ask? $150? Why do you do that? Is it because you know you will have to move, so you add a bit to knock a bit off? In fact, you are lying, because you don't want $150, you want $100. You have started your business dealings with a lie. Your opponent—I use the word deliberately, because that is exactly what they have just become—will probably value the item at $100 as well, so they offer $50, knowing that they too will have to move. They too have started with a lie. So now we have two liars across the table; a great basis for an honest and productive business relationship.

The danger of believing your own lies

You are a liar. How do you feel if someone says that to you? It's pure human nature to reject this accusation; all of us will justify ourselves rather than admit dishonesty. As we rush to the defense of our integrity, we find that the best justification is belief, so we then start believing that whatever it is *is* worth $150, and our opponent likewise argues himself into believing his offer of $50 is very generous. Disaster is looming.

If you don't believe me, try this exercise, which we often use. Take two people with strong and opposing political beliefs, and ask them to take part in a role play. The left-winger is given the role of wealthy company chairman, the right-winger that of communist union representative. The union man is told to ask for a $100 a week pay rise, despite agreeing that $50 would be fair. The boss also agrees that $50 is fair, but is told to refuse any rise at all. Off they go. They usually start lightheartedly, jokingly putting on what they believe to be the appropriate caricature accents, but after some time the good humor wears off and they become genuinely abusive towards each other. When they are interviewed separately afterwards, each condemns the intransigence of the other and hotly justifies his own position, in complete disregard of their original and genuine political views.

This should convince you that the stating of positions can be very destructive and has the negative effect of making the parties dig in. As the whole raison d'être of bargaining is supposed to be the movement of both sides, that is counterproductive to say the least. And yet a great number of the current high priests of negotiating skills state that the preliminary skirmish is an opportunity to clarify positions. I'm tempted to say that all it clarifies is the ease with which normal, happy people become pig-headed bigots. My own preference is to state nothing and do my utmost to get at the other person's true agenda. Listen, and gain information.

Whichever scheme you follow, the next step in the bargaining process is to make a proposal or offer. The other party responds to this (not, we hope, with personal violence). This response in turn should give us a clue as to how to proceed. An emphatic and unqualified "no" at this stage is in fact quite rare. Often there is a hesitation or ambiguity in the reply which can give you an indication of your best next step.

"No, the way things are at present, we can't..."

"It is not possible considering the standards of reliability of our current supplier."

"I don't think so, based on the figures you've shown me."

Faced with one of these, you don't say "Oh, okay, pick up your stuff and go." You say: "Are you saying that if our figures were adjusted, you may reconsider?"

As you go through this routine, it should begin to become clear to you what is needed to reach a deal. This is the time to start making realistic suggestions; but don't get carried away. Every offer you make must be conditional on a concession from the other party. At the risk of repeating myself until you are screaming with the torture of it, you must keep control, and keeping control of the whole thing means controlling every step. If you say, "Oh, okay, I'll give you my pen," they say, "thank you" and pocket it. You've just lost a pen and gained nothing.

The key here is the simple words "if" and "then": "If I give you my pen, then will you sign the agreement?" If they say no, you can say without embarrassment or conflict, "Okay, then you can't have my pen." Then nudge them on to the next stage.

"What do you want to make you sign?"

"A thousand dollars."

"If I gave you a thousand dollars, then would you sign and give us exclusive rights?"

"Not exclusive rights."

"Then I couldn't offer a thousand."

A tip to bear in mind while all this is going on is to try to gauge the real value to the other party of what you have to offer, and don't assume they will value it as you will. I love roller skating, but have nowhere to practice, and one of my clients has a huge empty factory. It cost him nothing to let me skate there, but it was of great value to me. Do you have a hotel? The accommodation is worth hundreds to the other party and may cost you virtually nothing. Understand the value to yourself of what you possess, and then understand its value to others.

A compromise is a dead end

So where is my problem with this standard bargaining routine? It starts with the claim that, ideally, this is win-win negotiating, as opposed to win-lose, lose-win, or even lose-lose. The theory states that if both sides get stuck in, the best that can be hoped for is that they both win something. This is called a compromise; I call it an impasse, or, more bluntly, a dead end. If the two trains are on the same track, where they touch is where they stop. The actual point at which this occurs may vary according to which is going faster, which manages to kid the other that it's already stopped and then put on a late spurt, which has got three extra engine-drivers aboard, but once they've stopped that's the end of the line: the other train is now in the way of any further movement. Both have won mileage, and you could say they have reached a destination, but it is a destination that has been forced on each by the obstruction of the other.

The man on the training video I was abusing at the start of this chapter, who taught his skills as a tough negotiator, was just showing how to push harder on his piece of track. His own smug complacency prevents him from seeing any alternative. He accepts that he's unlikely to get all that he wants, but he'll get as much as he can at the expense of the other party. Oh, yes, it would be nice if the other party got some of what they want as well, but ideally *we* should get what we set out to get, and that has overriding priority. It is his hardline attitude that blinds this man, and countless others like him, to opportunity, because his whole effort is put into a tough defense of position, with its tacit acceptance that an agreement will require some element of surrender. Reference is made regularly in tough talk sessions to a mythical cake. This cake can, through talking, be made bigger, but it is always finite and the victor gets the lion's share.

Some of you reading this will be married. Would you, without being facetious, like to tell me who is winning in your marriage? The correct answer to this question is a bewildered silence, because "winning" is not a word that could ever be used of a successful marriage. Not win-lose, lose-win, lose-lose, or even win-win: the answer "we are both winning" isn't really acceptable because winning implies competition and measurable achievement.

The word that best describes a successful marriage, in all its infinite variations, is "synergy," the state of affairs in which the sum of the parts is greater than the whole. Marriage, after all, is the coming together of two people for great personal benefit to each that is not achieved at the expense of the other. What is more, when this kind of relationship works, it is often because of differences between the partners, both positive and negative. At the most basic level—assuming for a moment that you are one male and one female partner—it is the very different, indeed opposite, nature of your shapes that makes the relationship successful. This principle has been institutionalized in engineering, where parts that fit together are called male and female. To turn from physiology and engineering to folk tradition, we find agreement in difference classically illustrated by Jack Sprat and his wife.

One rare book on negotiating skills that has impressed me is *Getting to Yes* by Fisher and Ury. The line these two take comes very close to my own beliefs; and they have also made me realize that the alternative to "hard" does not have to be "soft"—but more of that later. For now, we should concentrate on the excellent way in which they deal with the issue of the cake.

Fisher and Ury don't accept that the cake is a finite cake. If you had this cake and you gave someone half of it, 50 percent, how much would you have left? Fifty percent, you say? If it is Fisher and Ury's magic cake you could well have 100 percent. They mention two sisters who are beating the living daylights out of each other; they are gouging and screaming and spitting and you are asked to mediate between them. You discover that what they are fighting over is a large, juicy orange. What would be the fairest and most reasonable thing to do? Cut the orange in half, of course, and give them half each. Their reaction may surprise you. The first sister says, "Yum, yum," peels her bit of orange, eats it and throws the peel away. The second sister says, "Thank heavens, now I can make my cake," grates the peel and throws the flesh away. You decided what the parties wanted based on your own preconceptions of what you would do with an orange if you had one. You have let your feelings become involved and this has led you into making the wrong decision; a preliminary investigation would have enabled each sister to have had 100 percent of what she wanted. In other words, this particular cake will divide to give 200 percent.

Oranges and cakes may seem trivial, but when these ideas are transferred to world diplomacy, we can see some very exciting results. When I try the orange exercise on people, I get a variety of answers. There is the classic "Divide it in half," which is well meant, but when translated into Vietnam, Korea, or Berlin is a recipe for future disasters. I also usually find one smartass who says that he would take the orange away from the two sisters completely and look after it himself. This translates into South Africa, Northern Ireland, and Cambodia—a great way to make both sides turn on you.

You will have to forgive my cavalier way with historical and geographical detail in the following example, but I'm sure you'll get the gist. The situation was that Egypt and Israel set about each other in a big way and Egypt made a strong attempt to launch a tank invasion of Israel. The plan failed, and indeed Egypt lost a lot of land to the Israelis. The fighting stopped and Egypt tried to jolly things along.

"Phew! That was fun; nothing like a bracing little war before breakfast to get the circulation going. Well, I suppose we'd better get on. Oh, by the way, could we have our desert back, please?"

Israel's reply was unequivocal. "No."

The Egyptians, realizing they needed help, got their Arab friends to intercede. As they didn't have much to threaten Israel with, they did the next best thing and cut off America's oil.

"Hey!" cried the USA. "What was that for?"

"They're your friends. We'll turn the oil on again when you persuade them to give Egypt its desert back."

The Americans then did what so many negotiators failed to do. Remember that orange. They visited both sides and simply asked each: "Why on earth do you want a desert?" It was the difference between the replies that gave the clue to a solution.

The Egyptians said: "It is the land of our forefathers. It has always been Egyptian, and it is a matter of honor that it be returned to the map of Egypt."

The Israelis said: "Before we got that desert, their tanks used to sit on our border, ready to roll just a few hundred yards from our population. Now we have a thousand miles of desert between us and the nearest tank."

There was the answer. The desert returned to being Egyptian in name, but was totally demilitarized, thus giving both parties 100 percent of what they wanted.

The truth has nothing to do with it

I should like to utter a word of warning here against misplaced idealism. A great feature of my hippie days was the so-called "search for truth." If you peered through the pungent clouds of burning incense towards the tinkling of temple bells and the sound of people calling, "Ommmmmmmmm," you would find us all, eyes rolled heavenwards, waiting for Truth to drop in on us. In negotiating, dear reader, truth has virtually nothing to do with anything. If you are in dispute with another party and you have both argued your case, based on your sincere beliefs and prejudices, the introduction of the real truth will do nothing to move either side.

Perhaps you sincerely hold a particular religious belief that conflicts with the belief held by a friend. Imagine receiving a sealed envelope from heaven that will reveal the truth if it is opened in the presence of both of you. Whoever was wrong would not accept it—and I bet even now you are imagining how your friend would react, because it couldn't possibly be you that was wrong, could it?

If you know that you are going to negotiate and that a straight bargaining session is not enough, then as we have seen you have to find a better way. This path starts with preparation. First, you need to prepare for the feelings that will be released. How will you react to their anger? If you were them, what would it be that has made you angry? The bath is a very relaxing place, and if I have a big agreement to make, I get into a sort of trance-like state, surrounded by hot soapy bubbles, and picture what it would be like to explain my decisions to my boss if I were the other party. In this way you can get inside the other person's mind and appreciate how their situation and prejudices have colored their thinking.

It always frightens me when I see a politician on the television stating their case categorically, followed by their opposite number stating the exact opposite point of view. It's like one of those situations where there is a monster behind either door A or door B—but it's me who is expected to open the door. Always remember that it is more than likely that the person who contradicts you sincerely believes that they have right on their side. You can't just shrug and say "Well, they're wrong," because that way an impasse is inevitable. Before you condemn the other person's position, certainly before you can try to alter it, you must try to think as they do, to understand what they feel. Perhaps a concession to you would mean a major loss of face. Remember the classic tale of Carnegie trying to swallow up the Pullman company? The point arrived where Mr. Pullman said,

"But what will the company be called?"

Carnegie replied: "Why, Pullman, of course."

He saved the other man's face and gained the company.

The next aspect of preparation to consider is the question of what to do if the negotiations fail—and, indeed, of how to decide when this failure has taken place. If you don't know where to stop, you can really negotiate yourself into a hole.

You've decided to sell me your piano. You want $800 for it, so you tell me it is worth $950, but in your own mind you are determined not to take any less than $750. Therefore you come to the negotiation with a back wall of $750. I tell you that I cannot afford to pay a penny more than $750 and that is that. You reluctantly agree, and I fish through all my pockets for notes and coins. When the money is counted, there is $749.89: eleven cents short. What will you do? Will you take a mere eleven cents drop? What the hell, it's so near to $750 that it makes no difference— except that you have dropped below your absolute bottom line. How far will you go? Would you have accepted $749.51 if that was all I could rustle up? A forty-nine cent drop is still insignificant, surely? But where do you stop? So perhaps you should say, "No, enough is enough." I shrug and walk away. That is all the money I have, so that is it.

What has screwed you up here is your failure to prepare. The success of the whole project depends on your setting out with a clear objective and some sound alternatives. First of all, why are you selling the piano? It may be to make more room in your house; in that case a good price would be nice, but is not essential. Maybe you understand that it's a valuable instrument, though you don't play it yourself, and it may be the right time to realize this under-used asset. Maybe you do play it and love it dearly but are desperate for the money and have steeled yourself to selling it. If the last of these is the case, I might be more interested in paying a high price for your watch and you shouldn't just be thinking pianos (remember what we said about the relative value of things to you and someone else?). For the purposes of this illustration let's say that your objective is just to get the best possible price for the piano.

Second, where did the figure of $750 come from? Was it the

actual sum you needed, was it a figure pulled out from the air, or was it a figure arrived at through independent valuation—and if it was, would that valuer actually pay you anything like that for it? If you are selling the piano and you have a written offer in your pocket for $725, then that is your real back wall—and it is one you can show me to prevent me using tactics to twist your arm.

Whenever you start to negotiate, your situation is always strengthened by having alternatives. By this I mean real alternatives: it's very dangerous to bluff by saying, for example, that someone has already offered you $755, because I might turn around and tell you to accept that, and then you would really be in the cart. Let me remind you of my devastating secret weapon, the one that is completely incomprehensible to some salespeople: honesty. It has the value of being unexpected and is often impossible to counter. If the other party is not using it, they will always unravel before you do. It doesn't matter how strong they are, if you have real alternatives you have the high ground. A tough sales training book suggests that $50,000 in cash should be put in your pocket before you visit important potential clients. The book argues that it gives a mysterious psychological power; what it actually gives is a viable alternative, which is that you could afford to walk away.

Feel the benefits

When you get face to face with your opposite number, forget all you have ever learned about bargaining and don't adopt a position. Instead, investigate the situation: use your questioning skills to rummage out the other party's needs, problems, and interests. Remember the orange, remember the roller-skating and the factory. You are looking for real alternatives that will generate synergy.

"I want another $15 a week, boss."

Don't say: "No chance. I might offer you $5."

Say: "Oh, sit down, Mike. Now, what is it you need this $15 for?" "Well, the buses have stopped running past my house, and where the bus only cost me $5 a week, my car costs me $20, so I need an extra $15."

"Our truck goes past your home every day. If I get the driver to give you a lift that will cost you nothing and will actually mean that you will be $5 a week better off."

By investigating, you have found what he actually wants—not $15 for its own sake, but transport to work without leaving him out of pocket. You have solved the problem by giving him this without any cost to yourself and in fact have improved his financial position at the same time.

My accountant rang me up the other day and said that I didn't pay him enough. I said that I felt I paid him too much. Here was a complete divergence of views that looked like a basis for head-on conflict, so instead of battering our respective heads against opposite sides of the same brick wall, we had to look for an area that would reward us both.

"I pay you ten percent of my annual earnings," I wailed.

"But I don't think that 10 percent is enough," he moaned.

"Look," I said, "my business needs some sound advice to make it succeed. I should think my potential turnover should be $3 million. If we get together and you show me how to do this, your 10 percent will be worth $300,000."

It is now the case that my accountant also wants my business to succeed and we work together to achieve this.

Whatever the negotiation you enter into, there will always be a benefit to the other party; it is just that sometimes the other party may need this benefit pointed out to them. Even if the opposing general is surrendering unconditionally, there must be a benefit in the fact that you are no longer shooting at him. A classic hidden benefit lies in the Hollywood cliché of the Nazi arresting officer: "For you, ze war is over." Music to my ears.

If, on the other hand, you are on the receiving end of all this, again you can call in the massive power of honesty, this time asking the other party to exercise that rare virtue. When they make a point or claim, don't respond with a personal attack ("Don't be stupid. Do you think I was born yesterday?");

remember, if you involve emotions, theirs or yours, you only muddy the waters. Greet the statement in a cheery, friendly sort of way, but then ask how they got their information. Back to the piano:

"Oh, $725? Of course, I'm sure that's a fair offer, but could you tell me how you arrived at that figure?"

If they start to bluster and talk about general market trends, you can come back, because you have done your homework, and say:

"It's just that the music shop has given me a written valuation of $745 and I wonder why you feel it should be less?"

If a surprise should be sprung on you, don't be afraid to stop the proceedings:

"Oh, you mean that mine might be an inferior model? The ones with all those black keys aren't so popular? Well, I think the best thing to do is to stop now and meet again tomorrow. You can go off and rustle up a bit more cash, and I'll get the music shop to confirm what model I'm offering you."

You might begin to make out here the shape of that little Tibetan monk and his puddle coming into view. Our gentle martial art is coming into play again: as we politely decline to adopt a position, our opposite number has no target to strike at, and in their frustration they will often try to force us into one.

"For heaven's sake, what *do* you want?"

Don't state a position; but you can state your objective.

"I just want both of us to be happy with this…"

"I just want my boss to think I've done a good job…"

"I just want a fair price for this piano."

"What's a fair price?"

"Well, if neither of us is sure, why don't we get an independent valuation?"

It's important that you remember the value of lying in puddles. If you have got what you want, tell the other person what a great job they did, how they got the best out of you. Let them have their honor, it's important to them; if they feel they've won, you can expect a comfortable future dealing with them.

Pure undiluted argument

If the going gets tough, resist diluting your argument. I learned this from trying to get out of doing the dishes.

"Come on, you lazy fat lard, do the dishes." My wife is a sympathetic soul.

"I can't, I've gashed my hand, and if I get it in dirty water I will lose my right arm, and I did the dishes yesterday, and I'm tired, and I want to watch TV, and there's a good *Tom and Jerry* just starting."

"You want to watch bleeding *Tom and Jerry* while I slave away in the kitchen?"

Instead of strengthening my argument by adding more points, I diluted it. I should have said:

"I can't, I've gashed my hand, and if I get it in dirty water I will lose my right arm," and then stopped.

So where does it all end? Happily, yes, but most important of all, clearly. Very often if we are too eager to get to that happy ending we will tend to gloss over little discrepancies, and out of little discrepancies do whacking great time bombs grow. You might say:

"Well, I think that's just about everything. Now, you are delivering it, aren't you?"

They reply: "Yep, it's looking good. I don't think delivery is going to be a problem," and I hear ticking start. Don't be afraid to nail this one down. It is highly unlikely it will jeopardize your agreement, much more likely that it will save horrible grief in the future.

"Can I just get this clear? I'm sorry if I appear stupid, but will you confirm that you are responsible for delivery?"

If you design a bridge and build it on flat ground, you would be well advised to jump up and down on it a bit before you push it out over the yawning chasm where you are intending to use it. If you have been smart, you will have been making notes and jotting down bits and bobs throughout the whole process of negotiation. Don't be afraid to summarize out loud and to leap up and down vigorously on any creaky bits; it's no fun if, after standing back to admire it and saying, "Well, that looks all right, then," the structure collapses under you and your heavily laden donkey 150 feet above a raging torrent.

"Now, I'm not sure about this clause, could you tell me precisely the extent of our liability?"

If they bluster, threaten and say that the whole deal is in jeopardy, then perhaps it's a deal you didn't want.

This brings us neatly on to the subject of dirty tricks. There are two distinct sides to this. Obviously we must learn to recognize and deal with dirty tricks that are used against us; but often when classic negotiating systems warn us against dirty tricks, what they actually mean is that the other person is not playing the game by their rules, or, worse, is not playing the same game; or, most terrifying of all, is just not playing. This says more about the idiocy of negotiating systems as often taught than about the dirtiness or otherwise of tricks. There is a big macho idea that two tough-talking guys will get together across a polished table and thrash whatever it is out within the tight guidelines of the game called "Let's negotiate like we were taught on the last seminar." I have actually seen poor misguided loonies ticking boxes on a checklist to remind themselves what phase they are into. When these dinosaurs encounter a switched-on woman who is playing by her own rules and not trying to be more macho than the men, they are dead in the water. Time and again I have seen that skillful, single-minded businesswomen have an alarming ability to cut through the crap and settle issues on their merits. Why should clear-sightedness be a dirty trick?

Stay cool

When I was a kid at school, the teacher would try the line: "Now you are young adults, I think I can trust you to remain silent." I couldn't understand how some of my classmates could fall for this, and such a blatant ploy would provoke me into a frenzy of bad behavior. Of course, that was my downfall; but I have always resisted playing other people's games and it has paid dividends. The hippie era was a golden age for me, as for many others, a time when we all did our own thing. If you wondered what happened to us all, I can tell you where a lot of the others are now. It often happens that I'll be talking to a dynamic captain of industry and when we shake hands at parting he says, "Stay cool," or "Hang loose." We catch each other's eyes and say, "The Haight? Woodstock?" He knows that I know that he knows what I know, and we are both reassured.

Refusal to play the game can give you a real edge, and as it's based on personal integrity, you have the bonus of a nice warm glow as well. A bunch of idiots masquerading as management consultants were once told by a client of both theirs and mine to liaise with me over a seriously big project. My preparation consisted of being convinced that I didn't like these people and that it would be them in the soup if the project failed. They had been warned of my famous vagueness and were determined to play by the book—their book, of course. I arrived at their offices. The head honcho laid his watch on the table and said, "I have set aside precisely twenty-seven minutes for this meeting, and this will be quite adequate if we stay within the following agenda." I got up and went home.

If someone is deceiving you or trying techniques on you, telling them you know what they're up to is devastating.

"What are you trying to do here, Mike?" Or:

"I'm not sure these figures are correct. I may be wrong, but I have an idea you are hoping this will put me under pressure."

It is a shame if you have to see the other party as an adversary, because the essence of great negotiating is that you are both going to get something really good that is much better than what you had before. A car salesman has profit, you have a lovely shiny new car that is your pride and joy. Your new customer has all the benefits your company can offer, you have made a living. Don't think about being across a desk, think about being together for mutual gain. You couldn't play the bloodthirsty adversarial game of chess if you sat side by side, because you would keep seeing the other person's point of view. A rotten game, but a great negotiation.

10

Benefits, Whose Benefits?

Welcome to the world of the mnemonic, the bane of every aspiring salesperson. If you have ever undergone any sort of training in sales or negotiation, you probably came out of it with your brain feeling like a Scrabble board. The first steps of selling usually bring in A.I.D.A.; then there is the benefits business, that's F.B.I.; gradually the strings of letters get longer and wilder, with objections dealt with though Q.U.A.L.I.T.Y. or even the trademarked L. A. C. P. A. A. C.

I have two basic problems with all this. The first is a practical one: who on earth is going to remember all these? The second and more fundamental one is that it is very dangerous to set things out in prescribed order like this, to try to force what should be an art of the mind into lists of rules to be followed in set sequences. The truth of the matter is that every successful technique or piece of information you acquire on this subject is like a splotch of color on an artist's palette: you are the artist, and if you decide that a bit of blue is called for, on it goes. No artist is going to listen to anyone who shouts, "No, no! You can't use blue before you've used red!" Moreover, if you are not very experienced you can produce a competent little piece of work in black and white, whereas you might have trouble getting down a ladder with most of the the rungs missing.

In this chapter I will look at a few of the mnemonics routinely trotted out in training sessions on the subject of "selling the benefits": not because they are the whole story but because they aren't, because most of them function best as illustrations of the disasters that lie in wait for people who think they can operate in the real world by clinging to rigid structures and clever acronyms. Successful persuasion, as we have seen time and again before now, depends like any martial art on flexibility, adaptation, control: each element should be separately and instantaneously accessible to you, regardless of which other element you were using the moment before. Lightning responses are of the essence, and no one responds like lightning if they have to work themselves through four preparatory stages first.

Of course, I have a problem here myself, because a book, consisting of words appearing on the page one after another, is inescapably a linear kind of thing. I have tried to avoid the worst constraints of this form—to the point where my tyrannical publisher complained on seeing the first draft that it was "just a great big mass of words." It is unfortunately unavoidable that I have to put things down one after the other; but that doesn't mean that you have to pick them up in the same order. You should be able to browse through it, picking up on ideas here and there as they attract your attention, rather than having to read it from page one onwards to get any sense from it at all.

Having said this, you will know that if I start here with A.I.D.A. it is not because it begins with A; also that I am not saying you should use it at any particular point in your persuasive efforts— or, indeed, that you should use it at all. A.I.D.A., the all-time classic sales mnemonic, stands for Attention, Interest, Desire, Action. It first appeared, I believe, in the United States, where it was the prototype of a hilarious myth called "Scientific Selling," a fairy tale based on the idea that if you know the formulas, you will get the results. Like many myths, it can't be altogether discounted, because some of the magic formulas have been constructed by dissecting a successful sale and naming the bits; but it's no holy grail, as we shall see.

Attention isn't ripe bananas

A.I.D.A. may have been the darling of the high-powered sales representatives, but to see it at its best we need to watch a street market trader. A very rich client of mine built his fortune on market trading, and was fascinated by A.I.D.A.

"It's great stuff, that, Geoff," he said, "but you know, attention isn't ripe bananas."

"No, it isn't, is it," I said sympathetically, trying to humor him. Guessing that I was a bit bewildered, he attempted to explain. When he started out with a market stall, he told me, he took to it like a duck to water. The money came rolling in and before long he was driving a Rolls-Royce while others were arriving on bikes or in beat-up old vans. This puzzled him. How could there be such diversity of income levels from basically the same pitches? Others were puzzled too, among them many of the less successful traders, and they watched him to see how he did it.

It became obvious that while most stall-holders just stood about and waited for something to happen, our hero called and shouted and performed. Aha, they thought, that's what we must do. We must holler a bit and gain attention. The next week on market day the fruit seller would be holding up a bunch of bananas and yelling, "Ripe bananas! Ripe bananas!" They were then most disappointed to find themselves being ignored just as they had been before. Why?

Watch a successful market trader and you will see why.

"Hello, darling. Got any kids?"

"Yes, eight."

"Do you want to keep 'em fit and well this winter?"

"Oh, yes."

"'Cause I tell you for why, I was driving my van to work and there was this great big bang. Do you know what it was? It was them oranges, so packed with vitamins, they was exploding like hand grenades. They'll keep your kids fit. I'll put a dozen in for you."

What this trader is doing is "selling the benefits"—in other words, what the product will do for the customer. I will be saying more about this shortly, but already you can see that no one willingly gives you their attention unless there is something in it for them.

The next step, according to the A.I.D.A. program, is to interest the person, and your selling textbook will tell you that this is the moment when a demonstration or presentation is offered to arouse that interest. Our market trader might say:

"Gather round, ladies and gentlemen! In this box here I have the finest bargain that has ever been offered. When I reveal my offer to you, not one of you will be able to resist."

He has aroused your interest. What is in that box? Will you leave before you know what it is? There are loads of street market tricks like this that play on the combination of inquisitiveness and greed epitomized by the old Indian monkey trap theory. The idea of this is that you take a heavy, narrow-necked vase and put a peanut in it. The monkey can work its empty hand through the neck of the vase to grab the peanut, but in grasping its prize it forms a fist which cannot be withdrawn from the vase. It can only get its hand back if it relinquishes the peanut, which it refuses to do.

The trouble with sales techniques based on this sort of principle is that they depend on human failings—failings that we all have to some degree or other but that we can control if the consequences of a bad decision are great enough to make us careful. I might not worry too much about being inveigled into making foolish purchases at a Sunday street market, but I am unlikely to fall prey to the same methods in the context of a major business negotiation where my future depends on the outcome.

Anyway, for the moment back to our market trader. With a flourish he whisks the bargain out of the box and holds it up for all to see.

"Here we are, ladies and gentlemen, a delicious and succulent ten-pound roast beef!"

What have we here? D for desire, created by the sight and

description of the object on sale. This is the specialist subject of the fast-order steak bars with their lavish descriptions on the lines of "plump, succulent pieces of tender beef marinaded in our own delicious piquant sauce, served with golden French fried chipped potatoes and a crisp garden salad." We're all so used to these descriptions now that we accept them as the norm and don't notice the exaggeration; but we'd notice if it wasn't there. I recently saw a hilarious example of what such a description would be like couched in severely practical terms:

"Lumps of dead cow flesh, seared in such a way that unclotted body fluids are preserved inside; or we can offer a lump of preserved dead pig flesh served with the congealed embryo of a flightless bird."

Hungry? Would your appetite revive if we said:

"Juicy steak pieces, cooked just the way you like them, or choose our gammon steaklet served with a golden fresh-laid egg"?

You may think this is absurd; but whenever a sales engineer is asked to describe his latest mechanical marvel, nine times out of ten he will take the dead cow route. A better idea is to describe your goods or services in an appetizing and attractive way, one moreover that relates to the customer in question.

Don't praise beef to vegetarians

Take another look at the model A.I.D.A. routine I just described. Our trader secured the customer's attention, aroused their interest and kindled their desire; then the vital action question was asked: "Ten pounds of the finest roast beef for only a fiver." What do you think?

"Sounds super value, but I'm a vegetarian."

Oh dear. Here's a problem and no mistake. Despite the great respect in which he is held by the whole industry, even the expert closer will be sinking fast. Try some of his tricks and see if they work.

"Did you want to take it now or shall I deliver it?"

"I don't eat meat."

"Take it on approval and if after a few days you are not delighted, we will be happy to refund your investment."

"I don't eat meat."

Failure is inevitable. Why? Because there is a bit missing from A. I. D. A. The bit I have in mind is represented by another letter "I," and a lot of people would agree with me thus far; but where we will part company is in deciding what that extra "I" stands for. Many would say that it stands for Identify. OK, then, identify what? "Oh," they reply, "identify a need." It is claimed that sales and marketing are about identifying a need and then satisfying that need with your product or service. In my view this is too narrow and just leads to another tunnel that might take us straight past our target or simply to a dead end. A slightly better explanation, though still hooked on to this idea of "identifying," is that we have to identify a problem and then offer a solution to that problem. This at least offers a somewhat broader horizon and therefore more scope, if we can accept just for a moment that everyone who buys anything does so to solve a problem.

For instance, the customer may say, "I can't open my front

door." The need identifiers would say, "You need a key." This is OK if you sell keys; if you don't, you will then have to say, "...but we don't sell keys. Sorry, can't help you."

The problem identifiers would say "Hmm, now, that's a problem. It can be solved by a key, or a hammer, or dynamite, or a crowbar. We sell dynamite; one stick, a fuse, and a detonator should do it."

The range of opportunities is a bit wider, but still pretty limited. My added "I" widens up the field a great deal more and puts you in a much more powerful position, but before I reveal what it is I want to pause to consider another aspect of "selling the benefits" that is often overlooked: what the customer actually wants, and whether even they know what that is.

What would it be like if doctors were sales trained? Imagine going in with, say, a badly broken arm to be greeted by a positive, smiling individual who would put the situation into an attractive package for you.

"Ah, hello, do sit down. Well, I've got some super news for you: I intend to amputate your right leg. What I intend to do is to make an incision just above the knee to expose the bone, which I will just saw through as neat as a new pin. Then we will tack all the flesh back in to make you a lovely tidy stump. And do you know the really exciting part? I'm so thrilled for you, because you will save, and I mean really save, in cash terms, 50 percent of your total sock washing costs." And the closing question: "Well, shall we go ahead?" Did you agree? No? I'm not surprised; but a lot of salespeople believe that such a saving, even if it bears no relation to what the customer actually wants, should be attractive, and often translate their offers into such terms.

You know that you would refuse that offer, but do you know why? To answer that question we should look at what a real doctor does.

"Ah, Mr. Smith, hello, what seems to be the trouble?"

"I've broken my arm."

"Really? How did you do that?"

"Fell off my bike."

"And when did this happen?"

"Oh, a couple of days ago."

"Can you move your fingers?"

"A bit."

"When did it swell up?"

"Only today."

"Well, it may be broken, but we'll get you to hospital for an X ray first and then I'll decide what will be the best treatment."

Now here's a surprise: not only did she not try to sell the unwanted amputation, she is not even accepting the customer's word for what he wants. If that seems unreasonable to you, consider what it would be like if a doctor did accept what you said at face value.

"Doctor, I think I've got appendicitis."

"Okay. Hop up on the table and we'll whip your guts out."

Just the same misunderstanding can happen in sales; it is so very easy to take the customer at his word and screw the whole thing up. Some time ago, we were working for a fastenings company and I happened to be in the office when a customer called.

"Hello," he said. "What price are your strongest half-inch bolts?"

My client replied with cheery confidence:

"Fifty dollars each, sir."

Both he and I could hear the sharp intake of breath at the other end of the phone and the loud crack as the would-be customer fell out of his chair. I grabbed the phone.

"Would you just hold on a moment, sir, there may be some mistake." Turning to my client: "What half-inch bolt on this earth costs $50 a pop?"

"That's a product we're very proud of," he explained. "Just four of those tiny bolts hold the engine on a huge airliner. They're small, to give the prodigious thrust of the mighty engines some movement, but they're massively strong because the passengers tend to get a little alarmed if the engine goes whizzing past the windows on take-off. Anyway, it's only $200 a motor, and that's hardly a lot on a $50 million airplane."

I turned back to the phone. "Would you mind telling me, sir, why you want bolts so strong?"

"Well," came the reply, "we make sheds with corrugated iron roofs and the little galvanized bolts are brought from the Far East; only takes a gust of wind and they snap like twigs."

By this time my client was doing a little war dance of excitement.

"Ooh, ah, oh, what he needs is high-tensile Allen cap screws."

"How much are they?"

"Five dollars a gross."

The first answer was not what the client was asking for. A classic illustration of the same point concerns watches. If I asked you what a waterproof watch was, you'd probably say: a watch that doesn't let in water if you get it wet. Not so, apparently; that is a water-resistant watch. If you asked to see a waterproof watch you would most likely be shown something very expensive indeed.

The missing link

After this lengthy preamble I can at last reveal what my extra "I" stands for: Investigation. Thorough and painstaking investigation, with which you can navigate around, past, or through all these problems that lurk in the gaps between A., I., D., and A. To go back to our person who can't get through her front door: the need people have said she needs a key, the problem people have said that dynamite will solve it, and I think we should investigate.

"I can't open my front door." What conclusion can we draw from that statement? Well, for a start, we shouldn't draw any conclusions. Any conclusion we draw at this stage will be based on our own personal prejudices, and as we saw in the story of the sisters with the orange, that can get us into a lot of trouble. We have assumed that this person wants to open the door (she might have been trying to block the entrance); we have assumed that it's the door that is at fault (she might have a disability that makes it impossible for her to reach the handle). Why does she want the door open, if indeed she does? Perhaps she had forgotten her old umbrella; we could sell her a better one, but we would be unlikely to guess that the statement "I can't open my front door" would lead to the sale of an umbrella.

What is actually happening here is that the other party is giving us a fleeting glimpse of their current situation, where they are, and what they are doing at some split second in time. Some chain of events has led to this position and a further chain will lead away. Obviously it is the leading away journey we want to take part in, because we want it to end up at our products, services, and ideas; but we should still see the chain of events as a single process, because the past can be most useful to us. It is the past links in that chain that have brought the customer to the point where we meet them, and they will influence the customer's feelings and attitudes towards what we have to offer them.

In practical terms, too, the past is extremely useful: if the customer is the tiniest bit prickly or suspicious, talking about the past is a very good way of putting them at their ease. Most people are happy to talk about the past—it's happened, it commits them to nothing—and we can extrapolate from the information we thus gain.

"We need a new vacuum cleaner."

"Oh, right. Could I just ask you what you have been using up to now?"

"A Hoover upright, we've had it for twenty years."

Well, you tell me, what is it they might want to buy now? I hope you won't tell me, because if you do you are still jumping to conclusions. Further investigation will reveal more.

"And why have you decided to change?"

The answer could be "It's a great old machine but it's worn out; we'd like to find another like it," or "We're moving to a retirement flat and want something smaller and lighter."

This brings us on to a very powerful technique which I thought of describing in the next chapter on making major decisions—but, as I said earlier, all this information should ideally be at your fingertips simultaneously, and it works very nicely with vacuum cleaners and garden pests as well. The mnemonic I have created to go with it is I.S.I.S.: investigate, sympathize, implications, and solution. You are quite at liberty to forget this; it's more important that you follow the thread of what you are really up to here and how investigation puts you in a very powerful position for what follows.

A customer comes to you and says: "I have greenfly."

You reply: "Try a can of new Megasplat, this will kill them stone dead."

"Stone dead! I don't want to kill them, they're my little friends. I just wanted to tell you about them."

All right, that's a bit unlikely, but remember: don't jump to conclusions. More likely is this:

"Stone dead? Smashing! How much is it?"

"Thirty dollars a can."

"Thirty dollars to get rid of a few dismal greenfly? You must be joking."

A classic mistake has just been made. The subject has made a statement that has only told us about their current situation. In other words, this is where they are now. They have greenfly. This is a simple statement of fact that we are all eager to interpret as a statement of need; but it isn't. Someone comes to me and says: "Ah, Mr. Burch, my salespeople underperform." I hear: "Ah, Mr. Burch, we need sales training."

What we need to do is to take our customer on a journey from their factual statement of their current situation to a clear statement of acknowledgement that they need our offer.

"I have greenfly."

Investigate: "Is that a problem?"

"Yes, they're ruining my roses."

Sympathize: "Oh no, they're horrible things, aren't they?" Further investigation bubbles along meanwhile: "What have you tried to get rid of them?"

"Oh, everything: dishwater, sprays, the lot."

Implications: "Have they spread to any other plants?"

"Yes, they're on my apple trees."

More sympathy: "Oh dear. And nothing is stopping them? Sounds terrible."

"It is; I'm at my wits' end."

Solution: "I know how you feel. I'm not sure I can help, either; once they get established like that they are so hard to shift. Hang on, though, there is one thing: it's a super product, it'll kill them for good—it's not cheap, but what value do you put on the pleasure and hard work that you have put into your garden?"

"My garden is my life."

"Then take a can of Megasplat, it will solve your problems."

Thirty dollars to save your life's work is chickenfeed. As we will see in the next chapter, with the very high-value products this is the only way to go about business.

You may think some of the examples I use are facile; perhaps they are, but it would require a play the length of *Hamlet* for each illustration if I were to make them realistically complex, so I have to trust to your tolerance and powers of imagination in extrapolating to your own sophisticated transactions.

What you have just done is to elicit enough information from the customer to enable you to present with him with an offer appropriate to his need, his feelings and his circumstances. We did just the same with Genghis Khan, when what we sold him was not a tank but what the tank could do for him. It may disappoint you to hear that this is not a new discovery, and indeed that this concept had occurred to salespeople when they hawked the "New Acme Giantfelling Pebbles" to David. The bandwagon has been rolling ever since and has in more recent times taken on the aura of a holy crusade that marches under the ragged banner of "Selling the Benefits." Again, I'm ambivalent about this: when I sit in on training programs and hear the course leader shout "Sell the benefits, kid, always sell the benefits!" I can see his point, but there are horrible hidden dangers lurking that you need to know about. Once more, then, let's study the accepted practice and then look for the pitfalls.

More alphabet soup

The mnemonic dished out here is F.B.I., which stands for Features, Benefits, Incentives. Just to confuse things, there is also F.A.B., standing for Feature, Advantage, Benefit; this one is used by a certain kind of pedant for whom some benefits are only advantages. This distinction has more to do with semantics than real-world situations, and to understand it you have to appreciate that the sales training crowd fall into two major camps. On the one hand you have the finger-pointing, fist-banging, seminar-hawking, streetwise, university-of-life types, and on the other the pseudo-academic consultants who hover daintily above all this hysteria and have a fun time dreaming up new complications for the sake of it. To get a balanced view you need to know about both of them, but before you set out you must be armed with a chain mail of the purest cynicism. The academic types profit from the penchant of middle management for justifying their own existence; if concepts can be complicated to the extent that no one can understand them then their success becomes irrelevant because they perpetuate the art of managing for managing's (or managers') sake. The first bunch are just as dangerous, because they take the rapist's view of the act being the goal, with no past or future to consider.

As for me, I'm just an insecure neurotic who doesn't trust anything unless it seems to work with the minimum of dangerous consequences. So for now, we'll stick with F.B.I. Feature: these shoes are leather. That is a simple statement of fact, the answer to which is: so what? The magic phrase that we use to bring the product to life is "which means that...." Try it with the leather shoes and that brings you to the benefit.

"These shoes are leather, a natural breathing material, which means that they will stay comfortable all day."

Next we have to consider how this feature and its associated benefit will directly profit our customer to the point where they will buy our idea. We need, in other words, to offer them an incentive. This too has its key phrase: "and that means ..."

"These shoes are leather, a natural breathing material, which means that they will stay comfortable all day, and that means that you, as a person who makes their living on their feet, can keep going longer and make more money."

I can see the fork in the road inexorably approaching where accepted practice goes zooming down one track while I dig my heels in and go my own way. At this point in your training seminar, the presiding guru would ask you to list your products and/or services and then ask you to make corresponding lists of features, benefits, and incentives. He would then gather up these lists and give the person with the longest a toffee apple. However, as is so frequently remarked, size is not necessarily important. Consider the features. Have you noticed that advertisers have a disturbing habit of bragging about the fact that their product is "loaded with exciting features"? Is this such a good thing? Remember the dishwashing argument: the more points I added to my resistance, the weaker it became. It was diluted; in the area we are now discussing, we could say it was cheapened. Again, don't jump to conclusions: being cheap is no bad thing as long as you are genuinely cheap and stand up amazingly well against all comers. Features cheapen, so if you are cheap, have lots of features.

If that has got right up your nose, consider two types of car ads. Those strange, exotic East European and Far Eastern cars have ad copy which runs along these lines:

"Twin overhead cam engine, leather seats, galvanized body, 24-month guarantee, 25-year rust assurance, six-speed gearbox, stereo, exotic bird aviary, caviar dispenser, sunroof, rubber tires, electric windows, 8-liter engine, 80 miles to the gallon—and all this for only $7,500 on the road."

The list has led you to expect a bargain price, and you haven't been disappointed.

Now imagine a BMW or Mercedes advert. These people could provide a similar list, and it would be even longer, but they don't, because it would slip up at the end with "...and all this for only $165,000." Instead, they cultivate an image of understatement where the best of everything is taken for granted, and their copy reads: "The ultimate driving machine" or something similarly terse. Not a feature in sight. Beware drowning in features, then, unless you're undercutting everyone else.

We are about to venture into the real world to sell buckets, but before we set off let's just have a quick practice run to make sure we can link feature, benefit, and incentive in the approved fashion: "This bucket is plastic (feature), which means that it is light (benefit), and that means life is easier for you because it is easy to carry (incentive)." Brilliant.

Who uses buckets? We pick out our old friend Scroggits Fish and Chips. His bell tinkles merrily as we enter his shop with our shining sample plastic bucket.

"Ah, Mr. Scroggit, I represent the Acme Bucket Corporation and I would like to show you the new Thunderflash Mark 2 bucket. I notice that you use a large number of galvanized metal buckets, and the main feature of the Thunderflash is that it is made entirely of high-impact plastic which means that it is light and easy to carry. That would make life easier for you, wouldn't it, Mr. Scroggit?"

"Bless you, but no thanks. The wife does all the carrying and she's as strong as an ox."

Well, that fell flat on its back. Why? We did as we are constantly being exhorted to do and sold the benefits—but, as with the market trader's roast beef, we have attempted to extol benefits that are no benefit to the other party. I'm going to repeat myself again: don't assume, investigate.

Is the obvious problem obvious to you?

"Hello, Mr. Scroggit, I'm from the Acme Bucket Corporation— golly, you do use a lot of buckets. What problems do you get with them?"

"I don't get no trouble with my buckets at all. Except the obvious one, of course."

"The obvious one?"

"Yes, you know, finding a way of marking 'em so I can tell 'em apart. No label or nothing stays on in all this steam. Poured two gallon of vinegar in the hot fat this morning, cleaned my shoes in cod batter and pickled the eggs in strong disinfectant. Mind, I think they tasted the better for it."

"You see, Mr. Scroggit, I would like to show you the Thunderflash Mark 2, a bucket that is manufactured from high-impact plastic. This means that we can make it in thirty-seven scintillating colors. That would mean you could have a different color for each application. Say, shades of red for hot, greens for safe, yellows for toxic, and so on. That would stop these nasty accidents, wouldn't it, Mr. Scroggit?"

Here we have tied the benefit to a specific problem which we have uncovered by investigation. But our difficulties with this awkward term are not over yet. The dictionary defines "benefit" as "something advantageous," but who is to be the judge of that? Your average business guru will insist that you have a clear idea of the benefits of your product or service before you meet the customer; but what if the customer has a very different view from yours of what constitutes a benefit? What might seem a problem to you might appear as a benefit to one particular customer, and if you're too wedded to the benefits you've already learned by heart you might well miss the opportunity.

"I would like a plant for my mother-in-law."

"How about a fuchsia? Lovely, long-lasting plants."

"Mm...no."

"An African violet, perhaps? They're pretty."

"Mmm...no."

"Lily of the valley, then? Such a lovely perfume."

"Mmmm...no."

"Look here. Do you like your mother-in-law?"

"Mmmmm...no."

"Ah. Because I have here a fascinating climbing plant that has a beautiful display of white and yellow flowers in late summer and in autumn produces glossy black berries; but the real feature of the deadly nightshade is that the fruit causes inevitable and agonizing death, and the incentive to you is that it is undetectable in postmortems, meaning you won't get caught."

Don't be left flat-footed because you can't turn what has hitherto been putting everyone off into an attraction when you get the chance. Investigate, and be light on your feet.

Even this bizarre twist, however, doesn't show the extremes of convoluted reasoning that may be going inside our customer's head, making nonsense of preconceived lists of benefits. The best illustration I can find of this phenomenon involves a joke which I have never liked and which offends against all canons of good taste. Here it is.

A small boy approaches a Madam and asks if any of her girls have any sexually transmitted diseases.

"Certainly not!" exclaims the Madam.

"Oh, that's a shame," says the boy, and turns away.

"Hold on, sonny. Why did you want to know?"

"I want to catch something nasty. I have plenty of money."

"Oh...Okay sonny, I admit that one or two of the girls are a bit iffy..."

The boy happily pays up and goes in. Weeks later the Madam sees the boy again and can't resist asking him, "Did you catch anything?"

"Yes thank you, a very nasty case," he says brightly.

"Why did you want a disease like that?" she asks, puzzled.

"It wasn't for me, I wanted Nanny to get it."

"Poor Nanny. Why did she deserve it?"

"She didn't, but I wanted Daddy to get it."

"Poor Daddy. What had he done?"

"Nothing, but I wanted Mommy to get it."

"What has poor Mommy done to deserve that?"

"Mommy's done nothing, it's the milkman I've been after, ever since he backed his van over my bike."

How could you ever guess or predict a benefit chain like that? In this case the investigation took place after the event, whereas of course we should always investigate first; but you must see that the word "benefit" as generally understood almost ceases to

be relevant. I'm a motorcycle freak and once expressed an interest in a Russian bike. The salesman laughed and said that I would always be working on it. That was exactly why I wanted it; I was tired of the sanitized Japanese rocket ships, and wanted something I could tinker with. That salesman's prejudiced snap judgment got right up my nose, and lost him a probable sale—of something, moreover, that by his own standards he was unlikely to shift otherwise.

It is essential, then, to understand that "benefits" or "incentives" per se do not persuade, and that in some cases they can even put people off. Only careful and attentive investigation will lead you to what it is that will really match up with each customer. And while you are conducting your investigation, your questions should not just be finding out this information but should also be helping the other party to see the size of their problem and the value of solving it. Remember that a greenfly can be a trivial problem or the threat to a gardener's life-work.

Sometimes the size of the problem can be so obvious that the solution is eagerly accepted.

"I can't open my front door."

"Oh dear, that's a shame. Is that your child crying inside?"

"Yes."

"Does it disturb you that there are flames licking out of the windows?"

The benefits of our master key are obvious, and there is one task that it is expected to perform. There is no point explaining that it is manufactured from the finest bronze and that it has a ten-year guarantee. Nor, if we stand there driveling on about all these irrelevancies, should we be surprised if our unsophisticated competitor pushes past us and kicks the door off its hinges, subsequently selling several pairs of steel-toecapped boots. Our product may be superior; but theirs did the job. While you're investigating, you can jot down the information you get so that at the end you can remind them and yourself of what it was they liked and wanted; but whatever you do, don't sum up by reminding your customer of benefits they didn't want.

11

The Big Ones

Few people would deny that signing a contract to build five nuclear power stations is a bigger decision than choosing between two brands of flyspray for the greenhouse; but where do you draw the line? It's obviously crazy to think in purely quantitative terms, because what might mean a year's turnover to you might be just an afternoon's shopping for your biggest customer, so I suggest the following working definition. A big decision is one in which the other party is liable to show appreciable resistance to coming around to your way of thinking. You could even put it in pseudo-scientific terms, with increased mass causing increased inertia: in other words, if a lot hangs on the decision it will take more push to get it made; if there is a lot of weight behind the current situation, it will be more difficult to bring about a change of direction. A fully laden supertanker takes miles to turn around, even to stop. What we have to do in dealing with the special problems associated with big decisions is find ways of dealing with that inertia, that attachment to the status quo.

One response to this idea would be that more resistance calls for more pressure. This sounds logical; but it is a perfect example of how something that looks logical when put in terms of an "$x = y$ therefore $2x = 2y$" equation falls into very small pieces when you try to put it into practice. Take the starting point that sudden pressure used as a short, sharp shock against low resistance may produce success. The Nazis in the Second World War had great success initially with their blitzkrieg—the high-pressure version of warfare. But if it didn't work straight away, resistance to it began to grow and it got stuck. Look back a bit further, to warfare in the days of medieval castles: if you didn't catch them with the drawbridge down, when you could charge in with much shouting and clashing and general mayhem, a long and costly siege would be the result—and you might starve or die of plague before they did.

This whole area of pressure and resistance was well summed up a long time ago in the fable of the sun and the wind. For any of you who have never come across this old chestnut, apparently the sun and the wind were getting a bit bored one day when they saw a human being far down below them on the earth: a man wearing a new coat.

"I bet I could get that off him," said the wind.

"No chance," replied the sun.

"What'll you bet?" challenged the wind.

"You can't afford it," riposted the sun.

"Just you watch," said the wind. The bet was sealed, and the wind howled around a bit gathering strength before plunging down on the victim. The wind hit hard and fast, and within the first few seconds had the coat buttons pinging under the strain and the man snatching to stop the coat flying away. Having got a grip on it, however, he wrapped it around him and held on tight as the wind increased in savagery. It blew him bodily over a hedge, up a tree, and then into a brook. It ripped and whistled and screamed, but the man, frightened and bad-tempered as he was fast becoming, clung on. Eventually the wind, completely out of breath, had to give up. Wheezing helplessly, it returned to the sun, who was grinning fit to bust.

"Come on, then, pay up."

"I don't know what you're laughing about. You couldn't do any better."

"Oh, yes, I could."

"Go on then. Double or quits?"

The sun accepted the challenge and scampered off around the back of some mountains, where he spent a few minutes polishing himself up and practicing his sunniest smile. Then he rose into the air above the hills, and as he ascended the birds began to sing, the flowers opened, the puddles dried and the sky became a clear, calm blue. The man looked up at the smiling sun, realized what a lovely day it was, and took off his coat.

No place to hide

There's the catch. Not so hard to hide the occasional indulgence; but try hiding the new computer system that you bought for your company, or the fact that you have appointed new caterers for your entire conference season. The results of your decision are there for all to see; the spending was no fun at all, and the consequences could be dire. Here we have a clue to the identity of our biggest competitor—in fact, the bigger the deal, the bigger this competitor is going to be. When asked who their major competitors are, people tend to list other companies in a similar line of business: as we noted earlier, if we make drills, we'll think of other people who supply holes. All the clever marketing slogans, however, hide a fundamental truth which hit me one day like a garden rake: your real competitor is your target's current arrangements. If you sell cars, you are not selling against other manufacturers or dealers so much as against the level of satisfaction and resistance to change among car-owners.

Once this dawned on me, I realized that the problem is a massive one, the true size of which remains hidden from us. People in the business of selling cars only see those who are starting to be dissatisfied with their current travel arrangements: all the others driving round happy with the motors they've got don't even go anywhere near the showrooms. So if you actually have to go out and find new customers from among the contented millions you are likely to encounter a high level of initial resistance. If you are going to try to persuade them to make a change which has important consequences, that level is going to be even higher; and if that resistance is displayed in corporate form as a committee or something similar, you'll have a real fight on your hands. In this chapter I'm going to try to show you how to handle this sort of resistance, but it should be clear from the word go that achieving your goal is likely to take some time. Steady progress towards an inevitable outcome is what you're after; blitzkrieg is out.

If progress is going to be steady—even, to be blunt, slow— the first imperative is to be sure you're going in the right direction. One of those wonderful Zen sayings I remember from my hippie days pronounced that even a thousand-mile journey must start with a single footstep. Very profound; but if that single footstep is in the wrong direction, you then have a thousand miles and one footstep to go. This doesn't sound too bad; but you might carry on for five hundred miles before you realize you should have been pointing the other way at the outset, and at that stage the repercussions are a bit more serious. The problem here is that it's more difficult to see that you're going in the wrong direction after one footstep than after five hundred miles. When do you start asking, and how do you know?

Some time ago, a client of ours decided to hawk a nuclear power station to a Far Eastern government. Given the nature of the product, a quick sale wasn't anticipated; but after ten years they really weren't sure how things were going, and approached us for a bit of guidance. We sat in on one of their presentations.

"How did we do?" they asked us eagerly afterwards.

"Hell if I know," came the cheery reply.

It'll end in tears

This is a common problem. Companies learn how they should be going about things, then enthusiastically put all their newfound wisdom into practice to apparent good effect—but until the client says yes or no, no one can say how well they are doing. The problem is even more acute if there is no clearcut end product and therefore no tangible endpoint. The advertising industry is a pattern case. The sums involved are huge, the resistance is high, and the end-product—being appointed as a client's chosen agency—is not a clear decision to buy a particular product. One ad agency came to us in floods of tears, so far gone that even after a couple of boxes of tissues and lots of hot sweet tea all they could come up with was the old joke: "Half of our presentation budget is wasted, but we don't know which half." What made this even less funny was the fact that they were losing a lot more than half.

Ad agencies have to play a kind of insane poker game called "the pitch." For the uninitiated, this means that a potential client will call maybe five agencies and ask them to "pitch" for their business—in other words, to present their ideas of how they would handle the account if they won it. These presentations can be quite formal and very lavish affairs: for example, it's not unknown for an agency to construct a complete sample television advertisement entirely at its own expense. This particular agent spent around $7,500 a time on presentations; being no better or worse than the competition, this resulted in a one in five success rate, which of course in turn meant that the lucky client got to pick up the tab on the $25,000 cost of the failed pitches. If you're that expensive, you have to work hard to keep your customers, which costs more money, and so the pressures on you mount and you end up in our offices sniffling into Kleenexes.

To go back to that serene Zen saying about the thousand-mile journey, if you were to take that first step and then turn around to me and holler, "Hey, Geoff, how did I do?" I wouldn't know. When the stakes are as high as they are in a major persuasion situation, we have to know; we have to find a way to measure progress on even the most mist-shrouded journeys.

It's fascinating to think how international commerce was conducted in the nineteenth century. If you were a London merchant you could, with complete confidence, send a cargo from Rotherhithe to New York and be pretty sure it would get there. Imagine the mind of the sea captain as he sails out of the docks with your cargo aboard. It is quite likely that he has never seen New York; how does he know it exists? He certainly won't see his goal from his point of departure. Nevertheless, without drama, every morning he gets up, has a bit of breakfast, and commands his crew to take certain actions—actions that he knows will, without fail, take him eventually to his destination. There may be a storm, or an unexpected headwind, and these will affect the instructions handed out from day to day: but while they may change the time of arrival, they don't change the fact of arrival itself. (We'll leave out icebergs and hurricanes; we're not talking about what happens if your chief accountant is suddenly run in for fraud, sending the company bankrupt.)

If you picture this sea captain in your mind, you will see him considering the crew's next batch of instructions, and one of the images you conjure up will probably involve him looking at a chart. The secret, of course, lies in navigation. At any time, the captain knows where he is, where he has just come from, where he is going, and how long it will take him to get there (a) in calm weather, (b) with a couple of storms of the kind that normally blow up at this time of year, (c) if he has to take evasive action to avoid one of the privateers that might be around after the last war with the French. You are currently in various positions vis-à-vis people you are trying to persuade. Do you know exactly where you are in relation to the destination? If you don't, you may be lost, or even going in quite the wrong direction.

We have already noted the frightening habit salespeople have of writing "V. Interested" on their client visit reports. This is tantamount to our sea captain writing "Doing very nicely" in his log. The only way you can keep track accurately of a long and complicated journey, whether to New York or to a major deal, is to be accurate and to be honest. Success must be measurable at each stage. In the ship's log, an obvious complete lack of success would be indicated by an entry (dredged up later) that read: Sank. A salesperson's equivalent would be: Thrown out by security, no sale, no appointments. A slightly less terminal but nonetheless serious lack of naval success would be: Sailed round in circles. For the salesperson this would be: Customer evasive, no sale, no appointments. But he is very unlikely to be so honest, and writes instead: Will call us soon, or: Liked our offer—or even the dreaded: V. Int.—despite the fact that he is clearly getting absolutely nowhere.

As each contact or visit ends, we should have a clear understanding of where we are and a definite commitment to a forward movement. The captain's log reads: Two degrees south of Paradise Island, good headway despite strong sidewinds, aiming to make landfall six bells tomorrow. When your customer says, "I think this looks good. I just need to speak to my managing director. I'll try and call you tomorrow, or soon anyway," you respond, "That's great. Let's set up our next meeting, then, and perhaps the managing director could sit in. Do you have your diary?"

If you can get that date down in your diary, you will leave the building with clear-cut, written evidence of progress.

The ratchet effect

When I first discovered this way of establishing where I was and moving a step forward, I thought that this was all there was to it. In fact, essential though that task is, this technique does much more than that. To see how, we have to look back at the pressure v. resistance equation again. Say you have a small car, and it had a puncture; as long as you were reasonably robust, you could grab the bumper, pick up the car with one hand while removing the wheel with the other, and slap on the spare. The stronger you were, the easier this would be. Bucked by this success, you might decide to run some puncture repair classes; as not everyone there is as well-built as you, you encourage attendees to undertake a program of bodybuilding exercises. This sort of training affects the mind as well as the body—or perhaps it just appeals to people with a particular sort of mind to start with—and the result of your classes is a group of large-chested, swaggering individuals whose motto is "Success through strength." Watch any "hard-hitting sales team" being trained, and it will be obvious that their role plays, benefit searches, and trial closes are all geared to the confident application of strength.

They are also taught that benefits can literally outweigh objections. Suppose you have a puncture on a large truck. You try to lift the bumper like you did on the small car: nothing moves, except something in your back that shouldn't. So you call one of the fully trained toughies in to help; flexing his pecs, he shoves a heavy pole under the truck and over a handy log as a fulcrum, then applies his massive physique to the other end of this lever. You see his muscles bulge, the veins stand out on his neck; as he gives his all, he starts to vibrate with the very effort. A look of brutal triumph steals over his face as the truck begins to rise, proving that sheer weight of argument can overcome any resistance as long as you are strong enough. You go to release the offending wheel and find to your horror that the truck is not quite high enough to get it off.

"Hurry up," grunts our straining hero.

"It's not high enough; can you lift it a bit further?" you reply.

He strains and strains. "I can't," he gasps.

Now what? He's piled all his strength, every resource he has, into this situation and it wasn't enough. There is nothing for it, he has to let go. And what happens to the truck? It collapses to right back where it started, probably with a broken axle to boot, which means that any subsequent attempt will involve not only starting all over again with no guarantee of success, but a bigger problem to solve. And this happened with Mr. Muscles on our side. We are just puny mortals; even if we got a longer lever or something, we would have no chance.

Try this scene again, with different props. You are driving along in your monster truck and you have a puncture. What would you really do? What tool would really help? Yes: the jack. What a happy little device. You jump from the cab, slip a jack under the axle beam and with a minimum of effort, pump the handle. The jack contains a ratchet, and if you've ever used one you will know that each click means that the truck is being lifted upwards, even if you can't see any movement. After a while, its ascent becomes obvious to the naked eye. Even with a jack, it can be tiring work; so if you need a rest, you leave the jack locked in position and nip off for coffee. When you get back, the truck is just where it was; because of the ratchet, no ground has been lost.

Surely a jack with a ratchet is just what we need in our long-term persuasive activities. Mr. Muscles, once in a selling pose, is paranoid about leaving the situation for even five minutes, because he knows it will all fall back to the ground if he's not there applying brute force. "I'll think about it" acts on a traditional salesperson like garlic on a vampire. In fact, you can pay good money to go on a seminar that is almost entirely devoted to dealing with "I'll think about it," when the truth is that "I'll think about it" is created by the pressure of leverage selling.

Another great sales taboo is the importance of seeing the decision-maker. Armed with our ratchet, let's see if we can't lay this ghost to rest by skillful application of the jack. Imagine you want to sell consultancy to the largest corporation in the country. Decisions don't come much bigger than this: vast budgets are at stake, the product is a continuing service rather than a tangible item, the commitment is long-term. Obviously, then the chairman is the one you want to see. You ask for an appointment and get a flat refusal. Plummeting through the hierarchy, you find the only person who will see you is Aggy the tea-lady. According to the traditional wisdom, anything you do now will be regarded as a waste of time; but just let me have a go with the jack and see what happens.

"Hello, Aggy."

"Oh, hello, what can I do for you?"

"Well, Aggy, I'd like to discuss a ten-year business plan."

"You ought to have a word with my supervisor."

"D'you think you could give her a buzz on the internal phone and ask if I could see her for a minute?"

I succeed in getting the *entrée* to the head tea-lady. She tells me I really ought to talk to her friend Derek, who is a junior in the marketing department. She makes another internal call and introduces us. Can you hear something? The sound of a ratchet clicking, perhaps? With persistence but no sudden pressure, the jack will take us right to the top. We ask each contact for the maximum they are able to give us at that moment. It is like a sequence of mini-sales, where each click of the ratchet is an intermediate goal on the way to the target. We are quite firmly asking for some kind of action, thereby achieving measurable forward progress, but only the action that person is genuinely qualified to take. How do we know what this is? Of course: by investigation.

How to find the back door of the castle

A great master of investigation, and without doubt the greatest of all the philosophers of persuasion and conquest, was Machiavelli. I'm not sure whether the jack had been invented in the sixteenth century, but Machiavelli certainly had an eye for how to get your own way with best use of available resources. For one thing, he had the problem of the medieval castle down pat. As we noted at the beginning of this chapter, if you screw up the initial attack of a fortress, it shuts up tight as a clam and you're stuck there outside for the winter with nothing more appetizing than a lot of salted herring sandwiches. It comes down to a simple trial of strength and endurance. Machiavelli suggests that even if you won in the end, the victory would be hollow because the relative strengths of you and your enemy would remain the same. Once the vanquished warlord had gone out and pressed a few more barons and their underlings into service, he'd be back and you'd have the whole thing to do all over again. So, even if you manage by brute strength to defeat the opposition by a factor of, say, ten to nine, an effort of ten will always be required to maintain the status quo.

To translate this into modern business terms, if you have made huge promises and offered vast discounts to win a customer away from the opposition, those concessions will be a millstone around your neck and the contract will always suffer from that dynamic tension of potential conflict. So, if victory is gained by the application of great pressure, equally great pressure will be required to maintain the victorious position.

Machiavelli suggested a cunning alternative that is of great historical importance. If you find a minority in the target area who are outweighed by your intended victim, say, by a factor of ten to nine, you can then add your power to theirs and crush the victim's resistance by a factor of nineteen to ten. Having done this, you need only leave 20 percent of your forces in place along with the resident minority to maintain that position of power. The minority who helped you know that if you ever leave they will get their throats cut in short order and are therefore very eager for you to stay; at the same time your forces are never large enough to be seen as an army of occupation. This is a situation that can be maintained without dynamic tension.

This solution does not translate so directly into our own business practice, but the principle of alliance is highly significant. If we can find a reason to be needed, in a situation where mutual benefit and reliance are apparent to both sides, we can form an alliance with a client that has every prospect of durability—and, as we saw much earlier, it is durable relationships with our customers that give us the best chance of continued and increased commercial success.

I'm not done with history yet, in fact I'm now going to ask you to cast your mind back even further than the sixteenth century—much further: to the Stone Age. The cave man was probably the first human to work for a living. His job as a rule consisted of leaving the cave at the crack of dawn to search for buffalo to whack on the head and bring home for supper. As long as there were plenty of buffalo and not too many cave men, this was a steady job and the social economy worked rather well. Again, though, the quality of the catch is in direct proportion to the physical strength of the hunter: another situation fraught with dynamic tension. As time passed these arrangements began to become less satisfactory, for as the numbers of humans increased there was severe competition for the available buffalos: the weak cave men rarely caught anything and the quality of the animals that were caught declined. In fact, the really big, juicy, healthy ones were now far too sharp to be caught.

There was, however, one little cave man (probably a distant ancestor of Machiavelli) who had been watching the buffalo as he crept about the edges of the herds, not strong enough to charge in and grab one, and his investigations gave him a brilliant idea. He realized that if you got a mommy buffalo and a daddy buffalo and gave them lots of affection and nice sweet grass they would produce tiny buffalos on a regular basis and your suppers were assured indefinitely. This was called farming.

As a great number of salespeople are fairly Neanderthal in their outlook, it is not surprising that commerce is widely viewed as a hunt: but again, looking at the relative results of rape and courtship, it doesn't take much to see that farming is a much more fruitful model. It should be clear by now that our historical excursions are generating some very useful concepts: if you can get your customers, union bosses, or staff to trust you in alliances pursued for mutual benefit and future sustenance, life becomes a dream. You can get to the stage where your relationships with even really big customers have become so close that you forget that they are still buying from you: so far have you come from that teeth-gritted straining of the pressure sale that it no longer feels as if you are selling anything. We get phone calls from major clients who say, "Hey, Geoff, our northern teams are underperforming. What do you think we should do?"

I discuss some ideas with them and as we have a pleasant chat, I realize with some shock that they are buying.

To reach this blissful situation, where a partnership of true synergy exists between provider and client, you have to put a great deal of effort into making your deals so equitable that you and your customer are genuinely interdependent. Does this sound a bit idealistic for the rough world of commerce? Well, think what you do when you are lost. You ask someone for directions. Do you suspect the person who gives them to you as you would a high-pressure salesman? Why not? It can't be trust, you've only just met them. It must be that the directions are to your benefit and you are unaware of any benefit to the other person of handing out false instructions.

What this means in terms of your major business relationships is that you must sit with your customer—and I mean with, not opposite behind a large shiny desk—and steadily and thoroughly work yourself into an understanding of their situation. This requires a lot of gentle probing, sensitive questioning, and active, understanding listening to absorb not only their aspirations and concerns but also any lurking anxieties, potential problems, and underlying difficulties. As you think things through with your customer, you will both discover ways in which your company, your service, or your products can provide the means to achieve the objective. Together you will then be able to formulate a clear plan of action to achieve this objective.

It is important throughout this process that you do not think in terms of a sale to be made or an agreement to be sealed: those are short-term images and what you are doing here is building the foundations of a long-term professional relationship. You and your client are together constructing the skeleton of a process which you will then flesh out with your products or services to realize your mutual goal.

Big expensive solutions need big expensive problems

Obviously, such a sophisticated and intricate method is not best suited to selling chocolate bars, and even with very high-value products it is fairly useless unless the other party appreciates the size of the problem. Imagine this scenario.

"Tell me, friend, do you ever get punctures?"

"Yes, I sure do."

"Tiresome, aren't they?"

"Sure are."

"Tell me, how would you like never to have another puncture ever again?"

"Hey, that would be just dandy."

"Well, with the new Thunderflash Inflatorator you can be puncture-free for life."

"Gimme, gimme. How much?"

"$10,000 a wheel, shall we proceed?"

"Stick it in your ear."

What went wrong? That should have been a great success. We identified a trying problem that our product would solve, and we provided the means to solve it. We fell flat on our face because the customer did not put a value on the problem commensurate with the value we put on the solution. In a more modest transaction, the triviality of the perceived problem is no obstacle to success.

"Oh dear, it's raining."

"Don't you want to get wet, sir?"

"Bright lad."

"Try an umbrella, sir, only five dollars."

"Thank you," and money changes hands.

In a low-expenditure decision the whole process can be condensed into a couple of sentences. The potential customer stated no need or problem, just the current state of the weather, and from that we were able to create the desire for an umbrella—a low-cost solution to a mildly irritating problem.

If an umbrella cost $1,000, there would need to be a better reason for buying it than simply avoiding getting wet. Perhaps if the customer was convinced that he would dissolve, he might see the need for such expensive protection. In other words, expensive solutions require expensive problems, and it may be necessary to enlarge the problem to enable the other party to appreciate the real value of our offer. What about the Thunderflash Inflatorator? I feel a nasty bout of greasy salesmanitis coming on, but it will illustrate the point.

"Do you ever get punctures?"

"Sure do."

"Do your family ever ride in this car?"

"Sure do."

"Well, I know you're a really great driver, but could you be sure that your partner could handle a high-speed blowout?"

"Oh. I don't know..."

"How much is it worth to you to have the peace of mind to

know that your family will always be safe if that were to happen?"

Once again, I've made this sickeningly blatant to get the idea across swiftly, but once you have suppressed your nausea you will see that, toned down and used more subtly, it has the bones of a great method. Also, you will see that like so much in successful persuasion it is based on a series of questions. It is the questioning that grows the problem in the customer's mind. We saw back in Chapter 4 the amazing power of questions to make the other person's mind work in such a way as to do your job for you; here it is again. You don't exert the pressure on the customer; you encourage them almost to put pressure on themselves by making them work out the size of the problem—making them do your persuasion for you.

In a business situation, this is without doubt the finest technique to make a customer aware of the value of your offer. Ask about where they are, and where they have been (remembering that talking about the past can have a useful side-benefit in relaxing your opposite number); ask about the difficulties they may have and then about the consequences of those difficulties.

"So, what if the people in Scotland haven't heard of you?"

"Scotland represents up to twenty-five percent of the market and without it we could lose our competitive edge."

"Mm. What's the market currently worth?"

"Forty million."

"Golly. So you're saying that without Scotland you could be ten million down? How big a problem is that?"

"A ten-million-dollar one! It could cripple our entire investment program."

If you get the feeling that things are getting rather too somber, you might lighten the mood a little by asking a positive question. You don't want everyone to end up in a depressed heap, too miserable to take any decisions at all.

"So, if you did secure the Scottish market, what else might be good about that?"

"Well, I would sleep more easily; and a nice fat promotion would come my way."

A bit more of this and you should be well on the way to securing the full budget for the Scotland marketing project.

If the point isn't quite clear to you, imagine it backwards: in other words, see how the price of a service is actually used to devalue it. Many of us have recourse to the services of lawyers from time to time, and their skill and knowledge may save our business, home, or job; but when the bill arrives, we cry:

"Ten thousand dollars to write four letters!"

Lawyers would laugh this off; but how often do we devalue our own products, services, or talents in this way? Concentrate on the value of what the customer receives, and don't be paranoid.

What you want is dissatisfied customers

According to the great sales legend, passed down by word of mouth in a thousand seminar rooms and lovingly inscribed in generations of textbooks, there will be resistance to whatever we offer, and the teaching of the elders will show us how to overcome it by superior force. The favorite metaphor used in these tribal education sessions is that of the seesaw, with the customer and his resistance plonked on one end and the salesman and his benefits plonked on the other. Once you have enough benefits, the resistance is outweighed and the customer goes whizzing up into the air to land softly in your lap.

I admit that we have played along with this idea to an extent in the last example, where we grew the problem to outweigh resistance to the cost of the solution; nevertheless, as I picture the seesaw in my mind's eye a very frightening scene begins to appear which discourages me from wholesale allegiance to the principle as taught. There is the customer at the far end, sitting on a large crate of rocks labeled "Resistance"; and here at this end am I, sitting perched beside an empty crate labelled "Benefits." As we are talking specifically about big decisions here, the customer's crate is enormous and we have to work very hard to fill our crate with "benefit" rocks. You can see what is going to happen: as we pile in the rocks to match and then exceed the weight of the customer's "resistance" rocks, the customer's end begins to shift slightly—but there is so much weight on each end that the plank of the seesaw is bent into a twanging, humming arc of tension.

The whole structure is under such fearsome tension that just to be on any part of it is to be very frightened indeed. It might snap, in which case all is lost beyond repair; but even if it doesn't, that tension is there forever because the threat of rupture is always there. We saw in earlier chapters the value of long-term relationships in business, and the above example demonstrated their especially large role in major decisions; as we all know from personal experience, relationships tend to suffer when under permanent tension. You will get statements like:

"OK, we'll use your delivery service, but you'd better be good: slip up just once and you're out."

It's like facing a coiled spring, wondering every minute if it's about to take your eye out. So why are such situations allowed to occur? One of the reasons is that the people who prime the spring, coiling it tighter and tighter, and the people who have to live with it, an existence analogous to treading through a minefield, are generally not the same people. So we get salespeople howling, "I worked my butt off to get that contract fixed, and Service screwed the whole thing up in the first five minutes!"

Very sad; but this was because, through making extravagant promises, he handed Service a ticking bomb. (This, incidentally, shows again the damage that can be done by viewing "selling" as something done "over there," by someone else, with which we would rather not soil our nicely manicured hands. If Sales and Service had gotten together and worked out with joint commitment to the end result what promises could be met, the story would be somewhat different.)

To start looking for a solution to this difficulty we should go back to first principles again and ask ourselves why people make decisions. We noted earlier that no one makes a voluntary decision to change if they are perfectly happy with what they already have, and accordingly they start moving towards a decision when they start feeling dissatisfied with the status quo. The television manufacturers fall over themselves to tell us how advanced their sets are, but we don't start looking at them until our own telly has become unreliable or we notice it hasn't got the features we think we want. We start becoming interested in the prospect of change not because the new one has all these features, but because ours doesn't.

If you think this is a distinction without a difference, apply it to the seesaw. If we can get some of those heavy rocks— prejudices, misconceptions, resistance to change, satisfaction with the status quo—out of the customer's crate, we can swing the balance with a featherweight and shift the structure in our favor with no tension whatsoever arising. This situation, with its overall lightness and lack of stress, can be maintained indefinitely. We must examine our customer's crate of rocks and see how it can be lightened; in other words, we must create dissatisfied customers.

12

The End Is Nigh:
Close or Launch Pad?

Every interpersonal transaction must have some kind of conclusion, just as at the end of every cycle of cultivation the harvest
is gathered. Among traditional salespeople such soothing rural
metaphors are eschewed and all eyes are on "the close," the
arcane mystery at the core of the sales-shaman's art. As noted
earlier, it is not unlikely that you will see recruitment ads for sales
jobs specifying "must be good closer." This is about as intelligent
as a fruit farmer looking out sadly at bare trees and believing the
answer would be to advertise for good pickers. It's all a bit late.

This is not, however, to say that an excellent harvest cannot
be ruined by poor or clumsy picking. If the cultivation has been
done thoroughly and well and you have remained in control of it,
your questioning and negotiating should have produced a nice,
firm, juicy crop that will virtually fall into your hands; but it is a
sad fact that many of us, through a lack of courage or experience,
will at this point walk away, allowing our well-deserved harvest to
rot on the branch. Every persuasion must conclude with a
definite, firm action that benefits us; this is when we must grasp
that objective that we have held so faithfully before our mind's
eye right through the process. Nor is this all: it is near the end of
the process that we need to be especially alert to opportunities
that will emerge to capitalize on the work we have already done

by achieving even more than we set out to do. If your orchard produces an unexpectedly large crop, you don't go round it carefully picking only the quantities of fruit you predicted would grow, leaving the rest dangling to tempt thieves: you make the most of it.

You may feel that throughout this book I have been a bit hard on the so-called high-pressure sales people: but my venom is directed only at the destructive and dishonest aspects of their practice. Where many of the traditionalists might have a lesson to teach the rest of us is in the matter of commitment to the outcome, without which no persuasion, however lovingly conducted and sensitively nurtured, can come to its proper fruition. To illustrate how sheer motivation can beat all theories and techniques hands down when it comes to getting results, I will tell you the tale of Fred.

Fred the traveling salesman

I met Fred in the course of my research into sales methods. Back in the 1950s he had been a traveling salesman hawking washing machines. This job was on commission only, but included a valuable and unusual perk: the then almost unheard-of luxury of a vehicle. At the beginning of each week Fred was sent off in his van with five washing machines; so long as all five were sold each week, Fred could keep the van. This he succeeded in doing, week after week. It was a matter of honor, he told me, that if the demonstrator was taken from the van, it was never put back. Just as a Gurkha's *kukri* knife, once unsheathed, must draw blood, so the demonstrator, once unpacked, must be sold.

Eventually a week came when Fred's magic seemed to have abandoned him, and to his horror he found on Thursday evening that he had three machines left in his van. He felt that the midlands area where he normally worked was played out, and so, although he had only twenty-four hours until his van turned into a pumpkin, he was determined to find new pastures. A moment's thought convinced him that the naval bases on the East Coast would be his best bet, and, despite savage winter weather, he turned the van east and set off that same evening, so he could be on the spot first thing in the morning. Disaster struck when the van hit a patch of black ice, spun out of control, left the road, and hit a tree. Fred was flung through the windscreen (these were the days before compulsory seatbelts), severing an artery in the process. He says that he remembers watching his life's blood fountaining into the cold night air and thinking his end had come. Fortunately for him, two farmers' wives heard the crash and ran across the fields to his aid. Between them they called an ambulance and stemmed the flow of blood as Fred drifted in and out of consciousness. The ambulance arrived, Fred was loaded in and taken to the hospital; in the meantime each of the farmer's wives had signed up to become the proud owner of a shiny new washing machine!

"You see, I did it," Fred told me, "and when I came out of hospital, there was a new van waiting for me."

"Hold on," I said, "what about the third machine?"

"Oh," said Fred, "that's still going strong. It belongs to an ambulance driver in Southampton. I think he's retired now."

It is that determination to finish, that commitment to getting the customer's commitment, that so many of us seem to lack. Knowledgeable and accomplished as we are, we have little trouble creating a good, comfortable atmosphere between ourselves and our opposite numbers, but when the time comes to extract a firm decision we all seem to get a bit twitchy. It is this twitchiness that closing techniques are supposed to cure. The people who peddle these techniques will tell you that the measure of a good sale is the close. One would suppose, then, that the measure of a good sky-dive is the way you hit the ground. If you have to be hosed off the runway, then one would conclude that your technique requires some examination. As with the fruit farmer and his bare trees, it's a bit late by then. Your terminal velocity is determined by a lot of things that went before: the quality of your equipment, the altitude at which you pulled the ripcord, and so on. What needs examining is a whole chain of events; a seminar on hitting the ground is unlikely to help the next person who has to jump out of the plane.

Legend would have us believe that there exists some kind of pinpoint of light which is the precise moment when we must strike to close the deal: try it before or after and you will be lost. To identify the right pinpoint of time, you must look for buying signals. As with so much of the received wisdom, I don't entirely disagree with this idea; where I do take issue is on the question of what a buying signal actually is. It is said that as people become more interested they will ask more questions—about care of the product, details of the service, or the price of the deal. They may ask for a particular point to be repeated; if there are two of them they will exchange glances before turning to you with a sickly smile and saying, "Yes, we'll take it."

Finding fault is a good sign

Perhaps this does happen sometimes; but it is also the case that when people become picky, tricky, difficult, and argumentative, they are often ready to buy. Does that sound silly? Suppose I go to a Rolls-Royce showroom. I climb into one and the salesman oozes over.

"Good morning, sir, I see you are admiring the Silver Spirit."

"Yes, lovely, how much is it?"

"This particular model, sir, $190,000; but that does include the royal blue hide interior and the crystal decanters."

"Oh, that sounds great. If I could have a brochure, I'll show it to my wife and we might have a test drive."

He writes V. Int. in his little black book. You know as well as I do how accurate that is.

Later that same day I see a beat-up old car in Honest John's Autos for $500, and I tell my wife, "That would suit our boy; why don't you get it for him?"

"I haven't got $500."

"Well, let's go halves."

Later I wander into Honest John's with $500 scattered about my person. I amble around and kick a few tires, but I wait for them to come to me.

"Good morning, sir, can I help you?"

"Nah, not really—oh, except how much is the old car?"

"Price is on the windshield, sir, $500."

"I can see that, I mean the real price, for cash."

"Well, if you twist my arm, sir, maybe $400."

"Mmm. What about the bald tires?"

"Bald, sir? Maybe a little low, but..."

"Low? I can see my face in that one. And what about this scratch? I hope you're leaving the radio in."

Why am I being like this? I wasn't with the Rolls. It's obvious, isn't it? I want to buy. I've made the decision and there is nothing to be lost in getting the best possible deal. As we saw in Chapter 9, it's after you've decided to buy that the negotiating starts. If you choose to buy a valuable watch or camera, when you are first taking a look at it in the shop as you cast around various possibilities you enjoy its overall feel and appearance; but when you are on the brink of handing over the cash, you will notice the tiniest scratch or blemish, even a slightly crooked sticker. This is because you have now decided to buy and you want perfection. So be wary of the customer who loves everything you show them; their sincerity has to be in doubt.

Serious dangers lurk with the customer who has decided to buy but is pushing for that last concession from you. There is a tradition among gypsies called "luck money." If you ever trade with gypsies they will haggle, harangue you, and argue with you until you are driven by despair into giving them the very best possible deal. The agreement is made, money changes hands, and you are left drained and exhausted. At this point they come back at you and ask for "a little bit of luck money, just a fiver, to bring you gypsy's luck on the deal." What does it matter to them if you refuse? They've come out of the deal very well as it is, and the luck money if you do shell out will just be a nice bonus.

A commercial buyer will do just the same, even if slightly less blatantly. Perhaps they have received your very competitive proposal and their boss has not only approved it but has said that there is great urgency in proceeding. With this in mind, the buyer summons you to his office. You knock and wait. Eventually the buyer calls, "Come in," and looks up at you in surprise as you enter.

"I'm sorry, was I expecting you?"

"Yes, it's about the new press."

"Oh yes, I remember. Now, remind me, how much was it?"

"We did send you a proposal and quotation."

"Oh…did you? I seem to have mislaid them. How much was it again?"

"Well, altogether it was $48,000."

Tell you what, do it for forty-five thou and I'll take a risk and sign your order now."

What do you do? He could be bluffing, but he might not be, in which case you could lose the deal. The main thing to remember is the sheepdog: you need to stay in control. Always carry copies of quotes and other documents you have sent to customers; and minute meetings so that you can send contact reports to prevent convenient amnesia. Sheep will sidle off in all directions if you take your eye off them for a minute.

Having said that, it has to be admitted that a customer who has made a firm decision to buy is often in the driving seat, and it takes real nerve to test their resolve with a take-it-or-leave-it attitude. I still get caught out in these situations; you have to decide in each case how badly you want that agreement. It might help if you have lots of customers, enabling you to say something on the lines of "If you don't want it, thousands do"; but don't try that unless thousands really do want it. Honesty can help you, but dishonesty will turn very nasty given half a chance.

If people are going to be difficult with you, then there has to be a way of dealing with objections. The received wisdom on this subject is almost childlike in its simplicity. Little kids reckon that if they can't see you, you can't see them, and hide by putting their hands over their eyes. The sales trainers have a theory that as all failed sales end with some kind of objection, if you could remove or negate that objection the sale would succeed. This might at first glance sound more logical, but it isn't. They won't give up easily, though; if you tell them that often when you have decided not to buy you say nothing, they look smug and tell you that that is a case of an unspoken objection. This proceeds by way of yet more false logic to the claim that for a salesperson to deal effectively with an objection it must be clearly stated and the well-known seminar topic "uncovering the hidden objection." Yes, that's right; if you don't buy and don't object, they will try to make you object so that they can then trample down your objection and make you buy.

Don't create objections

People do object; they object about price, about need, about quality, about timing, and so on; but where do these objections come from? Tell me right now what objection you have to the next idea I'm going to offer you. You haven't got one? Well, of course you haven't; how can you object to something that you haven't even been offered yet? The point I'm making is that the objection can actually be generated by the offer.

In his wonderful book, *Games People Play,* Eric Berne described a psychological game which he called "Yes, but." (Please don't confuse this with the objection-handling technique also called "Yes, but," which we will come on to a little later.) Berne's game is played by two people, one who apparently has a problem, and the other poor fool who has to try to solve it. A typical example would go like this:

"My husband beats me."

"Then leave him."

"Yes, but I love him."

"Then persuade him to get help."

"Yes, but he would never go."

"Then threaten to leave him."

"Yes, but he would beat me more."

Eventually the game ends when the one suggesting the solutions has to admit defeat: "Well, I'm stumped. I don't know what else to suggest," leaving the obstinate victor smiling smugly at being beyond assistance.

Berne then suggests how to turn this around.

"My husband beats me."

"That's really sad. What do you intend to do about it?"

This should ring some bells. We have already seen that skillful use of questions can make the other party do your work for you. You will have noticed that the first example of Berne's game contains no questions, just a sequence of proposals to each of which an objection is raised: the solution, however reasonable, creates the objection. In the second, the potential objector is coaxed into articulating the solution herself.

Let's see how this might work in a sales situation.

"My factory gets too hot to work in."

"We can install a ventilation system that will deal with that."

"Yes, but that will be very expensive."

Your response, though expected and reasonable, generated the objection. Try Berne's other tack.

"My factory gets too hot to work in."

"That really is bad. What do you plan to do about it?"

"Well, I suppose ventilation is the only answer."

"Can you afford that?"

"Can I afford not to, with the production I'm losing through overheating?"

All right, it's a bit tricky and it isn't easy to do; but once you get the instinct for how far you can go while maintaining control you will see how valuable this technique can be. Simply by not provoking them, you should be able to reduce the objections offered by at least two-thirds; but of course you will still be left with some, and it is those to which we must now turn our attention.

There is, naturally, a popular repertoire of classic objection-handling techniques, the main feature of which on first sight is their extreme oiliness. However, loath as I am to admit it, if they are dried out with a bit of paper towel and carefully modified in line with the principles of persuasion we have been exploring, some of them actually work. I therefore reproduce here, with general and grateful acknowledgement to whichever of the thousands of sales textbooks I found them in, five of the best. Suspend your disbelief for a page or two and try them.

The first one involves asking about the objection.

"I'm sorry, that's just too much money."

"Too much money? In what way is that too much?" Before you giggle, see how it can work. A woman came into a furniture shop that was a client of ours and asked about wardrobes.

"Oh, that is nice, but I'm afraid it's too big." She was shown lots of smaller ones, but didn't like them. We leaped in.

"When you say too big, madam, what exactly do you mean by too big?"

"Well, it's lovely, but I won't get it in the car."

The salesperson started to do a little jig of excitement.

"We deliver, we deliver," he squeaked. And of course she bought it.

The next technique we should consider is "set-aside" (not to be confused with European agricultural policy, which owes even less to considered logic than most sales textbooks). There are two lines of thought behind this one: first, that if the objection can be set to one side, a further hidden objection may be uncovered; second, and more usefully, if we set the objection aside we give ourselves time to generate more desire for our product or service in the other party, to the point where the objection can be sidelined permanently. Let's take that most basic of all objections again.

"Oh, that's far too much money."

"Just set aside the price for a moment and tell me if this is exactly the pack mule you wanted."

Again, stifle your sniggers while I give you an example. I was negotiating a training deal with our biggest client of all when the question of cost came up.

"Okay, Geoff, we may want you to do this training, but before we go another step, we will have to deal with the issue of your ludicrous day rate."

This job was going to be so much fun that I would have done it for nothing, so in all innocence I said, "That's not going to be a problem, forget my day rate for a moment, I assure you we will come to some agreement. Let's talk about the project instead. It sounds really exciting."

Hours later I left with a signed contract at my full daily rate. The issue of cost had been set aside and I didn't even know I had done it. Perhaps it was something to do with sincerity. I hope so: it's so nice to have the warm glow of the moral high ground as well as the money.

Next, is the objection important? With characteristic smoothness, the books tell us that if an objection is important it can be positively handled, and if it isn't—it can be positively handled. We'll take the unimportant one first. Back to that atomic power station we were selling in Chapter 11. The buyer is viewing the control room. His eye lights on a door handle.

"That handle is a horrible shade of blue."

"No it isn't, it's most striking."

"I couldn't stand working with a handle that color."

"But it matches your eyes."

"How dare you!"

The right way might be:

"That handle is a horrible shade of blue."

"It is a bit bright, isn't it? Anyway, are you ready to see the reactor room?" Not so much set aside as quietly ignored.

Now, if the objection *is* important, you give the impression for a while that you can't solve it, thereby enticing the customer towards a commitment.

"I really wanted red."

"Is that very important?"

"Yes."

"Oh dear, I think blue ones are all we can get in this size. No, look, we're in luck, here's a red one. That'll be ten bucks please."

Again, seasoned with a generous ladling of honesty, it will work.

The last two are a bit sneaky, and yet in one form or another we use them all the time to negotiate our way around our families, our colleagues, our friends; if they sound implausible, just listen to yourself for a few days and see if you don't find yourself doing a little of the same thing.

The first of this pair is another kind of "yes, but" game. The idea here is that if the other person disagrees, it is fatal to contradict her, so agree and then turn it around with a nice fat "but":

"I'm on fire."

"Yes, but how nice it must be to be warm at last." The second is a variation on the same theme. The customer may make a disparaging comment on our product to accompany her objection; here we must again agree, and then reword the statement to change its meaning.

"Urghh, pooh, that smells utterly disgusting."

"Yes, it does have a distinctive aroma, but if you consider the advantage of a prescented product, I'm sure you will agree..."

The problem with all these, you might think, is that they rely on the caricature human being beloved of the sales trainers, the one with "Gullible" as a middle name. You can see right through these ploys, so the customer will as well. This is quite true, and brings me back to my favorite point that you cannot hope to be effective if you just learn techniques and phrases like gymnastic exercises and repeat them by rote. All these ideas are just raw material that you can trim, hone, cut, and apply as appropriate. It is the principles that are important; the practice must always be tailored to fit.

Just shut up

As we were fiddling about with our training methods one day, trimming, honing, and so on, a new client appeared. They made very special and very expensive chocolates, and they had a very specific problem.

"Now listen," they said, "in your seminars you have a bit on dealing with objections. We want you to come and tell our staff how to do it."

"Well, we will include that in our complete training program."

"Include nothing. All we want is dealing with objections. You can take the rest of your exorbitantly priced nonsense and…"

"Yes, I can understand your desire to insert our prestigious program in the appropriate aperture, but when you consider the advantages of a full and thorough modular approach…"

They explained that their premier product was a heart-shaped box of chocolates bought mainly by guilty husbands and priced at twenty-five dollars. There were of course objections to the price, and as this was their only problem this was all they wanted dealt with.

The classics were tried.

"How much are those heart-shaped chocolates?"

"Twenty-five dollars, sir."

"My heck, that's expensive."

"Expensive, sir? I'm sorry, what do you mean by expensive?"

"What do you think I mean? They're too expensive!" We tried set-aside.

"Putting the price aside for the moment, are these exactly the chocolates you wanted?"

"Yes."

"You'll take a box, then?"

"No."

This wasn't getting very far. Then we looked at the client's figures and found that there was one shop that was bucking the trend and selling loads of these prime goodies. Whoever was behind the counter here was clearly a megastar and worth seeing. Off we rushed to see this grandmaster in action. When we arrived, we were hugely disappointed to find no one in the shop but the archetypal dolt, gazing blankly into space. Before we could shut our mouths, let alone open them again, a customer entered. Guilt written all over his countenance, he homed in on the heart-shaped box.

"How much are those?"

The dolt gradually brought his eyes into focus.

"Twenty-five dollars."

"What? Twenty-five dollars? Are you mad? Twenty-five dollars for a stupid box of chocolates? You could buy twenty-five boxes of chocolate mint creams for that. When I was a kid, that was the price of a vacation in Europe. I really don't know how you people have the nerve to ask that price. I'll take two."

We were dumbstruck. How had this been achieved? The dolt had said nothing. Of course: that must be the answer. The candies were unique and could not be bought elsewhere. The customer may have felt that he was almost being blackmailed and had to let off steam; any comment would just have stoked him up and kept him going longer. As it was he gradually fizzled out and made the purchase. You see exactly the same thing happening in auto parts stores, when the customer is told that the ignition computer is $900. They shout and scream and bite the carpet, but they have to buy it. From this you may deduce that the first line of defense with objections is silence. At least wait until the other person has finished their tirade without interjecting; you might well find that by then the problem has solved itself, whereas a well-meant and

good-humored intervention will probably just remind the customer what they are so steamed up about.

Suppose that objections have evaporated or been overcome.
Now what do we do? This is it: we are supposed to close. What we
more often do is fidget about, not really daring to risk everything
by asking for a decision. It isn't unknown for salespeople at this
stage to tell a customer to go away and think about it. We have to
propose some kind of action; we want to gain, but are afraid to
lose. Some of the old closing techniques can in fact be a help
here, not so much for the effect they have on the customer as for
the moral crutch they provide for the nervous salesperson. Take
the classic "alternative close," for instance:

"Did you want red or blue?"

"How would you like to pay, cash or check?"

"Shall we say tomorrow, or would some time next week be
better for you?"

It all makes it easier to ask for a decision: but decision to do
what? It's not always clear-cut: acquiring a new client or moving
towards a major long-term deal is not like hawking an umbrella,
as we've already seen. Selling consultancy involves all sorts of
convoluted arrangements and often means contacting a number
of people and going through various stages with each of them, so
I don't really have an endpoint at which I can say to myself: This
is the close. In these circumstances it's necessary to look for
those clicks on the ratchet again—to achieve some kind of
action, take some intermediate step. This might be the awarding
of a major contract, or it might be just an agreement to meet the
next member of staff up the line. I find it helpful to use the notes
I've jotted down during the investigation stage as a basis for this
interim proposal, because in doing so I can refer back to the
point that concerned the other party most and to the solution
that they found most attractive. This, by the way, is one of the
reasons why it is a good idea to write things down; it can be very
disarming, not to say disconcerting, when you remind people of
things they said they didn't like, so you need to be accurate or
you might be accused of putting words into someone's mouth—

and to be sure of this you need a written record to which you can refer.

"So you felt the sales team could do better and that a preliminary discussion with them would help. Do you have your diary?" As we've already agreed in the course of our discussion on the nature of the problem and the preferred solution, there should be no difficulty in getting agreement to the action proposed.

"Then why don't you and your sales director come and see us next month? Or would the month after be better?"

Common ground has been established and confirmed by reminders of what has already been agreed.

The other important feature of exchanges like these is that we have invited the other party to give the maximum that they are qualified to give at that moment. Recognizing how far your opposite number is authorized is crucial in keeping the momentum going without losing the deal. Salespeople who are too pushy ask for more than the customer can give and therefore fail; at the other end of the spectrum, if you ask for too little or, worse, nothing at all, inertia sets in and no progress is made. For example, if you were just starting to look for a new car, then this would not be the day to ask you to buy; but just as bad would be to let you amble off with a brochure. Your next step might well be a test drive with your partner, and it would be correct to ask you to commit to a date for that. Exactly the same principle applies in major negotiations. If you ask the other party to commit to decisions beyond their authority, you only humiliate them and thereby sour the atmosphere for future discussions. To avoid this, find out where their limit lies through gentle and alert investigation and then propose your next click of the ratchet.

Sell more

We now have some kind of agreement: the job's in the bag, the money's in the till, and big cheesy grins of satisfaction are on faces. Now what? This is the time really to celebrate, but not by loosening ties and pouring the gin and generally putting feet up. This is the moment at which the real opportunities for profit start to appear. So far, all our time and effort have gone into finding and convincing this person; now we have them alongside us, and, to quote a sales trainer I heard recently, the easiest person in the world to sell to is a customer you already have. This, in other words, is the time to sell more.

Those of you who work in, or run, departmentally structured organizations might balk here and say: but the customer isn't mine any more once she's signed up—the customer contact is taken over by a series of other people. This should not make any difference. As I have said before, it is my firm belief that everyone in an enterprise can and should participate in selling whatever it has to offer. The faces the customer sees and the voices she hears on the phone may change as engineers, drivers, and managers become involved, but the continuous process of keeping the customer, and keeping the customer buying, should flow through the whole series of interactions. Instead of five sales staff and a thousand other employees, you should have a thousand and five salespeople.

This is why all your staff should learn enough of the principles and techniques of persuasion to help build profits. It does not mean that all of them have to spend every second Tuesday in the seminar room. In a retail environment, for example, where unskilled part-time staff form a large proportion of the workforce, simple politeness and taking a little trouble works wonders in bringing about positive buying decisions from customers. An elderly man in a group to which I was explaining this phenomenon told me that it had been noticed and exploited years ago by one of his former employers. Apparently this firm sold Philips wireless sets just after the war, and each shop had a stock room full of them. One set only was put on display in the window, where it would be surrounded by batteries and various accessories to make a most ornate display. If a customer came in and asked to see a Philips wireless, the assistant would smile and offer to get him one immediately; he would then go, not to the stock room as you would imagine, but into the window display. Clambering over the "for sale" sign, he would bang his head on the window, rip the backside out of his trousers, and knock over the pyramid of batteries. Eventually he would arrive back in front of the customer, breathless and disheveled but proudly bearing his prize. Well, would you ask him to put it back? When someone goes to a lot of trouble for you, they invite commitment.

So: all staff can sell, they can sell more, and they can get commitment. Armed with these powerful truths at a conference of garden center owners, I was brought up against the Shrub Boys.

The delegates had listened with interest to my message that everyone can sell, and several of them approached me afterwards just to check that when I said everyone, I meant everyone.

"Yes: every member of your staff," I said cheerily. "You mean…even the Shrub Boys?" they asked incredulously. I hadn't a clue what a Shrub Boy was, but I had confidence in my view.

"Yep, even them," I said.

When I visited one of these centers subsequently on a research trip, I found out why my audience had been a bit reluctant to accept my all-inclusive promise. I don't know if you used to watch the old horror movies, the ones where you never actually saw the monster? If they were going to frighten you, they couldn't let you see it, because the make-up in those days was so rudimentary that it wouldn't take you long to realize that the Beast was just a guy with an egg box and some plasticine on his head. Therefore the tension was generated by things that snuffled and grunted just out of sight among the shrubs and bushes, disturbing the foliage but remaining invisible. Someone would say, "What was that?" and a beautiful woman would go out into the garden with a guttering candle to investigate. She calls in a brave but shaky voice, "Who is there?" and seconds later we see a shot of her horrified face. Her piercing scream leads into the next scene, which is shot in daylight and consists of Peter Cushing looking at her mutilated corpse and saying, "My word, what on earth could have done this?" If he had ever been to a garden center, he would have had a fair idea, for they actually have these strange snuffling grunting creatures. Known collectively as the Shrub Boys, they have heavyboned foreheads and tend to walk in a rolling style that involves their knuckles bumping gently on the ground. You have probably seen them, or had one "help" you by bursting a jumbo bag of soil in the trunk of your car.

True to my word, I agreed to give these frolicsome youths some training. They had never been on a seminar before, and seemed to enjoy it rather. They were very attentive, anyway— apart from a spot of mutual grooming—in fact, almost too attentive: from the looks of revelation that spread over their faces as they gazed at me in awe, slack-jawed and immobile, you would have thought that they were discovering the secret of fire. In fact, at that moment they were discovering the secret of selling more.

It was explained to the Shrub Boys in the simplest possible terms that everyone who buys a tree should be asked to buy a stake to support it, thus adding 30 percent to the value of each sale. Subsequently, as unsuspecting customers browsed around the shrub area, the second their fingers alighted on a tree the leaves parted and out leaped the missing link, howling, grunting, and brandishing an eight-foot sharpened wooden stake. We knew that we had slightly overstepped the mark when analysis of the figures showed that sales of stakes had in fact outstripped sales of trees by a considerable margin.

The Shrub Boys, along with all the other staff, were also introduced to the concept of commitment. It had been noticed that previously, if staff were asked about the location of something, they would tend to mumble and point, sometimes without even looking up from what they were doing. Sales soared once we had persuaded them not only to give directions clearly and politely, but if possible to go off and fetch the goods mentioned. The customer is delighted by the attention, and also feels some obligation to buy, after such trouble has been gone to on their behalf. One girl who tried to be extra helpful would always come back with two plants to offer a choice; we and the center's owner alike were delighted to see that the customer often took both.

This idea was duly presented to the Shrub Boys, and shortly thereafter I saw one of them being asked about compost shredders. These cost about $350 and weigh about a hundred pounds. My pupil turned to me, gave me a huge wink and before I could restrain him loped off into the store, grunting, "I fetch it." You guessed it: he came back dragging two, and to my surprise and glee not only did the customer buy one, but the man standing next to me bought the other. The Shrub Boy jabbed his thumb in the air as a victory salute and gamboled away.

As so often, the principle is the same whatever the scale of the transaction. If you sell power stations rather than begonias, you can still get commitment by, say, building a model of the plant; if the client country's president is Mr. Lung Po and you call the project the Lung Po Power Station, it might be deemed churlish to look elsewhere.

Soup from the bones or icing on the cake?

What the Shrub Boys were attempting with the tree stakes was retail's greatest cliché, known as the "add-on" or "linked sale." It used to be a great profit-maker; but now, when we are leaped on with the shoe polish, the extended warranty, or the "selection of delicious sweets from the trolley," we do indeed feel as though we have been ravaged with a long, sharp stick. The problem is that the sellers are viewing the transaction from the wrong angle. It has come to be seen as a way to wring more from the customer, like making soup from the bones of the animal you've just slaughtered and eaten. If, on the other hand, we ask ourselves what extra bits and bobs this person might need to get maximum enjoyment from their basic purchase, the whole thing is seen as a compliment to the customer. And if you see it this way, the customer will feel it this way.

A client of ours who sold women's fashion accessories complained that the average sale was only about one dollar; when we watched a sale, we weren't surprised. A very bored girl, without even interrupting her conversation with another very bored girl, would take the money and fling the goods at the customer. We put in one of our staff who is a supremo of high-level corporate sales. Not long after she had started to apply her skills to this small-cost retail environment the value of the average sale had risen to eight dollars: an 800-percent increase. How? Simple. She was attentive, she asked questions and made suggestions.

"Oh, yes, these are lovely. Are you going anywhere special? Have you seen the matching tiara, and these long gloves would go well."

More surprising, perhaps, than her achievement was the reaction of the customers, who—even when told that they had spent eight times as much as they had meant to—declared what a wonderful experience it had been, and that they would certainly be back. Those of you out there who spend your lives conducting high-level negotiations may find it such a relief when the agreement is finally in the bag that you look no further than getting out of the building with the signed documents. In truth, this is the time to investigate how you can increase the customer's pleasure and your own profit. Perhaps that huge machine should have a maintenance contract, or a set of special tools and service spares. While you are on such good terms with the union, it might be the time to sort out the holiday arrangements. You can literally double your profits by selling to the customers you already have, and the wonderful paradox is that they are actually happier when you do.

12a

And Finally…

Although I don't agree with his argument, I have some sympathy for the film-maker Stanley Kubrick in his refusal to allow *A Clockwork Orange* to be shown in Britain lest it provoke, or be deemed to provoke, crimes of violence. If just one person was said to have committed a robbery, rape, or murder under the influence of the film, there would be fingers pointing at Kubrick—to say nothing of his own feeling of possible responsibility. If you have read even some of the preceding chapters you will know that the ideas and techniques I have been proposing are designed to provoke effects as far as it is possible to imagine from violent crime—enduring, amicable, and profitable relationships, happy customers, fulfilled colleagues, valued employees—and yet, as I emphasized earlier, no powerful tool is without its dangers, and I have been showing you some very powerful tools indeed. You will understand, then, why I share some of that sense of trepidation and responsibility for the possible effects of what I have written here, and why one of the things I want to do in this short final section is to stress the spirit in which this book should be read and used.

Back in Chapter 8, we noted how most people find a neutral or unresponsive face much more off-putting than either a happy or a sad face. One of the hardest things about writing this book has been the sense that I am conducting a one-sided conversation, whereas ideally I would have been able to hear and see you reacting to what I was saying, and you would have been able to chip in where you disagreed, or where something I said gave you an idea of your own. This raises a very important point which echoes much that I have written here. The advice that I have gained from books—and I have read and benefited from very many—has never been so valuable as the new ideas they have generated which I have subsequently tailored to my own working needs and circumstances. Moreover, these ideas have borne fruit irrespective of whether I loved or hated the books that sparked them off. Therefore, as you mull over what you have read here and perhaps dip in and out of it and go back over some sections or chapters, even if you are apoplectic with rage at some of the things you read, do please look on the principles outlined as infinitely adaptable tools, not as a rigid structure of scaffolding to be clung to at all costs; or as springboards from which you can perform whatever sort of dive you like rather than as cannons which will shoot you out forcefully in one direction only.

It is because this fluidity and adaptability are so crucial to successful persuasion that I am not ending this book with one of those summary lists so beloved of some business writers—Ten Golden Rules of Selling, or The Five Best Ways to Keep a Customer, or Six Stages to Successful Negotiation. One major drawback of this approach is that it encourages you to think in compartments. As I said earlier, a book is a linear kind of thing and it's unavoidable that subjects get tackled in some sort of sequence, but you will, I hope, have noticed that in this book the ideas discussed earlier keep coming back and feeding into the discussion in later chapters. None of them exists in isolation, any more than a purchase, or a complaint, or a sale exists in isolation. If you're going to build a continuing relationship with your clients and employees, there will be many facets to that relationship, and they will exist and function simultaneously, in all sorts of permutations, not in a neat prescribed order. Your approach to that relationship, and to nurturing it for your mutual profit and benefit, must be a holistic one. What is the point of taking care of customers you haven't got, getting customers you won't take care of, and getting and taking care of customers from whom you can't profit?

To pinpoint another fundamental objection to the Ten Golden

Rules approach, let us return to the star sheepdog of Chapter 5. Well, quite apart from the fact that so far as we know dogs can't count, can you imagine a Border collie learning Seven Rules for Penning Fifteen Sheep? The sheep certainly won't have learned them, anyway, so what use are they to the dog? As we have seen, he has to observe, to react, to adapt. He has learned the principles— he doesn't rush the sheep, doesn't scatter them, doesn't let them wander off in all directions—and he knows exactly where they're going; but given a very few general principles and a clear fixed objective he can coax, cajole, and encourage his targets from a variety of angles and with infinite shades of patience and firmness.

The sheepdog's skill—just like the martial art of the Tibetan monk—can be summed up as flexible control. I can perhaps illustrate the equal importance of the two elements of that phrase by explaining to you how it is that, while I loathe flying, I ride a large and powerful motorcycle. The accident statistics, of course, tell me that I am far more likely to come to grief on my bike than I am in a jumbo jet under the command of a skilled team of pilots; but on the motorcycle I am in control. I have to know what I'm doing; I have to be alert, I have to know what the bike can do and what the rest of the traffic is doing, but it's my hands on the controls. And because I am in control, I have a great time. If you are in control of your business transactions, and are flexible enough to adapt your tactics as required, you will not only make some healthy profits but will also have great fun doing it.

I will leave you with an illustration of the principle of mutual benefit that I have been propounding throughout this book. All of us know the *schadenfreude,* the guilty pleasure of seeing people slip on banana skins of one sort or another—even those closest to us can have ambivalent feelings about our success, while our enemies will be waiting with eager anticipation for the fatal slippery step. This book will only succeed if you succeed in what you do after reading it; in other words, my success depends on your success. Therefore, even in your darkest moments you can be sure that there is someone who is rooting for you. I wish you good times ahead.